The North Avenue Irregulars

A Suburb Battles the Mafia

by the Reverend Albert Fay Hill

COWLES

CONTENTS

Introduction iv

Chapter One 1

Chapter Two 12

Chapter Three 33

Chapter Four 53

Chapter Five 61

Chapter Six 94

Chapter Seven 110

Chapter Eight 142

Chapter Nine 161

Chapter Ten 178

Chapter Eleven 201

Chapter Twelve 232

INTRODUCTION

This book has been written for several reasons. One is a desire to give some tangible expression of gratitude to the people who worked with me on the campaign to rid New York's Westchester County and city of New Rochelle of Organized Crime. We called ourselves the North Avenue Irregulars in jest, but our purpose was serious. The men who risked their lives to acquire important information, the women who spent hours watching and following hoodlums, and the advisers who met with me for many hours to plan strategy, all deserve recognition, but if they must, for security reasons, remain anonymous, at least I can tell their story.

I have also written this book because I want to tell others what I have learned. I firmly believe that our nation faces a major threat to its welfare in the form of Organized Crime. Newspapers, orators, and commentators constantly call attention to the rising problem of "crime in the streets"—often committed by disillusioned victims of our affluent but cruel society or by addicts desperately looking for money with which to buy drugs. But legislatures are noticeably slow about passing legislation designed to curb the depredations of the Syndicate, the Organization, the Mob, the Cosa Nostra, the Mafia, or whatever one wants to call it. Jurists send to reform school kids from the slums who in their agony have thrown a brick through a window, but are mysteriously reluctant to give jail sentences to men whose entire lives have been devoted to flouting the law. Businessmen are deeply shocked by the civil disobedience of

Negroes who are trying to win a place for themselves in our economy, but think nothing of placing a bet with the corner bookie. I contend, however, that it is the Organized Criminal (and the official corruption that goes with him) who is the real threat to law and order in our nation. He is the bad apple that will cause the whole barrel to rot.

I do not know of a single authority in the field of law enforcement who will contend that Organized Crime is declining today. It is growing in size and in influence in the United States. Of course, nobody knows exactly how big or how tightly organized it is, but nobody any longer denies its existence. Its revenues are enormous. Comparing its revenues against figures taken from *The National Industrial Board Economic Almanac, 1967–68*, they are equal to the combined gross national products of Austria, Denmark, Ireland, Holland, Norway, Portugal, Sweden, Turkey, and Switzerland, if liberal estimates of the Syndicate's income are correct, or the equivalent of the gross national products of Taiwan, the Philippines, Venezuela, Guatemala, and Argentina, if conservative figures are used.

No nation, however rich and strong, can long tolerate such a malignancy. A nation must either do something to reduce that growth, or perish.

Wherever Organized Crime exists, there must of necessity be corruption. It cannot carry on its activities in real secrecy. Unorganized crime, such as burglary or forgery, is, by its nature, carried on in maximum secrecy. This is not the case with Organized Crime. It provides services that cannot be performed entirely in the dark: gambling, loan sharking, prostitution, narcotics, labor racketeering, extortion, and the take-over of legitimate business. It is possible for almost anybody with the desire to do so to find out if Organized Crime exists in his city. And if *he* finds it, he may be sure that the police know about it and have done nothing, for some reason. Not only the police, but politicians and courts and minor public officials as well know of its existence. In order to operate, Organized Crime must pay off the police and other officials in order to function without harassment and prosecution.

This corruption does not stop with winking at the activities of a bookie. The policeman who takes money from a bookie will soon expect it from the motorist to whom he gives a speeding ticket. The politician who accepts large campaign contributions from gangsters will soon want money from citizens asking for zoning variances. If we do not soon get effective control over Organized Crime, corruption will proceed until we are unable to deal effectively with any of our problems.

It is in part to call attention to this situation that I have written this book. In doing so, I do not mean to imply that New York, Westchester County, or the city of New Rochelle are sinkholes of crime. Although our county is certainly not the "cleanest county in the United States," neither is it the dirtiest. Nor is New Rochelle the dirtiest town. Indeed, the amount of Organized Crime here is somewhat typical of areas surrounding big cities. I say *somewhat typical*, for there *are* cities and counties that do not have any major problem with Organized Crime. As a result of my experiences and conversations with qualified law enforcement officials it was clear that gambling in New Rochelle was controlled by Organized Crime and used to finance other activities of the Mob.

I have written this book, too, to dispel some of the myths about Organized Crime. I have heard some learned men say that gangsters no longer resort to violence, that they have become "respectable." That is sheer, unadulterated nonsense. There has been an epidemic of gangland murders in the New York area. Most of the victims were men engaged in narcotics or gambling ventures of one sort or the other. The Mob also slays prosecutors, lawyers, witnesses, and anyone else who threatens its hold on a community. Nor do the hoodlums specialize only in murder. They also resort constantly to mayhem of one sort or another, though the incidents do not always appear in the newspapers; loan shark victims who have had their legs broken or their faces slashed seldom go to the police and file complaints. Thus, violence, after money, is the second source of power for the Organization, and it is still used lavishly, even if somewhat more "privately" than before.

Another myth says that the Mob is invulnerable. This is far from true. Twelve women and a Presbyterian minister proved that, where there is a will, the Organization can be seriously harmed. If amateurs can do it, so can the police.

Gambling plays so large a role in this story because it is an activity more vulnerable than some others of the Mob. It is hard to catch a loan shark, but relatively easy to snare a gambler. Many, if not most, of the convictions of even high-level mobsters have been on gambling charges. It is also safer for amateurs to work on a gambling case than on, say, a narcotics one. If a gambler is caught and convicted he will probably receive a light jail sentence, even from a judge in a federal court. A narcotics conviction, on the other hand, carries a long sentence, so the Mob will maim or kill to avoid narcotics convictions, but will seldom resort to such extremes over gambling charges. Thus, it was relatively safe for our women to work on the gambling problem. We also provided law enforcement officials with information on more serious crimes, but nothing will be said of these in this narrative because of the greater danger to informants.

This book, let me add, was *not* written to maintain that we "cleaned up" Organized Crime in Westchester or even that we hurt it seriously. We only pricked the Mob, barely drew blood. If it had not been for the decision by the Supreme Court that the gambling tax stamp law was unconstitutional, we might have done more serious damage.

Needless to say, the story told here is true. The names of all informants are fictitious, and some of the incidents have been changed to protect the informants. The girls' names are also fictitious, but their exploits are described accurately, though some exaggeration may have crept in at times. In dealing with others, I have used real names except for persons involved in incidents that were not reported by the press. Where an arrest was made and related by the press, the real name has been used. The dialogue from the SIC (State Investigation Committee) hearings is quoted from the transcript. Months have passed since some of the incidents described here took place, and my memory has clouded, but wherever possible I have checked for accuracy by talking with other people who were involved.

In a book such as this, where many persons have been associated in the work, the dedication poses something of a dilemma. One obvious possibility is the special agents of the Intelligence Division of the Internal Revenue Service. They richly deserve whatever praise I can give them. This is especially true of the agent I call "Marv" in the story. His energy, brilliance, and keen sense of honor have increasingly impressed me. Another possibility is Samson Gordon, who has helped and advised me constantly, and whose friendship during difficult times has been of great comfort to me. I have also thought of dedicating this book to the many people who did undercover work, gathering information and assisting Treasury agents. And I have considered "Anne" and the other girls of the North Avenue Irregulars who worked on the project. They are some of the finest women I have ever known and they deserve public recognition, a recognition they cannot have without being endangered. A still more obvious choice would be my wife, Grace, and our children. During the illness described in the text, Grace was indomitable in spirit and a source of encouragement to me.

I have decided instead, however, to dedicate this book to the congregation of the North Avenue Presbyterian Church. It has a tradition of calling to its pulpit ministers who are determined to be relevant to community life, and its members themselves have, individually and collectively, worked in every area of the city for its improvement. Furthermore, at a time when the church has been called the most segregated of American institutions, this church has been thoroughly integrated for more than a decade. And it maintains this policy with pride. It has also been meticulously faithful to the Gospel. Yet its fidelity to the traditional faith has been free of the anti-Semitism and anti-Catholicism that have been the shame of so many Protestant churches. The North Avenue Presbyterian Church is the kind of church that makes one proud to call himself a Christian. It has been a great privilege and honor to serve this congregation, and I proudly and gratefully dedicate this book to:

The Congregation of
THE NORTH AVENUE PRESBYTERIAN CHURCH

CHAPTER ONE

Heavy Eddie was nervous. It wasn't the weather, because it was a perfect spring day, warm and breezy. It wasn't that his business was slipping, because it was about the same as usual: some coffee and sandwiches sold along with a heavy volume of numbers and horse action. Actually Eddie's nervousness was a regular thing, associated with the hour of the day. Every day, shortly after the lunch period, Heavy Eddie had to get the numbers action out of its hiding place and put it together into a package for the pickup man. And this was the tricky part of the day. If there were a sudden raid at this point, all the guile and cunning he had exercised for so many years would not be able to keep him from arrest.

It wasn't that Heavy Eddie had a jail sentence to fear. A light fine was the usual punishment. But there was a new police commissioner in the city who had been distinctly unfriendly. And there had been more federal activity in New Rochelle ever since that minister sounded off. In fact, there had even been a raid by T-men, and Heavy Eddie had suffered the supreme indignity of being arrested, an experience rare in his life of crime. So Heavy Eddie was nervous, and he sighed for the old days when the town was friendly and cops slapped him on the back and had coffee in his place. He moved about his luncheonette, staring out the window, mopping the counter with a greasy rag, arranging chairs.

A tall, thin, swarthy man with a thin moustache and a mouth full of decayed teeth came in. "Give me a sandwich to go," he said.

"Sure, Dino, sure," Eddie answered. He went to the backroom and, partly hidden from view, he began to slice ham. The sandwich completed, he reached under the table and took out a packet of numbers slips and put it on the bottom of the paper bag, the sandwich on top. "Here you are, Dino," he said, handing over the sack. "Have a good lunch."

Dino grunted and pushed through the door, got in his car and immediately gunned the old rattletrap toward Main Street, where the light was conveniently green. He crossed the intersection and vanished in traffic. Inside the luncheonette Eddie became his usual jovial, loud, and crude self again. He was safe from arrest for another day at least.

Down the block several persons stood at a bus stop. As Dino drove away, one woman turned and walked quickly toward a big Pontiac station wagon, nodding twice as she came. I switched on the engine and at the same time spoke into a radio.

"OK, girls, he just left and is heading out across Main. Let's go." Immediately a car out of sight around the corner roared past with two women in it, big-eyed children in the back seat.

"Take it easy, girls, you'll alert the whole neighborhood." Anne had taken over the radio and was snapping out orders while I drove. As we rounded the corner to pass the luncheonette, another car full of women came up behind the first car.

"The light's turning red. He's going to get away again!"

"Relax, Alice," said Anne. "We'll get him. We know where he's going. He must be headed either for Church Street or the Daitch store. You and Sue take the Daitch, Grace and Honey take the Arnold Constable lot, and Fay and I'll take the Church Street location."

All three of us drivers raced our engines and thundered ahead the moment the light changed. The other two screamed around the block onto Main and disappeared in the traffic. I sent the white station wagon down Centre and then cautiously nosed out onto Church.

"See anything, Anne?"

"Nope, he's not here, Fay. Let's get to the Daitch."

I stepped on the gas, careening around corners toward the lot of the Daitch store. As we came to North Avenue where the store was situated, we met the pickup man head-on.

"Good grief! He'll see us. Hide your head with that newspaper—

No, he's going on, he didn't notice us. . . . Look, he's turning into the lot again. Get the girls and see if he has been there yet."

"This is Able to Baker. Has our man been there yet?"

The radio crackled. "He came in once, saw his contact, but couldn't find a parking place and left," Honey reported. "Now he's pulling in beside his man. The number two man is driving the T-bird. Now he's making the pass. They're talking for a moment."

Anne's hand trembled as she picked up the microphone, but her voice was steady. "Beautiful! Stay where you are, Baker, until he passes you. Charlie will pick him up in front of the church and we'll go around on Main and get in front of him."

Honey said, "Ten-four," and then giggled self-consciously at being uncharacteristically businesslike.

Anne and I drove around to Main and got through the light on Locust just in time to hear Sue gasp into the radio, "Able, he's right behind you and the two of us are behind him. The poor man can't move without running into one of us."

"And what could be more beautiful? Just don't let him see you using your radios. Oh, oh, he's passing us."

The blue T-bird saw a hole in the traffic and shot away at high speed. I roared after him. "I hope he didn't recognize me," I said.

"Your own mother wouldn't recognize you with that cap, the dark glasses, and that horrible shirt," Anne scoffed. "These bums have never seen you in anything but a black suit and clerical collar."

Over the radio we heard a mournful complaint, "I'd hoped this car would last for another year, but at this rate it'll be burned out today."

We were racing through traffic after the T-bird, leaving behind us a string of annoyed drivers honking their horns and shaking their fists.

"He's turning left on Stephenson—and the light's changing. We'll lose him," Anne almost screamed.

"The heck we will."

I gunned the Pontiac and went right through the red light. The T-bird was speeding ahead; apparently the driver was unaware he was being tailed by a contingent of the North Avenue Irregulars.

"You girls wait at the light and we'll let you know the direction he goes. But you'd better move, because he's going like a bat out of hell. Oh, oh, he's turning right on Palmer."

"We've got the light now and will catch you soon."

3

My hands were sweaty and my stomach as hard as a ball bearing as we rounded the corner onto Palmer. Anne was clapping her hands and shouting, "We've got him, we've got him, we've got him! If we can only stick with him long enough to pick up number three. Don't lose him! Get closer! Step on the gas—don't get too close—drop back a bit."

The radio crackled and we could tell by the voice it was Sue. "Baker, did you see that?"

Honey came over clearly, "What?"

Sue again. "That woman? She came out of that duplex in the kookiest pajama outfit and picked up her mail and—."

Anne grabbed for the microphone. "Will you girls stop that and keep your minds on crime? Get up here fast. We're going to have to dròp back or he'll know we are following him."

"We're coming, we're coming. If you wouldn't drive so fast, we'd have caught you by now."

"But, Sue, we'd lose the man if we drove more slowly."

At that point the T-bird made a sudden turn onto Potter Lane, where there was a construction site. I yelled, "There he goes, Anne! Tell the girls so they will know where to turn—*oh, no!*"

Ahead was a sign that said, "Blasting, turn off two-way radios." Now, I have never understood just why it is that blasting requires a cessation of radio transmission in the area, but I had visions of some workman setting a dynamite charge and then being blown to bits as we radioed back to the girls to make a left turn on Potter. So we snapped off the radio and followed the T-bird over the hill and right onto Fifth Avenue. Just as we topped the hill we heard Honey say, "OK, Able, we are on Palmer. Where are you? Able, Able, where are you? Come in, Able."

The moment we were on Fifth Avenue and away from the demolition men, Anne flicked on the radio and said, "Baker and Charlie, this is Able. Do you read me?" Silence. "Baker and Charlie, do you read me?" Silence. The hills between us blotted out radio transmission, and two of our cars were on their way to Palmer, lost to the effort. Anne groaned. "If that bum only looks in his rear-view mirror once he'll know we've been behind him on four turns and we're through with this tail."

But the fat Negro driving the car wasn't looking in his mirror. He was enjoying the experience of driving a powerful car and smoking a cigar, which he seemed inexplicably to enjoy. I say inexplicably because it was so foul that we could almost have followed him from the smell alone. We saw him through his rear window taking long drags on the thing and blowing out clouds of smoke as he cruised through the City Park section of New Rochelle and into Larchmont.

"Oh, oh, he's coming to the Thruway entrance—no, he's passing it—look! He's going into the lot of that supermarket. Don't let him see us."

I wasn't sure what Anne wanted me to do about not letting him see us. We had no choice but to drive past the lot as he pulled into it and swung around, facing us. But he was looking for his contact and didn't even glance at us. I drove past the lot and swung around behind a bar on the corner.

Anne hopped out immediately. "There's a telephone booth in that store. I'm going back and watch from there to see what happens. The Green Pea Kid ought to show up pretty soon, and when he does I'll come back and we'll tail him. While I'm gone, see if you can raise the girls on the radio."

I muttered something like, "OK, OK, chief," and obediently began to say, "Baker and Charlie, this is Able. Do you read me?" Silence. "Baker and Charlie, do you read me? This is Able. Please say you read me. We need you."

I don't know whether that entreaty had anything to do with it, but suddenly there was static and a garbled message that went something like this: "Sputter sputter Baker to—sputter sputter Charlie—where—sputter."

I punched the button again. "Baker? Charlie? This is Able. Do you read me?"

This time the message was clear. "This is Charlie. We read you loud and clear. Where the devil are you?"

"I'm behind the Thruway entrance in Larchmont and we've still got the guy. Get over here fast."

"Roger."

"Okay, Able, we've pulled into a shopping center lot right beside the Thruway entrance. Where are you? Good Grief!"

My heart turned cold. I had a vision of some thug walking over to the car and slugging one of the girls in Charlie. "Charlie! What is it? What is wrong?"

Sue's furious voice sputtered at me over the walkie-talkie. "Why, some Italian-looking kid in an old green Plymouth just pulled right into my parking place. I'm going to get out and give him a piece of my mind."

"SUE!" Silence. "SUE!"

The radio sputtered again. "I wish you wouldn't yell on the radio. Someone will hear you."

"Sue, for heaven's sake, that kid in the green car is the Green Pea Kid, the number three man. Leave him alone and get into another place."

"All right, all right, but he certainly is rude. You should have seen the way he—why, there's Anne. Shall I call to her?"

"Sue, are you out of your mind? Sit still and wait until we find out what is going on."

"The kid in the green car is back now and is backing out of his place. He didn't use it very long after wanting it so badly."

"SUE! Will you forget that! Is the blue T-bird leaving?"

"You mean the blue car with the man in it you tailed? He left a couple of minutes ago, and now the green car is leaving, too."

I snapped on the ignition and screamed at Sue, "Charlie! Stay in the lot until Anne and I pass you, and then you girls follow us. Don't leave until you see us pass the lot. That kid might have noticed you."

"He'd have noticed me if you hadn't called me back, I'll tell you."

Anne came around the corner at a dead run and jumped into the car as I stepped on the gas. From the back seat a plaintive little voice said, "Mommy, Mr. Hill talked so loud he woke me up."

"All right, dear, it's all right. Mr. Hill is excited."

"Is that why he yells on Sunday mornings?"

"Hush, dear, and go to sleep again."

"OK."

We hurtled around the corner and saw the Green Pea Kid pulling onto the Thruway headed southwest.

"Beautiful! Beautiful! He's heading for Yonkers as sure as anything. Oh, is this perfect! He has no idea we're behind him. Play it loose and drop back as far as you can." Anne was flushed and squirming with excitement. She clicked on the radio. "Charlie, I saw you girls turn into the lot and thought you were going to run over the Green Pea Kid. Where is Baker?"

"I would have run over him if Fay hadn't stopped me. Baker went to check out the diner and is out of radio range. We'll have to go it without them."

After a few minutes, we dropped back and let Sue and Alice take over the tailing.

"He's exiting onto Pelhamdale Avenue."

"I read you. Stick with him until you feel he may have looked you over in his rear mirror. Remember not to get too close at red lights and try to keep a couple of cars between you and him."

"Check."

Eventually, after passing through Pelham, our quarry turned onto the Hutchinson River Parkway and then onto the Cross County Parkway. By that time the girls were squealing with excitement. It was obvious that he was headed for Yonkers. We had always suspected it, but now we knew: the New Rochelle numbers operation was no local thing—it was part of a syndicate, an all-county organization.

A little head appeared over the back seat. "Mommy, how can I go to sleep when everybody is yelling?"

"All right, darling, you don't have to sleep if you don't want to. You can go to bed early tonight."

"Able! This is Charlie! He just looked me over in his mirror and he's exiting onto Yonkers Avenue. You'd better catch him. Hurry!"

"But, Mommy, I don't *want* to go to bed early. I want to watch TV tonight."

"Well, you can't watch TV tonight. There he goes—turning left on Yonkers Avenue! Hurry! We'll miss the light."

"You told me I could watch 'Maverick.' Waaaaa!"

"Able, this is Charlie. Do you read me?"

"All right, you can watch 'Maverick.' Yes, Charlie, I read you. What do you want?"

"What's *your* trouble? You don't have to be so grouchy. I forgot to get gas. I didn't realize we would be driving this far and I'm running out of gas."

"You're what?"

"Well, I'm awfully low. Can I stop and get some and catch up later? Alice has to go to the bathroom anyway."

"You are not permitted to go to the bathroom until we are finished and you may not run out of gas."

"Mommy, *I* have to go to the bathroom."

"You do not. You just heard her talking about it. Careful, Fay, he's turning on that next block. And I think he looked back at us."

"OK, have Charlie come up and take over for a block or two."

"Charlie, this is Able. Will you take the guy for a block or two?"

"Roger."

We turned off onto a parallel street as the little blue Plymouth with the two women in it dashed past us after the green car.

"He's turning down toward you again. Pick him up down there and we'll get him at the next block."

And so it went through a maze of dead-end and one-way streets in the Little Italy section of Yonkers. Now we were behind him and, because the other car was stuck at a light, had to stay on him for two turns. He looked twice in his rear-view mirror and we were certain that he was suspicious. So we turned off and called to the other car to pick him up. But the section was strange to all of us, and the women weren't sure where they were or where we were. Then, suddenly, the radio went silent, apparently because of interference. We were sick. To be so close to finding the headquarters and then to miss it! Our only consolation was that the Green Pea Kid might show himself again and we could pick up his trail.

We turned around a circle through the area, hoping to see him. Fat women stood on street corners yelling at dirty little children. Trucks and cars jostled through the streets honking at each other. Shopkeepers stood outside their tiny stores staring at passing autos, and we were convinced that everyone was a lookout watching for us. We tried to raise Charlie on the radio but got only silence. Finally, we turned a corner and heard this message:

"Able, this is Charlie. Do you read me?"

"Charlie, this is Able. We read you loud and clear. Where are you?"

"We're at a gas station. Alice had to go to the bathroom and I had to get gas."

"You're *where?* But did you ever see the guy?"

"We sure did. We caught him right after you turned off and followed him till he stopped. The address is three-six-oh Old Broadway."

Anne was beside herself with joy. "You *found* it, you *found* it. No wonder you had to go to the bathroom. It's a wonder you didn't wet your pants when you saw him go in."

From the back seat a little voice said, "I *have* wet *my* pants." Anne turned around and found Rachel standing in a pool of water. "Oh, you poor child, I'm so sorry."

We soon joined the other car at the gas station and stood talking in subdued but excited tones of our coup. Passersby stared as we chuckled and guffawed and giggled. Months of work had come to fruition and we could hardly contain ourselves. When Anne came out of the restroom with her little girl, we got ready to leave. But first I called the girls together and sternly lectured them not to talk too loud while we were driving through this section of town, because many of the people were involved in the numbers game. "And, by the way, you might as well turn off your radios so no one will hear us talking and wonder what is going on."

As we got into the cars, however, I remembered that none of us knew our way and that we ought to stick together until we got close to home. Until now, I had been the model of masculine coolness among a bevy of excitable females and they had marveled at me. But when I realized how important it was to stick together, and that I had to tell the other girls before they drove away, I turned quickly and shouted at the top of my lungs, "Hey, you'd better leave your radio on after all. We don't want to get lost—."

"Shhhhh, you idiot." Anne was laughing so hard she collapsed into her seat.

Outside, two men with granite faces and the inevitable fedoras looked blankly at each other. "Radios? Lost? Oh, yeah, the traffic reports."

Somehow we managed to get back to New Rochelle, amid talk of champagne and calling all our friends. When we arrived at the North Avenue Presbyterian Church, we tried to avoid seeing anyone and to be very sedate about getting upstairs to my office. We almost made it, but one dear friend, an elderly woman, caught sight of me. "Mr. Hill—it *is you* isn't it?"

I stopped. "Er, yes, Mrs. Hutchinson, how good it is to see you. How is the arthritis today?"

"Oh, much better, thank you, but I had a bad day yesterday. The cold weather always does that to me. But on a day like this I feel fine. You seem to be enjoying *yourself* today," she said, glancing at the girls stealing quietly upstairs.

"Well, I am taking the afternoon off and have been doing some errands."

"Yes, of course." She thought for a moment. "Well, I *did* want to talk to you about our circle and the Bible study we are doing but perhaps I had better wait until, uh, anoth—."

"Why don't I give you a call first thing in the morning, Mrs. Hutchinson?"

"That would be fine. Now, don't forget an *old* lady."

Her smile was innocent, but I was a trifle shaken by the time I got to the office. When I opened the door there was pandemonium, all the girls talking at once, one child crying, another saying, "Where is the bathroom?" and another sucking his thumb.

"Will you look at him?" my secretary, Jean, said. "The luck of the Irish! The first day he goes out and WHAM! You go all the way to Yonkers."

"You've got to be quiet and let me call Art," Anne said. "He's at home with the other kids and he's going to need the car."

While we shushed each other, she went to the telephone and called her husband.

"Art? Guess what! We—." Silence. More silence. "Oh, you expected me home and . . . Yes, well, I . . . Yes, I *do* know what it is like to get stuck with two kids all afternoon, but . . . I'm coming, I'm coming, but wait'll you hear . . ." Silence. "Well, I'll *tell* you where I've been if you will give me a chance. I'VE BEEN DOING THE LORD'S WORK!" And with that she slammed down the receiver.

"Should we call the other girls first, or Marv?" I asked.

"Call Marv!" said Anne and Alice, but Sue was musing to herself, "Boy! When I joined the church I thought I was settling down to a dull life. But doing the Lord's work can be fun!"

"Oh, come on, Fay, call Marv."

So I dialed the number of the Treasury Department's Intelligence Division.

"Marvie, baby. Fay. Got a pencil?"

"Of course, I've got a pencil. What are you up to now, Fay? What have you and that 'mob' of yours done?"

"Take down this address, Marv, kid. Three-six-oh Old Broadway, Yonkers. Got it?"

"Three-six-oh Old Broadway—Yonkers? What have you crazy people been doing in Yonkers?"

"Marv, old buddy, that's the address of either the bank or at least of some collecting point for virtually all the policy work from Westchester County."

"You're kidding! That's fantastic! What makes you think you've got it?"

I told him briefly what we had done, of the weeks of work and how we had slowly pieced together the system they used to move the work to the area we had discovered.

When I finished, there was a long period of silence. Then he said, "I don't believe it, I simply don't believe it. A minister and a bunch of women. I'll be over to the church Monday morning to get the full story and begin to plan. But I still don't believe it—women, babies—my God, the Mafia is doomed! They'll be laughed out of existence."

Such was the culmination of the painstaking effort by a group of us in New Rochelle to do something about Organized Crime in our city and county. It had actually begun a long time before.

CHAPTER TWO

After Elizabeth, New Jersey, the lovely suburban city of New Rochelle seemed like a haven of beauty and peace. For five years my wife and I had been at the Old First Church in Elizabeth, a city of smoking factories, teeming slums, and a miserable Negro ghetto. I had constantly been involved in a civil rights fight or in a campaign to force slumlords to clean up their hideous houses, and I must admit that, aside from stinging them a couple of times, I had not been too successful with the latter. But that fight did at least prepare me for the one ahead.

New Rochelle, called the "Queen City of the Sound" by residents, is much different from Elizabeth. It is on Long Island Sound and has many miles of shoreline, virtually all of it controlled by swanky private clubs that, of course, keep out the public. Hundreds of yachts bob in its marinas and its beachfronts are dotted with rows of mansions sitting like dowagers above their rolling lawns. The rest of the city is a study in contrasts, most of it acres and acres of magnificent, expensive homes occupied by tired executives and their scrubbed children and lacquered wives. The men arise each day, don their $250 gray flannel or blue serge uniforms, grab their attaché cases, and are driven by their wives to the decrepit railway station, where they stand under a roof that can hardly be said to leak any more than a tree without leaves leaks. Off they go to New York City to man vast businesses in air-conditioned palaces. In the evening, more often than not, these paladins of commerce stagger home at seven, eight, or nine o'clock to greet their children as they go up to bed and their wives as they leave for PTA meetings. On weekends, those who have not already flown to a meeting in London or a sales conference in Denver force their tired bodies out of their expensive beds and into old clothes to wage the perpetual battle with crabgrass. Having thus sufficiently punished themselves for their success in business, they bathe and go out for a night of cocktail parties. If they happen to be members of that declining minority called churchgoers, they will force themselves into their beautiful clothes once more and drive to church on Sunday. There they will either be endlessly congratulated by their pastor for having made it so good, or scolded by him for the same reason, depending largely on what seminary the minister attended. Such is life in one of those places newspapers refer to as "wealthy suburbs."

But that is not the entire story. New Rochelle is also an old, old city. It was established almost three centuries ago by Huguenots fleeing Catholic suppression and adventurers seeking a fortune in the New World. Not too many years later the city acquired a large Negro population, which it still retains. In the beginning most of them were servants, and many are still servants of the rich. This section of the population of the Queen City of the Sound has changed greatly in the past few years. Like Negroes everywhere, they were suitably docile for decades, even centuries. Then came World War II and the Korean conflict and the civil rights movement and all the strange ideas that came with them. The Negroes began to demand that they be treated like people and suddenly arose from their stupor and sued to remove what they charged was de facto segregation in the schools. That charge seemed terribly unfair and unkind to their white masters, even though the school district did have only a handful of white children and virtually all the Negro children. The courts thought differently. After a long, bruising fight the city lost, and an important chapter in the fight for full rights for all Americans was written. In the process, New Rochelle lost much of its fine reputation as the Queen City. People began calling it the "Little Rock of the North" and worse. Many white families sniffed, the women gathered their minks about them, and they silently stole away to new mansions, larger and with lower taxes, in other suburbs or exurbs.

New Rochelle also has other minorities—indeed, it is a city of minorities, for there is no majority. It is about one-third Jewish, one-third Catholic, and one-third Protestant, of whom at least half are Negro. Most of the Jews are well-to-do and live in the northern district. They tend to be culturally more sophisticated than their Christian brothers, genial, ferociously insistent that their children receive good educations, and effectively active in civic affairs. The Catholics are largely divided into two groups: the rich executives, and the Italians who reside in the West Side. The Italians are close-knit, colorful, hardworking, and, politically, probably the most likely to vote as a bloc. The Protestants, aside from the Negroes, are largely executives, local merchants, doctors, lawyers, teachers, and middle-aged secretaries living in the apartment houses that line Shore Road, Locust Avenue, and Centre Avenue. All the Protestant churches, with the exception of one or two ethnic ones, are declining in membership and prestige. Few Protestants have any interest left in community affairs, where they feel like interlopers among the Jews and Catholics.

The business district is somewhat disconcerting. It has a few of the grand shops one would expect in such a center of wealth, a few department stores, many rug and carpet merchants, and the usual pompous banks. Sprinkled more generously throughout the city are dozens and dozens of little stationery stores, luncheonettes, grocery stores, and bars that seem so poorly stocked and so indifferent in their treatment of customers that one wonders how they exist. I soon found out.

New Rochelle, it turns out, is a city to which many years ago the Syndicate sent its stubby little men with hard eyes, smelly cigars, and vulgar taste to open up illegal gambling establishments. Nobody seems to know when it began—indeed, the city managers, the police, the councilmen, and the city boosters spend a great deal of time denying that they exist, or that New Rochelle has any more of them than other towns as close to New York City. Periodically, for the past 30 years or so, there have been exposés and demands for a cleanup, a flurry of pre-election activity, and then the usual decline into pleasant civic slumber.

But in 1962 something happened to set off a chain of events that forced the officials to modify their cheerful myopia to the presence of the Syndicate.

The Presbytery of Hudson River had hardly proclaimed me duly installed as the pastor of the North Avenue Presbyterian Church when a speeding automobile paused long enough on North Avenue one night to push out the body of a young man by the name of

John Amorosano. Within minutes a motorist had found Amorosano in a pool of blood, his head hideously shattered by two bullets fired at point-blank range. The police immediately speculated that the man had been shot elsewhere and his body dumped here. Witnesses reported that Amorosano had been in a coffee shop in New Rochelle half an hour before the body was discovered, and that he had said, "There will be trouble tonight." Amorosano had previously been arrested on narcotics charges. The police had raided his home in 1958 and found a packet of heroin, a hidden revolver, and a quantity of jewelry they believed to be part of the loot from a Pelham burglary a month earlier. "Johnny Boy," as he was known, had been sentenced to nine months at the Westchester Penitentiary. Not long after that he was arrested by New York City police together with a Bronx man when 52 envelopes of heroin were found in their car. Still later, in 1959, he was arrested with a Yonkers man trying to break into a gun shop. The police said that the pair admitted stealing rifles and guns to pay for narcotics.

At the time of Amorosano's murder, rumors ran wild in New Rochelle. The most commonly believed one was that a local thug had killed him in an argument. It was said that Amorosano had been engaged in the narcotics racket and had not been paid as much as he thought he deserved. So he had threatened to go to the police and "sing" unless properly remunerated. According to this story, the local chief thug and two of his musclemen picked up Johnny Boy at a coffee shop on the promise that they would make a financial adjustment, but with the real intention of delivering him to a couple of professional killers in New York who would see to it that he vanished. Something went wrong, so the story went, and the "top man" whipped out his gun and killed Amorosano on the spot. Then, in a panic, the three threw the body out of the car.

The police labored long and hard on the case, but, like most gangland killings, this one was never solved. It did, however, bring onto the fair city of New Rochelle a "heat" that has never quite dissipated.

Rumblings of scandal followed the murder. Virtually everyone in town knew that the State Investigation Commission, commonly called the SIC, was looking into illegal gambling in five southern Westchester cities and the inability or unwillingness of the police to suppress it. At one point a newspaper reported that the three Republican councilmen of our city had been summoned to White

Plains by the district attorney, warned that the SIC was investigating, and told that the city had better be sure to get things cleaned up quickly. According to its story, the councilmen were told that the situation in New Rochelle was very bad and that, as the majority on the five-member city council, it was their responsibility to do something. When asked if the city manager knew of the situation, so the story went, the district attorney replied that she did. One report of the meeting said that one councilman asked incredulously, "You mean to tell me that police are giving bookies protection?" To which an assistant D.A. said, "We know of one spot that's been operating for 25 years—don't be naïve." The D.A. reportedly interrupted then to say acidly that one street was so bad that it would be almost impossible to run a wiretap because a gambler operated in front of each telephone pole. There was a flurry of activity over this and similar stories, with the Democrats objecting to the briefing and their exclusion from the meeting, and with somewhat conflicting accounts of what had transpired.

In March of 1962, a series of raids took place throughout Westchester County, some of them in New Rochelle, all without the cooperation of local police. Then on October 15, 1963, the ax fell on our lovely city and on four other Westchester communities. On that day, the State Investigation Commission began an open hearing in its headquarters on lower Broadway in Manhattan, and before it paraded a dozen and a half witnesses from New Rochelle —bookies and racketeers, policemen and public officials—whose testimony would soon lift the lid on a Pandora's box of crime and corruption.

The hearing began on a note of careful understatement. The commission's assistant counsel, Joseph Fisch, made a few introductory remarks, recalling that a special agent had already told the commission about placing bets in "some 26 gambling establishments in New Rochelle."

"There was no difficulty encountered, for these gambling places operated openly," Fisch declared. "Our men were strangers and they were in New Rochelle 'cold,' so to speak, with no suspect premises list to guide them. They needed no one."

The first witness was Wilbur Kittle, the balding Negro proprietor of a dilapidated taxi stand that fronted for a numbers parlor. He calmly told of having operated his numbers business there for 12 years without ever being arrested, despite the fact that his place was on the police list of suspected premises. He had been lured into the business, he continued, by Canio DiNapoli, since deceased, who had comforted him with the assurance that he had nothing to worry about from the police. Kittle also said he understood that Canio's labors were under the direction of Tommy Milo, Sr., of Yonkers, also deceased, thus indicating that the numbers operation was part of a large syndicate. When pressed to name the big boss in New Rochelle, he said he understood it was Joseph Tufo, Canio's son-in-law.

Twenty to 40 persons made bets daily with Kittle, who also received "work" from several runners. He took the work at the appropriate time to a parked automobile or on occasion, so he testified, passed it on to Luther or Rebecca Lane.

At this point, Fisch reported that Mrs. Lane had testified under oath earlier at a private hearing that she had been engaged in the policy racket at her stationery store with her husband, then deceased, for about 19 years. During that time she had never been arrested and her husband had been so only twice. Fisch went on to report that Jesse Harvey, another numbers chieftain who had also testified at a private hearing under oath, had admitted to having been engaged in policy in New Rochelle for more than 30 years. He had been arrested twice, only once by the local police.

Perhaps the most interesting part of Kittle's testimony was his statement that he had given money to members of the New Rochelle Police Department. He said he had met George Straehle, a detective, at the Pelham railroad station and had given him money for himself and for Det. Jack Murray. With some surprise in his voice, Kittle related that he had also sent money to Lt. Russell Moody of the Vice Squad but that it had been returned. In any event, the amounts were small, usually $25.

The next witness was a volunteer, an insurance broker whose name was withheld for reasons of security. He claimed to have been a compulsive gambler and to have lost great sums of money on the horses and in dice and card games. He told of participating in "cut" (professional) games with various police officers, including Det. Daniel Kraft, Det. William Skiff, Jr., Sgt. Adrian Rose (who allegedly wore his uniform in the illegal game on one occasion), and a Detective Capparelli. One of the several places where the games were held was a plumbing shop across from the police station. Another was a charming place nicknamed "The Hole" and run by a man called "Piggy" Rossetti. The businessman said he had taken part in the games for five years and had seen officers present throughout that time.

The games included bets as high as $500 at a time, and on one occasion, the witness said, he saw Detective Capparelli borrow money from a gambler in order to continue playing.

Asked if gambling was wide open in New Rochelle, the businessman said that it was and so far as he could remember always had been. Although he claimed to have given up gambling, he said that in the past few months he had visited 10 to 15 places that were operating openly.

Did the witness mean, Fisch asked, that "anyone with two eyes could see it?"

"With one eye could see it," the businessman answered. "In fact, I even once gambled with a blind man. He could find it."

The next witness, who was to have been one of the stars of the show, had recently had surgery and was unable to appear. However, he had shared some of his deepest thoughts with the SIC staff in private testimony that was read at the hearing. Peter Rispole had operated a candy store known as the Blue Room from 1946 until November, 1962. Rispole had been arrested in 1954, late in 1960, and again in 1962 by federal agents. His place was a suspected gambling location and the local police made regular inspections. They certainly knew what he was doing, he said— "they were in there enough."

Rispole said he gave some of his policy action to Vincent Matturro and Steve Corrado, whom he would meet in Mount Vernon, usually around Third Street and the park. He knew, he said, that Matturro was part of the Milo operation.

Rispole then told of one of those little contretemps that occur in the lives of the best protected bookies and explain some of their bitterness toward the police. On May 4, 1960, Sheriff John Hoy of Westchester County called New Rochelle's chief of police and reported the Blue Room as a suspected gambling place. Members of the Vice Squad, including George Straehle, raided the Blue Room and arrested Rispole. "I met him [Straehle] one day and I bawled him out," Rispole continued. "I asked him why he didn't leave me alone, 'Get off my back.'" The result was, Rispole said, that he and Straehle arranged a tip-off signal that Straehle would use to warn Rispole about police action—"cloudy weather." On November 2, 1961, according to Fisch, "Straehle did contact Rispole on the phone, using the signal, the prearranged signal 'Cloudy weather' to tip him off about an inspection or about some police activity the following day." The day afterward, the assistant counsel reported, the Vice Squad sent a special employee to the premises. "Pete Rispole was not there, his brother was there, and a bet was placed with him."

Interestingly, one of the things I have learned in my "studies" of Organized Crime in the past few years is the lack of honor among thieves. Pete had left his brother in the shop, thrown his own brother, as it were, to the wolves. Such treatment of members of the Syndicate by their superiors is commonplace. If it fits their purposes, a man is set up for an arrest or some incriminating fact is given to the police that will lead to his arrest. The picture we get from the movies of fiercely loyal gangsters refusing to tell anything that would harm another gangster is nonsense.

After a brief recess, and while reporters scrambled to get the story into their papers, the commission reconvened to hear the testimony of Detective Straehle, a member of the police department since 1951. Straehle denied ever having discussed any warning with Rispole. He denied calling Rispole at his place and ever having told him, "You better take a vacation tomorrow. You know what I mean?" I was not present at these hearings and have no idea how the witnesses reacted, but this must have been a dreadful moment for Straehle. He must have known from the nature of the questions that the SIC believed it had evidence to prove that he did give the warning to Rispole. (As a matter of fact, its agents had put a tap on the telephone and had recorded the warning about the raid. The SIC maintained that the voices were those of Rispole and Straehle, and eventually both were charged with perjury and brought to trial. The jury found Rispole guilty of having received the call, but was unable to decide whether Straehle had made the call. The trial, which ended in a hung jury regarding Straehle, was of more than usual interest because it was the first in which a "voice print" was offered as evidence. Still later, after a decision by the U. S. Supreme Court regarding the standards for admissibility of wiretap evidence, the case against Straehle was thrown out before a second trial could take place and, under civil service rules, he was reappointed to the police department.)

Straehle did not deny having met Kittle at the Pelham railroad station, but he said that it was to receive not money but information, that he used Kittle as an informant. He also declared that he had visited the home of the man described as "Mr. Big," Joe Tufo, for the purpose of receiving information about a murder.

After Straehle stepped down from the stand, the SIC called an unremarkable little man who had been a policy gambler. Alphonse Ciallela said he ran a one-seater shoeshine stand on Union Avenue and took policy action on the side. He identified his boss as Joseph Calandruccio, sometimes called Joe Cal. Ciallela took bets on policy, bolita, and horses, and had a half dozen runners turning in to him. He did about $300 of policy business on a weekday, $500 on Saturdays, for the astonishing total of $2,000 a week or $100,000 a year. People, he said, used to line up at his stand to place their bets, and he had been arrested only once and then on a fluke. For his endeavors, Ciallela, who worked a six-hour day, was paid $70 a week.

After the noon recess, a patrolman named Salvatore Quatrocchi took the stand, and there followed one of the most moving of the many tragedies being recounted. Quatrocchi had the reputation of being the toughest cop on the force when it came to the gamblers. He had applied several times for the position of detective, passed the necessary tests, but been turned down again and again. When asked why, he said, Mrs. Meagher, the city manager, had told him that a psychological report showed he was not "adaptable."

Quatrocchi fumed for weeks. He learned, he testified, that he had been turned down because he was too tough on gamblers. Then, one day, he saw Thomas Cestone, whom he identified in his testimony as a runner for Joe Tufo, a pickup man who carried the policy work from the betting establishments to the "policy bank." Quatrocchi said he pulled Cestone over and arrested him with the work in the seat beside him, but Cestone protested that Quatrocchi had no warrant and could get in trouble for improperly arresting him. Quatrocchi panicked and let the man go but kept the bag of slips. He drove around awhile, trying to decide what to do. If he turned in the slips, he would be reprimanded for letting Cestone go. If he had taken him in, he probably would have been punished for an improper arrest (patrolmen were not supposed to make gambling arrests). Finally, Quatrocchi said, he tossed the bag into a vacant lot and went home. Within a short time, he said, he received a call from Tufo, who wanted to see him. When they met, Quatrocchi testified, Tufo asked him for the bag and denied that any gamblers had sought to block the patrolman's promotion. Quatrocchi finally told him where the bag was.

In view of Quatrocchi's testimony regarding his own serious error in judgment, he was suspended from the force and ultimately dismissed. The tragic aspect of the case was that many residents who had not followed the entire story thought that Quatrocchi was a "crooked cop" who had been fired for cooperating with the bookies. I came to know this man and was fully convinced of his integrity and honesty. I read through his report book and saw many notes to his superiors that gambling was going on at some of the very places that were later raided by the SIC—including the Blue Room. I even went so far as to give him a sensitive psychological test to determine if there was anything to the claim that he was not "adaptable." I found him to be perfectly normal, with only a hot Italian temper that might be used as an excuse for not appointing him.

The next witness was James Pedicano, who freely admitted to having been engaged in gambling for many years in New Rochelle. It seemed that he once had a problem. "The police department," Pedicano testified, "was always bothering me. They were always going in front of my store, sticking around, see who was coming in, going out. Once in awhile they came in and search the place. People didn't want to come in to give me any play at all." (This incident is interesting because it shows what the police can do if they really want to get rid of a bookie: harass a known gambler out of business.)

Like any other citizen with a problem, Pedicano went to see the mayor, George Vergara. "I thought he could put a little light on the matter," Pedicano said. The mayor, however, refused to do anything and even turned down a $200 campaign contribution.

Vergara now took the stand and told much the same story. He then went on to tell about an uproar he had created in 1957 when he compiled a list of gamblers and gambling locations, 116 to be exact, and demanded action. He had handed over the list to Treasury Department agents, he said, because he didn't have confidence in the police department at the time.

Fisch had Vergara's list and, scanning it, found Kittle's place and many others among the names of those that were still operating six years later.

"Is it your impression," the assistant counsel asked Vergara, "that conditions have improved or changed in any way, in all these years?"

"I have seen no visible evidence of it," the former mayor answered.

Next to take the stand was Det. William (Billy) Franklin Skiff, Jr., a member of the police force for 17 years and a detective for 11. He testified that, among other things, he bought plumbing fittings from Hodge's Plumbing Shop, which was on the suspected gamblers list, had his hat blocked at another suspected place, played golf with a convicted gambler, had lunch at a suspected place, coffee at another, and bought his newspapers at yet another. All the suspected places, he acknowledged, were ones that he was charged with inspecting.

Had he, he was asked, ever caught anybody making a bet?

"They wouldn't dare," Skiff insisted.

"Not in front of you?"

"No, sir."

On that note the hearing was recessed until the next day. City officials, meanwhile, met to discuss the testimony and to assess the damage done to New Rochelle's good name. And in more than one candy store and tavern, racketeers gathered to discuss the "heat" and decide what could be done to keep any more "birds" from "singing." It was obvious that someone in the Organization had talked. Indeed, weeks before, when the investigation was still in progress, the Organization suspected that one policy gambler had squealed, so someone fired a shot through his store window, either to kill or scare him. It failed to do the first but certainly succeeded in the second. Apparently, however, it was too late to stop the flow of information.

The reaction throughout Westchester the next day was, generally, massive indifference. Most of the residents had little interest in their own community except as a bedroom for themselves and a schoolroom for their children. There were some residents, however, who were deeply wounded that the name of their county was being smudged. Naturally, instead of being annoyed with the hoodlums and inept police who had brought about the embarrassment, they took out their pique on the SIC. Justice Frank McCullough in White Plains stated solemnly that there was a "serious and substantial" question as to whether the four SIC members existed under law. All the commissioners' terms had expired April 30. They had not yet been reappointed, but had proceeded with their work anyway. The question had been first raised by a convicted Yonkers bookie, Anthony (Teddy Bear) Calise, who had refused on that basis to answer questions even though he had been granted immunity. At the same time as Justice McCullough made his statement of doubt, he did order Calise, a brother of a Republican member of the Yonkers Common Council, to surrender himself for contempt.

Another voice of outrage was that of Sol Friedman, lawyer for four Westchester police associations, who said that the hearings made a mockery out of law enforcement and held the police up to public ridicule. Before the hearings began the next day, Friedman again rose to say that he had received from the New Rochelle policemen named by Kittle as recipients of gifts sworn statements that they had never accepted any money from such a person. The city's police department, he declared, "has been publicized and pilloried from pillar to post."

The first witness that morning was Stuart Bottinick, who owned a restaurant on Main Street and had been a partner, he said, with Arlindo Fernandez in a luncheonette on Main Street where they accepted policy and horse bets. When their partnership ended, Bottinick took on a new partner.

"During the second partnership, were numbers still taken at the luncheonette?" Fisch, the assistant counselor, asked.

"Yes, sir," Bottinick replied.

"Who was your partner during this second period of time?"

"Anthony Capparelli."

"Anthony Capparelli?"

"Yes."

"C-a-p-p-a-r-e-l-l-i. At that time was he a detective on the New Rochelle Police Force?"

"Yes, sir."

"Was he aware of the fact that numbers were being taken there?"

"To my knowledge, yes, sir."

Bottinick went on to tell how he and Capparelli divided the money from the gambling at the end of the week. He also testified that the policy work was picked up by Cestone, the man identified by Quatrocchi as the pickup man, and said that Cestone worked for Tufo. He said he had the usual agreement with Tufo: in the unlikely event of an arrest he would be taken care of and the bail, lawyer's fees, and all fines would be paid by the Syndicate. He mentioned that a counterman who worked for him on occasion, a man whose last name was Figliuzzi, sometimes carried the action down to the drop.

He and the detectives, Bottinick said, once decided to shift their policy work from Tufo to Jesse Harvey. In fact, he said, Harvey paid them $1,500 to make the shift, but then they got the stern word that if they didn't give it to Tufo they would not be in action anymore. So they meekly changed back to Tufo's operation and returned the money to Harvey, he said.

Bottinick's activities were not restricted to his own restaurant. He liked to gamble on his own and had gone to card and dice games run by Piggy Rossetti. He testified that he had seen Capparelli participating in a game on one occasion.

Then came a more amazing story. When Figliuzzi, Bottinick said, found out about some butter that had been stolen from a Daitch Shopwell, it occurred to Bottinick that they might make a dishonest buck from the knowledge. In addition to using some of the stolen butter in their luncheonette, they went to the Daitch Shopwell officials and offered to tell what was happening to the butter if they were reimbursed $1,500. The person who actually handled the transaction—who, in essence, sold the name of the thief to the company—was, according to Bottinick, Capparelli. The money was subsequently divided evenly among the three, he said.

Bottinick further testified that, after Capparelli abruptly broke up the partnership, he suddenly found it necessary to make a $15 gift to Straehle of the Vice Squad.

Fisch then asked a mysterious question that was later to become important. "In the back of your store, do you have any equipment that wasn't used too much, like a coffee urn or a big coffee pot?"

"Yes, sir," Bottinick acknowledged.

"Was it something that you rarely had access to? You hardly went to and—."

"It was an old coffee urn, just sitting in the back of the store, which I never used."

The next witness was Richard A. Figliuzzi, Bottinick's counterman. In 1946 he had been convicted of second-degree robbery in California. He had also served time for possession of marijuana and for forgery. Figliuzzi confirmed what Bottinick had said about policy and horse betting in the store, and also told of participating in illegal dice and card games with Capparelli.

His version of the stolen butter story was about the same as

Bottinick's, but he added a few interesting details. They had entered the store where Figliuzzi worked and where he had found the stolen butter, but they had entered it at night and illegally. Figliuzzi went on to say that after they had arrived at their plan to disclose the name of the thief to the Daitch Shopwell managers it was Capparelli who handled the affair.

Figliuzzi then related a bizarre plan, allegedly conceived by Capparelli, to have Figliuzzi burglarize the home of Joe Tufo, whom he identified as the man who "owns a whole numbers operation in New Rochelle." Figliuzzi testified that Capparelli had told him that he had been to Tufo's house on various occasions, was on very friendly terms with him, and knew that Tufo kept a great deal of money in the house. The robbery, however, never came off. Figliuzzi said he had looked the place over and decided that it was too well lighted.

Under questioning, Figliuzzi told of how Capparelli had given him a Colt .45 and how he had kept it in that empty, unused coffee urn. He had intended to use the gun for a robbery, but had no ammunition. Capparelli, Figliuzzi further testified, had given him another gun as well, a sawed-off .22, but "I never fulfilled the original reason I got it for . . . [and] threw the thing in a bay, or whatever it was."

When asked where the detective had gotten the automatic, Figliuzzi said he did not know, but that it was in a manilla envelope with an inscription pertaining to the New Rochelle Police Department.

The witness had also talked with Capparelli, he said, about a woman who used to come to the luncheonette. She worked for a trucking company and, Figliuzzi said, the detective had informed him that she went to the bank on Wednesdays to pick up the company's payroll. Capparelli suggested, said Figliuzzi, that he arrange a robbery, but there was a complication: the woman knew him and would be able to identify him. So Figliuzzi got himself a partner, a Herb Martin, who was actually to make the snatch. Capparelli, the witness said, was to verify that the woman had in fact withdrawn the money.

The robbery never came off. Martin didn't show up at the crucial moment and, because of an SIC wiretap, the entire scheme was exposed. Capparelli was subsequently demoted from detective to patrolman because of his involvement, and, after the SIC hearing, dismissed altogether.

The commission next called Capparelli to explain his side of the incidents. He denied participating in the games described by earlier witnesses and denied knowing that Bottinick received any bets at his luncheonette. He said he had once observed a dice game at Hodge's Plumbing Shop, adding that Sergeant Rose, out of uniform, was there also, but said that the game had not been a professional one. Regarding his partnership with Bottinick, Capparelli said that it had been approved by the police chief. He also said he knew Figliuzzi and had been willing to have him help out at the luncheonette because he thought the ex-convict was "straightening himself out."

Capparelli denied ever having been at Tufo's house and having talked with Jesse Harvey about changing any policy action from Tufo to him. He admitted investigating the theft of the butter from Daitch Shopwell at an out-of-town warehouse, but said it was done in his spare time at the request of Bottinick's brother, who worked for the chain. He had checked with Captain John Meehan, his immediate superior, before accepting the job and had received his approval. When he had ascertained the facts, he said, he had given them to the president of the Shopwell chain and had received his money in cash, which he then divided three ways with his two partners in the investigation.

According to Capparelli, Figliuzzi asked him to cover for him in the aborted payroll messenger robbery. The policeman "wasn't too surprised" at the request—"He was an informant. They ask you a million things. Why be surprised at a pocketbook snatcher?"

Capparelli insisted that he "wasn't going to permit anything. I was going to effect an arrest." And he saw no element of risk involved to the woman. Asked if he had reported the plot to his superiors, Capparelli answered, "No."

As I reread the transcript of the SIC hearings in order to write this account, I was overcome with sadness about Capparelli's testimony. He was a much-decorated officer commended for his courage, and he had a fine wife and a large family. He could have had a splendid career. Sadness has often come over me in this fight. So many innocent people—wives and children—were destroyed. What must it have been like for Capparelli and Straehle to go home after these hearings and face their children? Psychologists have helped us to understand the social forces at work on the slum child and the emotional strains on the child from a broken home, but they have failed to explain men like Capparelli. Those almost unbearable biblical sentences about men choosing darkness instead of light and about the way that leads to salvation being hard and narrow are true, terrifyingly true.

About the next witness we need feel no sadness. Joseph Tufo is reputed to have been in the rackets all his adult life. He was once arrested for possession of a policy slip, but since then has managed to stay out of jail. One of the reasons is his refusal to talk. At the hearing he pleaded the Fifth Amendment against self-incrimination more than 20 times. Declining to say what his business or occupation was or if he knew the late Canio DiNapoli, the late Tommy Milo, or Vincent Matturro. One hears about these men who flatly refuse to answer all questions, and it is unsettling. The rest of us live such relatively open lives, chatting with friends about our work, sighing about what a tough day it was at the office, and grumping about not getting a raise from the boss. What must it be like to live all one's life in secrecy, checking constantly to see if there is a tap on the telephone or anyone watching your comings and goings? What is it like to be identified everywhere one goes as a gangster? What does it do to a man's soul?

To continue with the SIC hearings, Lieutenants Theodore Buderman and Michael Lynch followed Tufo to the stand to tell about the procedures in the police property room, which clearly had sloppy rules. There was no possibility, they acknowledged, of checking whether Capparelli did in fact give a pistol from the property room to Figliuzzi.

There were, in turn, followed by Mrs. Betty A. Meagher, one of the few female city managers in the United States. She had had a remarkable career, rising from secretary to her present exalted position. Mrs. Meagher said she had had a hearing held concerning the information received about Detective Capparelli, and that he had been found "not guilty" on the charge of gaming in a suspected place and associating with known criminals. He had been found guilty of failing to report a crime and of engaging in a game of craps in a suspected place. The penalty was loss of pay and allowances for three months. Subsequently, Capparelli was relieved of his assignment as detective and returned to duty as a patrolman. The charges against Capparelli, she declared, were "very serious." (Later, after the hearing, the city manager, who had immediately suspended and fired Quatrocchi for his gaffe, suspended and ultimately discharged Capparelli.)

An interesting aspect of Mrs. Meagher's testimony was her

response to questions about the Eastman Report. George Eastman, a highly respected police authority, had been hired by the city to study the management of the police department and had handed in his report to the city council in preliminary form in November of 1957 and in final form in February of 1958. He had found the department in dreadful shape, with serious internecine strife and low morale. He also said, although he was only studying the efficiency of the police, that "there is . . . substantial indication that gambling is a serious problem." Asked what she had done with the Eastman Report, Mrs. Meagher reported that she had asked her personnel officer to make a survey of it and make suggestions as to what parts of it should be adopted. (Later, when the controversy over police ineffectiveness boiled up again, she asked the city council for $10,000 to conduct a survey of condition in New Rochelle to see if the SIC revelations were true. Her proposal was much ridiculed as a study of a study.)

Mrs. Meagher told the commission she was satisfied with the police chief's enforcement of the gambling laws, but would have to re-evaluate his performance after reviewing the testimony of the hearings.

The next and last person to give testimony about New Rochelle was the police chief, Edward F. McCaffrey, who began as a police officer in 1940 and had been chief since 1958. He was closely questioned by Fisch about a written report, anonymous in nature. The dialogue between the commission's assistant counsel and the police chief went like this:

"It is a complaint, a written complaint, about police officers participating in a crap game at Hodge's Plumbing Shop. Is that correct?"

"That is what this letter states, yes."

"So you had official notice of this before the hearings, Chief. Isn't that correct?"

"Pardon me?"

"You had some written complaints about this before the testimony which was adduced at these hearings."

"Had I received this before the hearings?"

"Yes."

"Surely. It is a 1960 date."

"What police officer is mentioned in that complaint?"

"They mentioned 'your favorite boy, Murray.' I would assume

that they are referring to who was then Detective John Murray, now Sergeant Murray.".

"Who investigated the complaint?"

"The Special Service Squad."

"Who in particular, specifically? You have his name on the lower lefthand corner."

"Detective Murray is the signature here. But it is countersigned, and all investigations in that squad are supervised and directed by Lieutenant Moody."

"You had Detective Murray investigate himself, in effect? . . . There was testimony yesterday about Detective Straehle. Did you ever receive any complaints or read anything adverse, seriously adverse about Detective Straehle?"

"In writing, or in any manner?"

"Any manner which was serious enough to warrant attention."

"I believe at one time Mr. [Joseph] Gagliardi, who was then district attorney of Westchester County—and I have forgotten the years—it would have been in 1957, 1958, I believe—advised me that I should use care and caution and check my Special Squad, and I believe he at that time mentioned Detective Straehle."

"He warned you about Detective Straehle?"

"No, he admonished me that I should use care and caution and supervision over Detective Straehle."

"What care and supervision did you exercise?"

"I asked Mr. Gagliardi if he would offer me or present me with anything factual, with which I could conduct an investigation, which would be the basis of a removal or a recommendation for a removal or any other disciplinary action. And there was none forthcoming. I had a discussion with Lieutenant Moody, and at my next staff conference I discussed it with all the commanding officers."

"You weren't stuck with Straehle on the Vice Squad, were you? You could have requested that another man be placed in there?"

"I could have made that recommendation. Had I desired it, yes, sir. . . . The reason I didn't, sir, is because removal of a police officer from a position such as that would necessarily cast a reflection, and unless there was some justifiable reason or basis, I wouldn't feel that I could submit such a recommendation to my director, unless I could support the reason for my recommendation."

"In 1957, I believe, in the Eastman Report, a recommendation was made that men of the Vice Squad ought to be rotated. . . . Do you agree with that recommendation?"

"That was a good recommendation."

"Could you have rotated Straehle out, without casting any aspersions on his integrity?"

"That would be one way that that situation could have been handled, yes, sir."

Fisch turned to another issue, concerning Murray and Straehle again, who had worked as bartenders in violation of a state law. They had never asked permission to do such work, the chief acknowledged, and he had not instituted any departmental disciplinary action against them.

And so New Rochelle's part of the hearing was completed. Later, many citizens were to maintain that our city was no worse than others and, certainly, when compared to the cities of Port Chester, Mount Vernon, and Yonkers, they were correct. Which is a sad thing to say about *those* cities. This does not excuse the Queen City; it only shows what depths of corruption and inefficiency we have come to tolerate in many of our communities.

The city administration immediately suspended and later fired Quatrocchi and Capparelli and suspended Straehle. Eventually Murray was mildly punished. But on the whole not much happened. Of course, the Westchester newspapers carried the story in headlines, but it soon disappeared and residents of one of the country's richest counties sank deep into their cushioned apathy.

New Rochelle was in the midst of a mayoral and councilmanic election, and the hearings became grist for the mill, but almost nobody seemed to be very upset. An exception was former Mayor Vergara, who kept the issue alive for awhile. There was also the mild flare-up of anger by Democrats over the meeting with the district attorney attended by the three Republican councilmen. The most vehement protest came from the Liberal candidate for mayor, Louis Yagoda, who demanded an investigation, but nothing came of this either, because the Liberal party is not strong in New Rochelle.

On October 26, there occurred an incident typical of the Westchester approach to the problem. Instead of taking vigorous action against the police departments that had failed in their duty, many in the county turned their attention to attacking the people who had disclosed the corrupt situation. *The Standard Star*, New Rochelle's substandard news sheet, carried the headline, "D.A. ASKED TO PROBE 'EAVESDROPPING'." It seems that lawyers for Yonkers police groups had been infuriated to find that the SIC had verbatim transcripts of conversations between some of the persons whom the lawyers described as "these excellent citizens." Now, it is not particularly remarkable that such a probe should be requested, because in this day and age it is standard for any citizen who is accused of anything to attack the investigating body that makes the charge. There is a good chance that some time during any investigation the police will have made a mistake and thereby opened the way to an appeal or to having the charges thrown out of court. That is understandable. What is remarkable is that *The Standard Star* should give headline space to it. But, then, it was only the first of many remarkable performances by that sheet.

There was one fine response, by *The Herald Statesman* of Yonkers. In a splendid editorial on October 15, 1963, it said:

"No matter who is or is not punished, no matter who is or is not exculpated—the job of cleaning up the Augean Stable belongs to good citizens—and if they shirk the job it will never get done. Indeed, the jungle of crime will move in on us further.

"We hear outcries that the exposure of apparent gravest corruption in our police department comes at 'the wrong time,' that the lifting of the slabs to show what crawls underneath is 'just before municipal elections.'

"What better or more appropriate time for the sounding of an alarm clock with any hope of getting public attention and perhaps some remedial application?

"What is essential, what is imperative, if there is to be any relief, is some effective moral reaction in Yonkers and in Westchester, some clear indication that there is public anger, that there is public revulsion, that there is determination to weed out of government and politics those who have betrayed their public trust for personal or party financial gain.

"It is widely conceded that the individual who places bets with bookmakers and policy numbers gamblers is not only victimized by crooked operation and often crooked races but that his money is used to finance the rape of his daughter, the 'hooking' of his children into the wreckage of a life destroyed by narcotics, the burglarizing of his home and business, the robbery and mugging of his person, the community debasement of prostitution, and the incidence of murder.

"But the Gargantuan evil is silence—silence on the part of the ignorant patron of the bookie who likes to pretend that it is only the quarters and dollars of other persons who are corrupting his home and his community, not his own—the silence of public officials and of political leaders, who fear that the flood of green stuff to themselves and their parties may be interrupted—the silence of clergymen who are expected to provide moral leadership—the silence of physicians who know the deviltry of narcotics addiction among young people—the silence of leaders in industry and labor who might work wonders against organized crime which undermines and corrupts both.

"It is inescapable that, before there can be political reform, before there can be proper and lasting cleanup of the cesspools of crime and law defiance, there must come an expression of moral principles from the community—first from its leaders and then from the people at large.

"Without the moral expression, the state hearings and the tenderhearted coping with crime in the courts are but meaningless rituals which, indeed, may actually prove helpful to organized crime when the winds of inquiry calm down.

"So long as ordinary citizens—husbands, wives, and young people —sit by as silent onlookers, who refuse to believe that the massive invasion of crime and the corruption of our police and government and politics are real and menacing to the individual, so long will the situation grow worse and worse, without abatement."

CHAPTER THREE

I was relatively new in town and knew nothing about Organized Crime. I had read of the Appalachian conference, and Joseph Valachi's testimony was being given before the Senate Permanent Subcommittee on Investigations at the very time of the SIC hearings, yet I knew only that there was something called the Cosa Nostra or the Mafia that seemed to be a national or perhaps international organization. But in Westchester County? The sheer improbability was too much for me, as it was for most citizens.

One man in our city knew better. Samson Gordon, a local businessman and one of those citizens who are interested in everything about their community, from cultural to political events, knew many of the people involved and had developed friendships with others who knew every gangster in town. He began to call a few local leaders about forming a committee to do something about our police department. They met and decided to call in clergymen as a matter of policy—one rabbi, one Catholic priest, and one Protestant minister. I was the minister called because, although I was new in town, the North Avenue Church had a tradition of active interest in the problems of the city. A former pastor had tried to do something about the gambling problem, and other North Avenue ministers had lent their weight to programs of civic improvement.

The first meeting I attended was impressive. There was a lawyer who was cool, rational, and keenly determined to have a better police department. Another, older lawyer showed strength and intelligence. One man in his eighties, a militant reformer, was vigorous and bright. There was also a young banker who was obviously able. The others were civically prominent but displayed little zeal and less intelligence. We chatted awhile and only showed how little we really knew about the situation. Finally, we elected a temporary leader and decided to invite some of the SIC commissioners and their counsel to visit with us and give advice.

A week or so later Karl Vergari, chief counsel for the SIC, and Joseph Fisch, his assistant, came with two of the commissioners. Nothing they said went much beyond the testimony of the hearing because they were careful not to make any innuendoes or irresponsible allegations, but when they left we had a rather clear picture of how desperately bad our police enforcement was.

Then, the next Saturday morning, as I was working on my Sunday sermon, I received a call from Sam Gordon. He asked if he could bring a friend over to see me. When they arrived, I met one of the truly remarkable men of my life. He was a large Irishman, with incredibly blue eyes, a quick smile, and florid face. His clothes were poor and the condition of his nose clearly said something about his dealings with John Barleycorn. But his handshake was firm and his voice was of the approximate timbre and magnitude of a foghorn.

"Well, Rivrind, it's glad I am to meet ya. I have never met a Presbiteerian before—not that I was anxious to."

He roared at his own humor as I smiled rather stiffly.

"Reverend Hill," Sam said, "this is Pete. I wanted you to meet him because you seemed to be sincerely interested in doing something about this situation. This guy knows more about what is going on in our town than anybody else, including the police."

"Pah! The police. What do they know about it? Or on sicond thought, they know, until they are asked. Then they know nothing. I ought to know. I grew up with these bums and there is nobody, Rivrind, *nobody*, who knows as much as I do! For I am a gifted man, gifted indeed. I have a phonogenic memory."

It took me a moment to catch that, but I soon realized that the man was a gold mine of malaproprisms.

"Oh, you have a good memory?"

"Fantastic! I don't wish to boast, Rivrind, but a psychologist once told me that I have psyledelic imagery. Let me once meet a man or see a license number and I never forget it."

"He's telling the truth," Sam interjected. "I have never seen anything like this guy. He knows every gangster and every bookie joint in Westchester County."

So we sat down and Pete began to talk, and, although he couldn't have been as fabulous as he thought he was, his memory *was* fantastic. He reeled off lists of places, gave descriptions of men, told of their fronts, how much action they did a day in policy or horse betting. He told of police officers giving rides to bookies as they went their rounds picking up bets. He related incidents of beatings administered to informers, of robberies of homes, and of dope being pushed on the streets. At first I tried to take notes, but I fell hopelessly behind as he rattled on and on.

"Rivrind, you shoulda seen what they did to poor Angelo when he was late in paying back that miserable loan shark. Two o' their boys who look like Mack trucks came and found him standing outside their house. Now, Tony is big but not very tough. One good punch in his big belly and he'll run like a pregnant jackrabbit. But the other fellow, Al the Simp, we call him, he is tough, tough and nasty. So he walks up to this poor divil and says, in his own inimical way, 'Angelo, Fats wants his dough.' And when Angelo began to say something, he hit him in the belly and then began to kick and slug the poor fellow. Even after he fell down in the gutter they stomped him. It was awful. When they got him to a hospital, they found he had been beaten so awful that he culdn't pass his water. His plumbing was so crushed and twisted that they say to this day he can't have intersectional recourse with a woman!"

By this time the morning had passed and I knew that we had to get this astonishing man on a tape recorder. He could give nothing less than a complete picture of the Syndicate in Westchester County. But we needed someone to help us, so I suggested inviting a lawyer friend to join us and ask questions over lunch.

Pete talked into the tape recorder for three hours, about gangsters and cops and lawyers and bettors and beatings and killings. When he finished, we were dazed. If New Rochelle were half or even one-tenth as bad as he insisted it was, the situation was desperate. He told of brothers of city officials having run policy rings with impunity for decades and of businesses being taken over by the Mob, of payoffs, and of gangsters in politics. Of course, at that point we had no way of knowing how much of it was true. I was staggered.

Eventually, we took much of the information to men at the SIC, and they told us they knew most of it and that the local police did, too. But the SIC, strictly speaking, was not a police force. Its major function was to expose a problem and hope that the community would act on it.

Sam and I steamed and fumed all the way home from the SIC. Then at the next meeting of the committee, I got an idea. I had, at that time, a radio program on Sunday mornings at eight o'clock. It was a typical church program, devoted almost entirely to religious news. I suggested to the committee that I use the program to demand action from the city manager on cleaning up the city.

Nobody objected, or for that matter paid much attention, and that Sunday I made a sharp statement to the effect that it might not be amiss if the police would enforce the law against gangsters as well as they did against parking offenders. As I might have expected, there was no response, which was probably a good index of how many people listened to my program. All the next week, however, I was becoming angrier at the lack of reaction. So I made a still sharper statement, my words based entirely on testimony in the SIC report. The associate pastor of my church, Norman Stanton, suggested that if I really wanted a response I should release a copy of my words to the press. I mentioned to the station manager that I was giving a copy to *The Standard Star,* and he nodded absentmindedly. I made the tape for the broadcast on Friday evening and promptly forgot about it over the weekend.

I considerably underestimated the power of the written word. By the time I reached my office Tuesday morning, after the statement had appeared in Monday afternoon's paper, there was a message that the city manager wanted me to call her. Because I was on my way to a meeting of the presbytery, I decided not to make the call until after lunch. By the time I did call her, she was icily furious and informed me that she had been forced to release a statement to the press without talking to me. So I casually walked out to get the afternoon paper and found page one screaming, "Mrs. Meagher Hits Pastor's Criticism." The long article was among the first of several almost hysterical responses to the criticism I was to level at her administration. High up in it she made a statement that was a classic response to criticism such as mine:

"It must be pointed out that Mr. Hill and other citizens conferred in the Mayor's office early in February. At that time Mr. Hill made certain statements concerning gambling and was asked to furnish the City Manager with names of his informants and places to which he referred. He failed to do so. At the time he stated he would try to do so but as of today he has not communicated with the Mayor, the City Manager or Chief of Police, despite the fact the Mayor and I offered to meet with such persons on their own terms and at such places as they might designate."

Despite its pompous, magisterial tone, her statement was plausible and made headway against me. In essence she was saying that I was "playing Joe McCarthy," waving fake lists and making charges that I was unwilling or unable to back up. She was correct in saying that I had "made certain statements concerning gambling in the city." I had related two humorous stories. One of my parishioners had told me she was having a hard time paying her gas bill because her husband had been to "that bookie" around the corner and lost most of his paycheck. Her remark startled me because she was referring to a time after the SIC hearing and I had naïvely supposed that bookies were at least temporarily shut down. Only later did I find out that, far from shutting down, some of them had come home from giving testimony and opened up their businesses that very afternoon. The other incident concerned a friend who had told me of being in a luncheonette near his business and watching a cop have coffee and read his newspaper while bets were being placed two stools down from him so loudly that my friend could hear the entire transaction from farther away. When the cop had left, my friend asked the bookie if he wasn't afraid he would be arrested after all the publicity from the hearings. "Naw," the man answered. "We seen that kinda stuff before. It'll all blow over. The cops leave us alone."

Mrs. Meagher asked to speak to these two people and I had immediately called them. The lady was aghast. "Talk to her, to the police? Reverend, you don't know what you are saying. I complained to them before, and the next day that bookie asked my husband why I was trying to cause him trouble. You shouldn't have said anything to anybody, pastor. I'll get hurt." The friend only laughed at me. "Do you think City Hall doesn't know what is going on? Don't be naïve, Fay. Whom do you think they would send? Probably that cop I saw in there. Tell her I said to drop dead."

Before I could relay his message I had met Pete and come to see how right my friend was. The police had the information; they only lacked the will to do anything about it.

Mrs. Meagher's grave statement about wanting names and places, and especially to talk to informants, was to be repeated many times. Over and over again I would hear this cry, and then find that the very places I finally named were already on the police department's suspected premises list.

"Mr. Hill is not alone in his claims that gambling exists and should be eliminated," the city manager said at another point. "However, individuals who may gamble and operators of suspected premises cannot be jailed merely on suspicion." Another classic statement, common to every city where Organized Crime flourishes and where officials wish to deny it. A noble word or two about protecting the rights of the innocent and letting 10 guilty men go free, about the difficulty of obtaining evidence, and then just a hint that the critics wish to erect a police state with a gestapo breaking into the homes of good and true citizens merely on suspicion that some wrongdoing has occurred.

"Mrs. Meagher," the article continued, "repeated her offer to Mr. Hill, or to anyone with information on gambling or alleged police complicity, to meet in confidence at a time and place of their own choosing. 'Such a meeting is necessary to remove the cloud of suspicion which Mr. Hill has cast over present members of the police force,' she commented." Another chestnut with which I was to become lamentably familiar. To say anything about the department as a whole casts aspersions on the "many honest and hard-working officers who serve our city so well and often without the recognition they deserve." Of course, there is some truth in that statement. Innocent officers do suffer when the department is criticized, just as I suffer when some fathead of a Presbyterian minister keeps Negroes out of his worship service.

In fact, there was enough plausibility in Mrs. Meagher's statement that I found myself quite miserable for awhile. I wondered if I had been unfair. Then I began to think. Difficult to obtain evidence when an agent of the SIC had been able to walk into 26 places "cold" and place bets? Difficult to obtain evidence when a patrolman could in a moment of pique grab the pickup man and his bag of work? No doubt she *was* willing, as the police chief would be, to see informants. But was that necessary? The SIC had told us that she already knew everything we had discovered from Pete. So when reporters called, I merely said I would answer her on my regular Sunday morning broadcast.

A meeting of our committee was called for that afternoon. As soon as I arrived, I sensed that something was wrong. A few of those distinguished businessmen seemed cool, and nobody said anything about the articles. Finally, when we began, one man made a delicately phrased statement about how he felt that the work of the committee had been damaged by my statement in the press and that he and a couple of others wished to resign.

The tall, older lawyer said, "What for? Everyone knows that what he said is true and that nothing is being done. I think we ought to support him."

One little businessman with a long nose that dripped constantly said in a shaking voice, "When I joined this committee, I had no idea it would become unpleasant. I have a business to tend, and if the city should become tough about our trash collection it would cost us money. I can't afford to offend anyone."

Another pompous man said, "Well, I am not afraid of anyone. But I felt we would go about this in a quiet way, visiting the mayor and the district attorney and calling upon them for action."

"Don't be naïve," the tall lawyer said. "How many times have we already done just exactly that and gotten nowhere."

"Well, I play golf with the chief," said a bouncy little man with a small business and vague political ambitions, "and I am not going to be involved in anything that will make our relationship uncomfortable. We must do this thing without offending anyone."

"Nonsense! Nonsense! You're acting like children. You know perfectly well that we have a major mess on our hands and have had for some time, for years! And what have we done about it? What makes anyone think these rascals will calmly, meekly give up their corrupt habits because we meet with the city manager? We've done it a million times and nothing has ever come of it." The speaker this time was a small Kewpie doll of a man in his eighties, one of the best forces for better government in our city. Stanley Renton had learned about politics from Teddy Roosevelt and had never flagged in his zeal to clean up corruption wherever he found it—and he found plenty of it in Westchester. He had already, on at least one occasion, gone to see Treasury agents about what he personally knew about gambling in New Rochelle. He was one of the most respected and revered men in the city, head of the Charter League.

"Well, I hate to see anybody resign—," the chairman, a young lawyer with a brilliant mind who never lost his cool, began.

"One man has already dropped out!"

"Who?"

"The editor of *The Standard Star,* and you know how much we will need newspaper support."

"We'll need it, but I never for a moment expected to get it. In fact, I was surprised to see him here in the first place," said one businessman drily.

"Gentlemen, I think we should hear from the Reverend Hill."

I spoke for a few moments, giving some of my reasons for making the statement and the thinking behind it. Finally, after more comments about losing business, washing dirty linen in public, and bringing bad publicity on our city, the resignations were withdrawn and the committee went on with its work.

It was my first experience with the depth of the problem in doing anything about Organized Crime. Every businessman in the United States will pound his fist on the table and roar belligerently about "crime in the streets," about kids stealing cars, and about pilfering and vandalism. But mention Organized Crime and their tones become hushed and they begin to caution against getting bombed and having legs broken and about political reprisals.

And now began an amazing sequel to the broadcast. By the time I got back to my office, the telephone was ringing and I had a dozen messages about other calls. This caller—anonymous—yelled at me that everything I had said and everything the SIC had said was true, and everybody in town who was anybody knew all about it. The man reeled off approximately the same list of "wide-open" places as Pete had given and added one or two names of "distinguished citizens" who he claimed were either in the rackets or giving aid and comfort to them. When he hung up, a politician from New Rochelle was ushered in. He bitterly told me of knowing for years about the situation with the gangsters and city officials. Some of his talk was so intemperate that I suspected he was only expressing personal pique rather than objective truth, but later I came to know that everything he said was true. Twice our conversation was interrupted by telephone calls from someone else who wanted to tell us how right I had been and what a mess our city was. New names were added and the same ones repeated, the same places listed. I learned of a bookie named "Bootsie" who operated so openly and on such a large scale that bettors lined up to collect their winnings from him after the races every night. The woman who mentioned him said she had once gone into his stationery store for a newspaper while the payoff was being made and had been dumbfounded at how brazen everyone was. She said that when she asked for her paper the owner was furious. "A paper?" he said. "Can't you see I am busy paying my customers

their winnings? I don't got no time to give you a paper—beat it."
A teacher told me of going into a cigar store to buy a cigar. Inside
were three men busily and openly working on adding machines.
The place had no tobacco except for one cigar so old and dry that,
when the teacher lit it, it almost exploded.

After the politician left, a woman came in to tell me in outraged
tones about what she had seen. When I asked her why she didn't go
to the local police, she said, "Whatcha think, I'ma craze? Tella
police, tella gangsters, alla same." When I suggested the district
attorney, she also hooted. "Maybe he'sa honest. That I'ma don't
know. But everything you tella people in hisa office is known the
next day." She gave the same names and places as the others and
added a few picturesque stories about them, including one about a
man whose house was blown up because he had angered the
gangsters. Then there was the story about the man who had
gambled so heavily that the gangsters took away his delicatessen.

And so it went all week. Residents who were frustrated by what
they had seen called or wrote to tell me what they knew. Many
were anonymous, but many frankly told me their names. One was
a high-ranking official in City Hall, another an appointed, non-
salaried civic leader. There were teachers and writers and housewives and workingmen and police officers and firemen and City
Hall clerks and store owners and salesmen and even children. Each
had the same story, virtually the same names and places. Each
was furious over the inaction of local and county officials and their
denials that the situation existed. And each warned me that I would
be hurt or sued or framed or in some way punished for daring
to challenge the Mob.

"You son of a bitch," an anonymous caller told me one day, "if
you don't keep your mouth shut you'll get both legs broken and
your kids will be run over by a car. Who do you think you are?
A cop or something? We got along just fine until you opened your
mouth."

"Who is this speaking, please?"

"Never mind who this is. I'm telling ya that if you know what
is smart you'll—."

"Look, Buster, if you think I can be frightened by some clown
who is afraid to tell who he is, you're wrong."

"Clown, why you—."

I hung up. I later learned that my wife had received a quieter
threat, merely the warning that I was asking for a slug in the head.

Neither of us was particularly upset by such threats. We figured that, as long as they were talking, they weren't acting.

During this time my one-time secretary, a prissy little woman who resented every task I asked her to do, found her job unbearable. Mrs. Hobbs, as I'll call her here, once received a call from a gravel-voiced man who did not wait to talk to me but began to shout abuse at her. So she rang me on the intercom and said, "A threat for you on 86." Mrs. Hobbs found informants particularly hard to swallow. Often they would arrive early and wait in her office. Now, one takes informants where one can find them and it is rare for them to be distinguished businessmen or delicately perfumed, mink-coated matrons. They tend to be stubby little men with smelly cigars (Mrs. Hobbs did not smoke, detested cigarette, cigar, or pipe smoke, and was happy to inform anyone who did not catch on from her ostentatious coughing that it caused her monstrous pain), or women who were too busy working for a living to worry about deodorants. Mrs. Hobbs would come into my office to announce such visitors with her nostrils literally pinched together with disdain.

My second broadcast in answer to Mrs. Meagher's attack drew a larger audience than the first one. I denied the things she had said but promised to cooperate in any way I could. So, early on Monday, amid the flood of telephone calls from informants, there also came a request from her office to meet with her and the city attorney. That afternoon the three of us had a little chat in which I shared some of the names and places I had been given, and she assured me that swift action would be taken to check out the information. The city attorney, or corporation counsel as he is called here, was there to give advice. Murray Fuerst is a soft-spoken man of modesty that exactly corresponds to his abilities. Both he and the city manager gave me the usual treatment for zealots who wish the city to enforce gambling laws. I was piously assured that they personally knew nothing about bookies and betting operations because they never went into such places. Furthermore, they told me how difficult it was to gain convictions and how hard even to find out where the places were. The stormy waters having thus been properly oiled, I went back to my office to receive more calls and letters from people telling about our town.

Slowly the picture became clear. There was nothing new about the gangland activity. It had been going on for a long time, some of my friends told me, since the 1920's, and old Jesse Harvey, they said, got his "franchise" in the numbers racket from Dutch Schultz himself. As early as 1950, Sol Rubin, a brilliant lawyer, came out of a one-month assignment in city court as judge in a fury at what he had seen—wide-open gambling and inadequate police action. Among other things, he said that a month earlier he had given to Police Chief Walter L. Kirchoff information about the top men in the gambling rackets in the city, complete with names, addresses, and telephone numbers, that had been furnished by a subordinate member of the police department. The information, he said, was promptly permitted to leak out; the brother of one man named in the report knew about it within a matter of hours. Rubin made several suggestions, including one that the Vice Squad be transferred to other duties and that personnel charged with enforcement of antigambling laws be rotated every 60 to 90 days.

Charges and countercharges were leveled back and forth. The then city manager, Ralph D. Klebes, said he had "complete faith in the integrity" of the police department. Chief Kirchoff investigated Rubin's accusations and came up with a ruling of "not guilty."

By September of 1951, less than a year after Rubin issued his charges, Klebes felt it necessary to pledge "a thorough investigation into charges of police laxity in law enforcement here, particularly in gambling." But again silence returned and City Hall went back to its ordered rhythm of slumber and apathy.

I soon discovered that this is the usual pattern in corrupt cities. The police and city officials can afford to ignore charges because nobody pays much attention to them. On the few occasions when demands for action become too clamorous to be lightly dismissed, the police rouse themselves, make an arrest or two, and proudly parade before the public some hapless minion of the Mob, gravely stating that the arrest has been made after months of hard work—and adding darkly that the entire investigation was almost destroyed by the furor raised by certain "well-meaning but naïve individuals." There follow the usual clucks of sympathy and understanding, and people turn with annoyance against the critics, saying, "All you are doing is driving the bookies underground and making things harder for the police." So the reformers relapse into frustrated silence and things return to their comfortable status quo. Usually such storms last only a few days or weeks at most. The local newspaper can almost always be counted on to minimize the affair and to print solemn editorials about how it is more important to support the police in the performance of their dangerous and difficult duties than to make irresponsible charges against them.

However, in 1957 there occurred a disturbance that did not so easily die down. It started with the Eastman Report, the management survey of the police department conducted by George Eastman, superintendent of police for the Port of New York Authority and one of the nation's top-ranking experts in police matters. Eastman not only found internecine strife in the department and sloppily run operations, but also a strong awareness and passive acceptance of political pressures. And he found a serious gambling problem in the city. Mayor George Vergara had sponsored the Eastman study and quickly used it to support his claim that the police were permitting wide-open, large-scale gambling. The issue, unfortunately, was soon hopelessly embroiled in politics, even though Eastman reported that he had met four times with officials of a federal agency and had learned that the gambling was big-time, syndicated, and involved all of southern Westchester. The Eastman Report was accepted and its recommendations adopted, only to be "disadopted" later by the city council and permitted to gather dust until disinterred by the SIC six years later.

Meanwhile, in February of 1958, investigators from the district attorney's office and sheriff's deputies made an important series of raids on alleged policy operations and on a large policy bank, reputed to belong to Tommy Milo, Sr., that handled work from New Rochelle as well as other cities. Luther Lane and Jesse Harvey of New Rochelle were arrested and charged with possession of policy slips—their last brush with the law until the SIC hearings six years later.

There were again raids in the county in April of 1960. Nine men were arrested, some of them fairly important. And in 1961 a $10 million bookie ring was smashed in New Rochelle and for the first time electronic devices for avoiding the payment of telephone tolls were discovered. They were later to appear all over the country.

So, it was an old, old story that gambling had been going on with almost no interference by local officials for years, longer than anyone could remember. It would seem impossible for anyone to deny its existence or question the accuracy of the charges the SIC made. Yet people did—and they questioned what I was saying.

I continued to press for action against the hoods and a cleanup of the police department, and despite opposition I began to make headway. More and more people were paying attention. It was talked about at weekend cocktail parties, and commuters on the morning train asked casually about the minister who objected so strenuously to gambling. Most people misunderstood the issue, thinking that my campaign was against bingo and other forms of gambling as such instead of against Organized Crime, whose chief expression in our city, it was clear to me, was illegal, syndicated gambling. Slowly, however, with each broadcast, we made progress, gathered more information, and alerted more people. The district attorney's office called me in, and two Treasury agents visited us to pick up possible leads for their investigations. Various organizations, such as the Charter League, the Liberal party, Citizens for a Better New Rochelle, and the City Affairs Committee, joined the fray. I spoke at a mass rally of the Protestant Council of Churches attended by about 500 persons, urging prompt action by the city manager to appoint a new director of police.

The weeks ground on and support built up steadily. Even the venerable Woman's Club voted its approval.

But there was still massive opposition. Many, many businessmen were resentful at the bad publicity the city was receiving, and they blamed me and those who had gathered to work with me. Some liberals were scornful. They talked instead about working to eradicate the social causes of crime, such as slums. They do not realize that Organized Crime is not produced by society, as is unorganized crime, but that Organized Crime is one of the causes of such unorganized crime. Gangsters victimize the poor and lure youngsters into crime, giving them dope, and providing a climate of violence and defiance of the law that is devastating in its effect. Some conservatives were in flat opposition to the drive, claiming that nothing could be done and that, if I wanted to do something about crime, I should devote myself to fighting "crime in the streets."

Generally, my congregation was behind me, especially the young people, though some individual members accused me of spending time on crime that I ought to have spent calling on the aged or getting new members. A few said this was not a proper activity for a minister, who should instead be devoting himself to spiritual matters, such as bazaars, bowling parties, and money-raising efforts for the church. Of deeper significance was the feeling that a minister should be soft and gentle. It offended some people to think of a minister of the Gospel as being tough and stubborn. I argued that Amos and other prophets had fought for social justice and rectitude in government, that John Calvin had involved himself in the life of the city of Geneva, and that the early Presbyterians in this nation had been so active in fighting for freedom from England that some Englishmen referred to the Revolution as the "Presbyterian War." The Rev. James Caldwell, pastor of the First Presbyterian Church of Elizabeth during the Revolution, I told them, had been so determined in his work for independence that he was sure the British would try to murder him and had preached with pistols on the pulpit. All to no avail. The image of a minister that so many people have is of a timid, very nice, but rather weak and irrelevant man who indulges in pleasant dreams every Sunday morning so that his parishioners can join him in fantasy and escape the real world for one hour a week.

Of course, the most determined and heated resistance to my campaign came from city officials. The then mayor, Alvin Ruskin, was open to truth, but the city manager and corporation counsel became more annoyed with each day, and more insistent that the city had already been cleaned up. Gangsters talked constantly of how I would soon be transferred by my superiors, or run over by an automobile, or that they would get "something on me." Friends in Elizabeth called one day to say that discreet inquiries were being made about my life there.

Eventually, the city manager began to fight back more sharply. She issued a pompous statement about the inevitable "well-meaning persons" and "blackening the name of innocent people," and so forth, and finished by saying that gambling had been wiped out. To counter that, the next week I went on the air with a good friend and supporter, the Rev. David Coleman of the Salem Baptist Church, who told two interesting stories. He said he had walked into one of the "suspected premises" (which I had listed to the city manager as a bookie joint still operating) and said, "Well, how's the bookie business these days?" Even though he was a well-known clergyman, the chaps had sat down and freely discussed their trials and tribulations with him, grumbling about my "big mouth" and about the fact that you "couldn't trust cops no more."

The Reverend Coleman also told of going into a store near his church where he was known and of waiting to buy some oranges while the owner and another man discussed which horse the latter should bet on. Finally, when the bet had been made, my friend was able to pay for his oranges.

The first store figures in my memory for other reasons. My

sister-in-law, Bernie, came to town during the fracas and asked to see a bona fide bookie joint. So I took her to the suspected place, a stationery store, and told her to walk in and ask for a newspaper.

She found three men working there and finally got the attention of one of them to ask for her paper. He looked at her blankly.

"Paper? Hey, Charlie, you got any papers back there?"

"You know we ain't got no papers. Whyja ask?"

"Lady out here wants one."

"Yeh?" In disbelief he came out from the back room to behold this strange sight. "What kinda paper didja want, lady?"

"Why, a *New York Times*."

"Oh, well, we're out of them. We only got *The News*."

"Then I'll take *The News*."

"Oh." He searched the back room and then reported that he didn't have "no *News*" either, but she could have his copy. Bernie declined his offer and asked for a magazine instead. This time he was visibly embarrassed.

"Well, we don't sell magazines."

"Then I'll take some cigarettes."

"Well, uh, we don't have no cigarettes either, lady," he said, "but would you like a cigar?"

Another time, when city officials reminded me that they could not indiscriminately raid stores, I reminded them that I had given them a list, as had Mayor Vergara, and that it was simple to find the places on it. A blind man had once called and given me a good list. An arthritic, bedridden cripple had done the same, and a child in the second grade had told me of two places operating openly in his neighborhood. Once I visited the city manager with a group of ministers who wished to express their concern about the problem. When she played the "these-places-are-hard-to-find" tune, I offered to take her to one, suggesting it was so wide open that the bookie would probably take a bet from her. I also offered to take her to a place run by the brother of a city official, where a friend of mine was betting daily at my request. She colored mightily, but contained her anger. Within two weeks both of these places were closed.

Whether there was any connection between my remarks and the closings, I do not know. The fight, however, was reaching a crescendo. Each day and night was a nightmare, the telephone ringing so often that I was frantic. My mail was filled with letters about gambling. And through it all I was trying meticulously not to fail in my duties as pastor. I would dash from a meeting with an informant to the hospital to see a parishioner who had just had a stroke. I would have lunch with some associate over strategy and be called away to talk with someone having a nervous breakdown. Each week I lived with the fear of inadvertently saying something on my radio show that would enable my enemies to sue me for slander, or something that I would not be able to substantiate. The management of the radio station, WVOX, was sympathetic and never hinted that I should drop the campaign lest it get them into trouble. My wife seldom saw me, the children were neglected, the snow did not get shoveled as promptly as it should have, and odd jobs around the house went begging. My wife was in agreement throughout with what I was trying to do, but the pressures were great and she often wondered aloud where it would end, if someone would kill me, or if any good could ever come of it when none of the previous reform movements had ever culminated in anything of substance.

Mrs. Meagher at last released her report on the study she had made of the SIC charges and again stated, in essence, that gambling had been virtually wiped out in the city. So the next week I brought on the air a distinguished young Negro minister who told of having seen bets being openly received in two places on the very day the city manager had released her report. Furthermore, he said, he had reported both places to Mrs. Meagher months before but nothing had happened.

Several persons in town were whispering that it would be a good idea to get rid of the city manager, and still she didn't appoint a new commissioner of police. At one point she even called the city council together and asked for permission to spend $10,000 on a study of the SIC study. She was hooted at and ridiculed for this proposal, and we heard little more of it.

Then, one day, the police announced the arrest of a numbers runner, a figure of fun whom everyone hailed as he made his rounds, writing his numbers on slips that he stuffed into his gloves or hat. The police gravely announced that the arrest had come after months of arduous investigative work, which had been jeopardized many times by the public furor. The trick, however, didn't work. The public was too riled up, and only laughter met the announcement. Most people felt, rightly or not, that it was a setup, too obvious.

In an attempt to turn aside the mounting criticism, Chief

McCaffrey announced through the press that he was charging Detective Skiff with incompetence on the basis of his testimony before the SIC. The thought of Chief McCaffrey sitting in judgment on another man, however incompetent, was too much. He himself had a record unblemished by any act of competence or vigor. This diversion was also greeted with jeers.

The mayor became so worried about the tension that he proposed to the D.A. a grand jury investigation to clear the air, but the D.A. turned down the suggestion.

Further doubt about the integrity and efficiency of the police resulted when a group of Negroes, very much embarrassed about a particular bar that catered to Negroes and was the source of one scandal after another, began a campaign to have it closed. They gathered their facts carefully and presented them effectively. The bar was clearly a disgrace. The Westchester Movement, a Negro civic improvement organization, sent a letter to the city manager informing her that it had reported to the State Liquor Authority the shocking conditions surrounding the club. The police chief had earlier told the Westchester Movement that he already had reported all violations and arrests at the club, but the SLA insisted it had received only one report from him. After further inquiries the SLA discovered that there had in fact been 50 more violations that had not been reported over a three-year period. It refused to renew the license and the club was closed.

By this time the tension in the city was almost unbearable. Everywhere I went, people approached me about the situation, to tell me how stupid and wrong I was or how right I was. The original businessmen's committee was still meeting with city officials and with the D.A., and was calling for the appointment of a new police commissioner. Everyone was taking sides. Even my fellow clergymen were split in their sympathies. One Protestant minister said cynically that the numbers game was only the poor man's pari-mutuel and that we would never wipe out gambling, as if this were the point. Another informed me coldly that I was bringing disgrace on the city. (One of this cleric's parishioners is a notorious numbers runner who reportedly takes up the collection on Sundays and receives communion when he wishes.) A liberal minister assailed me for trying to "outlaw sin" while he, brave man that he was, worked for the eradication of the social *causes* of crime. Another minister, from another city but in my presbytery, scolded me:

"You should be doing *positive,* kindly things, helping people, not being so negative."

"As Jesus was so positive and kind with the money changers in the temple?"

I had called for the resignation of the police chief long before a commissioner was appointed over his head to do what he should have been doing all along. Apparently this struck some citizens as an unkind cut, especially because I read the chief's own testimony over the air to support my demand for his resignation.

Then I received a letter, an anonymous one, from a woman:

"Dear Rev Hill, I am sorry I cannot tell you my name. I have children in New Rochelle schools and I overheard some shocking facts about gambling and numbers, and it seems that these kids and all the kids at the high school know everything the cops are doing. . . . That luncheonette on Centre Ave near Main Street at the bus stop—where these kids have seen cops come in there and place their bets. One kid said now I have seen everything cops placing bets. that other luncheonette on Main Street near Drake Avenue has been taking bets and numbers for years, there is a man who runs or owns the place he has so much money from the horse betting he has it hidden on account of the income tax. another man who owns taxis has been running games in the cellar of the luncheonette for years every Saturday nite and that detective has been taking liquor from an eating place on Main Street. he has been so drunk that when he does not report in, his pals other cops go looking for him and carry him out of the taverns dead drunk. these kids seem to hear about everything before it gets in the papers. that boy who was arrested at high school for numbers, it is the biggest joke of the year to the kids. the cops know this is going on and who the kids taking numbers are so they arrested one boy big deal the kids other boys are taking bets said. . . If I had the money and could afford to I would take my family out of this town—we are hard working people and stay home and take care of our children. my husband never goes to tavern and bars. . . . I am a mother and I am afriad for other children besides mine. so maybe the places where they gamble and take bets and these men who do such things something can be done about it by people like you. I would like to believe this but I do not."

I had known about the people and places she listed, but nevertheless the letter moved me. Here was a simple woman and man trying to bring up their children properly, with a keen sense of right and wrong, and the entire environment was against them. That was the really deleterious effect should a town fall into the hands of mobsters, the real effect of having charming police officers look the other way while the bookies did their business. However it might hurt a slow-witted policeman or cast aspersions on the honor of efficient and honest police officers to keep up the criticism until there was improvement, the alternative—to permit our town to fall into the hands of thugs—was worse.

Things, however, began to look up. Mrs. Meagher suddenly announced that she was appointing Edward F. Carey, a high-ranking officer from the New York City Police Department, as commissioner of police. The day Carey arrived, television cameras and hordes of reporters were present. His appearance was not terribly reassuring—he was enormously overweight—but his record was that of a tough Irish cop, even if lacking in some of the finesse of modern public relations. He was reported to be an authority on narcotics but not too interested in suppressing gambling. He was also known as a tough disciplinarian, something our police force needed badly.

I immediately congratulated Mrs. Meagher on her choice and pledged my cooperation. A young assistant district attorney assured me that the new commissioner looked very good and that the D.A.'s office would forward him all the information about gambling that I had provided.

I sighed with relief. We finally seemed to have gotten what we had worked for. Some of my informants, however, were not so sure. "It's too entrenched," they said. "Even if he does want to do something, they can survive his presence for a long time. They'll just hunker down and wait till he loses interest. Furthermore, he has had the same department that has so assiduously avoided doing anything for the past 30 years. All his information will come from them and all investigations will be done by them. The prospect is not good."

All of us agreed, though, that we would give the man a chance and would remain silent until he had had a decent time to produce results.

Soon afterward, I received confidential information about some men who were causing a nuisance by buying and selling liquor illegally on Sunday mornings. Drunks would buy the liquor, get smashed, and shout and sing and urinate on the walls of the houses in the neighborhood in broad daylight.

I had a conference with the commissioner about this. I also offered to sit down and relate all I knew about the gambling rackets in New Rochelle and to use my own informants to get whatever additional information he might want. He nodded, and the next Sunday he personally led a raid on the illegal sellers of liquor and made seven arrests. But he never showed any interest in the gambling information I had offered.

CHAPTER FOUR

The first few months after Commissioner Carey's arrival were delightful ones for me. The lawn got mowed, odd jobs around the house that had piled up were gradually dispensed with, and I caught up on my pastoral calling. Norman Stanton and I prepared and executed many plans at the church, including a carefully studied and revolutionary worship service, a zone plan, a reorganization of the boards of the church, a new communicants' class, and some adult study groups. I was able to pay more attention to the presbytery and to civic affairs. It was a relief to turn to matters in which I felt competent and experienced. Those months after Carey came were halcyon, sleepy times.

I also discovered how many experts there are on Organized Crime. After the smoke had died down, people would come up to me at parties and meetings to talk about the campaign.

"Well, Mr. Hill, that was some fight you had there."

"You really made a lot of headlines. I said to my wife, 'Boy, that Hill fellow sure knows how to get his name in the headlines.'"

"Of course, I was with you all the way."

"I want to be honest with you. I don't think you'll ever get people to stop gambling. After all, life itself is a gamble. The numbers game is just the same as the stock market. Don't you think so? I suppose that you are shocked at my morality, but—."

On the first few dozen such occasions, I managed to be courteous and patiently explained my position, but soon I found myself sighing audibly, then my reaction became a wince, and by the end of the year I had developed a tic. It automatically began the moment such phrases as "stock market" and "life is a gamble" were uttered. The only way I could control the tic was by gritting my teeth until they hurt. That gave me an almost constant toothache, but at least I think I avoided offending people who meant well yet had no understanding of the problem of Organized Crime.

"No, I'm not shocked at all. I am not carrying on any sort of campaign against gambling, which I think is largely a personal matter, but against Organized Crime. Furthermore, the purchase of stock, even most forms of speculation in stocks, is constructive in that it makes capital available for plant expansion and . . ."

"Oh, now, Reverend, surely you don't think that some guy who takes his dough down to his broker and tells him to buy a few shares is thinking about plant expansion."

Sigh. "No, of course not. But that is the effect of it, and it is a system which for all its faults has been quite successful in its performance. If you are interested in the comparison of the stock market to straight gambling, Virgil Petersen, the noted authority on Organized Crime, has done a classic study, and it is published . . ."

"Well, anyway, you'll never get people to stop gambling. So why stop? There'll always be gamblers around."

Double sigh, tic begins, grit teeth. "Well, that's true, but I am not trying to stop people from gambling, whatever my personal view of it is. I am trying to stop illegal gambling that is the chief source of revenue for the Syndicate."

"Chief source of revenue? You don't mean that you think that our little town is involved in Organized Crime? I'll be honest with you. I know a few bookies. My stationer is one, and the guy from whom I get my afternoon coffee is one. But they are just local guys, making a few extra bucks on the side. I have known this one guy for years and he wouldn't do anything . . ."

Tic gone but teeth begin to ache. "Of course, I don't mean that he is a Mafia enforcer or anything like that. But I know the man to whom you are referring, and he is part of the Combination. He turns over his numbers work to a pickup man who takes it to the Bronx to a bank operated by some real thugs."

"Oh, Mr. Hill! You're dreaming. He handles all the work himself and has nothing to do with the rackets."

"No. You are wrong. The SIC hearings and other sources have

conclusively proved that there is a vast Syndicate here in West-chester, that it is part of the even larger New York City organization and that it . . ."

"I'm for legalizing it anyway, to take it out of the hands of the Mob. Look at what happened when you moralists voted in Prohibition. It was a windfall for the Mob, and it is the same with gambling."

Teeth aching down to the roots, shoulders drooping. "Again I will have to disagree. First of all, I am not talking moralistically and am not and never was in favor of Prohibition. But gambling is different. It is by nature corrupting on any organized level. It has been legal in almost every state at one time or the other and had to be made illegal because it became such a pest. It 'hooks' more and more people who would never have gambled if it had not become legal. Pari-mutuel betting is what started the current craze with gambling in the United States. Before it was widely legalized, gambling was not a major source of revenue for the Syndicate. But people became interested in gambling and when they didn't have time to get to the track, they turned to a bookie."

"Sure, but legalize all of it, like in England and Las Vegas."

"It hasn't worked there either, and won't. Gambling inevitably quickly becomes such a public nuisance that it has to be stomped out. You see, if a man is a big-time gambler, legal or illegal, and he has a lot of money bet with him on an athletic event or on a horse, the temptation to spend a few hundred or thousand to bribe a boy to miss a few baskets or to pull a horse in the final stretch is overwhelming. Gamblers trying to fix events almost ruined baseball, then basketball, then professional football, and they probably have ruined boxing. Even in horseracing there is a lot of hanky-panky. I have many times gotten tips from informants who got them from hoodlums and most of the time those horses win. Just the other day a driver from Roosevelt Raceway was beaten almost to death because he didn't throw a race the way they'd told him to. Do you think that he was the only one ever approached?"

"Yeah? Well, what about Las Vegas? There it is all legal and honest, and it has saved the state from financial insolvency."

By the time we reached the Las Vegas-honesty issue in one of these conversations, I was beginning to get dizzy from clenching my teeth and was probably a bit abrupt.

"Las Vegas, for that matter all of Nevada, is one of the worst examples you could pick. Many times mathematicians who have studied the games there have claimed that they are fixed so as to give the sucker a less than even break. Also, the city teems with crime of every type, with crime rates much above those of any city of comparable size. It's commonly known that most of the large casinos there are owned by the Mob, and federal authorities have claimed for years that they 'skim off' the profits before declaring their winnings. And just look at the number of scandals they've had in their state and city administrations. Gambling is a sort of marginal moral problem that cannot be properly controlled. It invariably falls into the hands of the mobsters."

"But the Mob isn't what it used to be. They don't kill anybody any more. They're very able men who could have made a go of it in any legitimate business but chose this field."

"They don't kill anybody any longer?"

"Nah. It's bad for their public image."

"Look, since you know the bookie down there on Main Street so well, how about helping me get evidence on him?"

"Oh, no, Reverend! I ain't no hero. I don't want to get shot."

There were also little catch phrases that slipped into a "typical conversation." There was "I like what you're trying to do, but I don't approve of your method," and another little sermon I listened to about 800 times was "You are washing our linen in public, blackening the name of the city, driving people away." There also was the accusing one, usually delivered from a lofty moral promontory and with a disapproving stare, "You should have gone to see the district attorney or given the names and places to our own local police." Then there were "It's narcotics you ought to go after" and "I believe in working quietly, without all the publicity, for the reform of the city." One of my favorites was "I think you should have taken what you had to city council." Another classic was "I believe that ministers should stick to spiritual things."

The city administration underwent some changes that summer. The most important was the resignation of Betty Meagher as city manager, after talking for months about retiring. For weeks the city council haggled about her replacement. Then one councilman suggested appointing the faithful corporation counsel to the position. There were immediate outcries. The city-manager type of government works admirably when the appointee is a professional, thoroughly trained for the job. When the position becomes a political football, used as a reward for valuable service to the party, the system falls apart. And that is what had been happening in

New Rochelle for years. Accordingly, the proposal to appoint the corporation counsel was bitterly fought by all the civic organizations and resisted by the mayor. The city council, however, rarely paid any attention to the public, and it didn't this time either. After an interval it went through with the appointment of the corporation counsel, Murray Fuerst.

As the months wore on, the police improved their performance somewhat, making more arrests than had been their custom, and there were constant boasts by city officials that our city was now "clean." Certainly things were better than they had been. Police morale seemed to be better. The officers actually ticketed cars that were parked illegally, caught some burglars, and in general performed more efficiently. But many of those who had given me information for my files were still disgruntled.

"Whyja stop your talks on the radio? Ya had 'em on the run. All the hoods useta get up at eight every Sunday to hear what you were going to say. Now things are wide open again."

I explained patiently that I had to give the new commissioner a chance to see what he could do, and that I had a few problems in my church and at home to tend to. Privately, I doubted that things had become as bad as they claimed.

Pete called me one night in a huff. "Rivrind, how much did they pay you? How much did it cost them to get to you?"

"Pete, for heaven's sake, cut that out. You know that no one has gotten to me."

"Oh, yeah? Well, I heerd some of 'em talkin' and they claim that you shut up because they paid you off."

"Pete, do you really think that is true?"

"You stopped for some reason. A man doesn't cease and decease for no reason at all."

"Well, now, I've told you that I'm giving the new man a chance before I start mouthing off. Besides, things are better now, aren't they?"

"Pfahhh! Heavy Eddie is running wide open. Mike the Mouse is still running his rounds. Union Avenue is like Las Vegas. Lincoln Avenue is like one big parry-mutual fund. All that big talk don't mean nothing. Things are wide open again."

I decided quietly to test things. I sent people whose objectivity I could trust into the numbers and horse parlors. All of them had the same report: things had returned pretty much to the old level, the bookies were more careful but back at work. I sat outside one notorious place on North Avenue myself and counted 15 persons going in and coming out in 18 minutes, only two of them with anything in their hands, cigarettes or newspapers, when they came out. It didn't require much imagination to know what was going on.

Still I hesitated. I dreaded getting back into that maelstrom again. It meant more midnight telephone calls, long conferences, the constant threat of violence to my family or me. It also meant once again annoying all the good people of New Rochelle who wanted only peace and quiet.

There was another reason, too, much more important. That summer, Grace began to cough ominously. Three years before she had undergone a radical mastectomy, and she knew that she was in danger of metastasis developing, most likely in the lungs or bones.

As it turned out, X-rays disclosed lethally cancerous nodes in both lungs. An operation was performed within days and she responded miraculously. All the doctors, however, cautioned against overoptimism.

Grace came home to take care of the children and carry a full load of housework, and then returned to the choir and her other church work. However, the preparation of a special diet, added to her daily chores, became horribly taxing. For me to drag her into such a bruising fight as I had been in before would be unfair. I feared that the emotional stress might trigger the cancer into returning.

But the rumblings about renewed gambling activity continued. I decided that I had to know for sure. I bought a miniature tape recorder and persuaded a woman to go into a couple of parlors, place a bet, and record the procedure. She was a great gal. Hazel had had a tough time in life. Although very intelligent, she had never had the opportunity to go to college or to land a very good job. She had married, but she and her husband were unable to have children. Their finances were constantly in bad shape, but she maintained a fine sense of humor. The adventure and the comic aspect of the expedition appealed to her. She knew there was at least a modicum of danger, but she loved doing it as a welcome relief from a life that was altogether too dull at times. She tucked the recorder into her purse and went off to her adventures.

"When I went up to the Lyn Sue, I felt funny," she told me later. "There was a cop parked right outside, but I decided, what the heck. So I went in and there was this guy in there and I said, 'Hi,' and he said, 'Hi,' and I said, 'A pack of Camels and a quarter on number 109.' He said, 'OK, what's your name?' and I told him and walked out."

Hazel was a tremendous find. She went from one place to another, collecting information. One was the cigar store where the Rev. David Coleman had had his chat with the bookies. Hazel walked in and said, "Hi. A *News* and a quarter on number 109."

"Hey, you ain't never been in here before," one of the guys said. "You might be a cop or something."

Hazel gave him one of her withering looks. "Don't be a fink. I used to bet with Bootsie."

We got some excellent tapes. One contained a conversation with a city official's brother who had run a numbers action in New Rochelle for as long as anybody could remember. He'd closed his operation so as not to jeopardize his brother's chances for advancement, but chatted freely about the perils and tribulations of the numbers business.

From Hazel's activities, it was evident that my informants were right: the town was not cleaned up. One by one friends brought in tapes of bets being placed in other places, until I had quite a collection of electronic entertainment. It was during this period that a reporter from a New York newspaper came to see me. He said that he was doing an article on how a city cleans itself up and had already interviewed various city officials, who had assured him that indeed a marvel had been wrought. He asked for my thoughts. I reached for the telephone and said, "Hazel, baby. Got a minute? Run down to the old Lyn Sue and place a bet with Mickey and let me know how it goes." The reporter and I chatted for a few minutes, and then I let him listen in when Hazel called back. "Hi, chief. Mission accomplished. No problems at all." The glowing article was never written.

I was still reluctant to make a move. A man can demand reform only a few times before he begins to sound like a cranky spoilsport. What could I do? Go to the D.A.? I had done that, and nothing had happened. Go to the police commissioner? I had done that, and he had all the information I had. Go to the SIC? It only did investigations and was not responsible for continuing law enforcement. Should I go to the committee of businessmen? No, they would have a conference with the city manager and express grave concern.

While I waited, a few aggressive, concerned people in town decided that some action had to be taken. After dozens of meetings and much vacillation, they decided to form the Reform party and run a slate of candidates in the councilmanic race that fall. I was asked to attend the meetings, but my wife's health was questionable and our anxiety too great. Besides, although I recognize the importance of politics, I have no flair for or much interest in the game. Nevertheless, during discussions of various city needs, the committee asked me about the crime situation, knowing that I had built up a system of informants. I told them there had been some arrests but little improvement. One of the founding members of the Reform party was Stanley Renton, who had once defended me before the committee of businessmen. He quickly asked if I were going to do anything about it, and offered me $500 to purchase a good tape recorder and pay expenses.

That evening I told Grace that I felt I had to do something. We talked it over, and she sighed and said to go ahead.

So began the second chapter in our efforts to rid New Rochelle of the Syndicate.

CHAPTER FIVE

This time the approach had to be different. We could not point to what the SIC had disclosed, because local officials would claim that, if it had ever been true, it was no more and everything was just dandy. This time we had to have proof.

I called in some of my informants and asked them to get more tapes. They did, and again we had a fine record of bets placed. In order to prove that prostitutes were operating in New Rochelle, I persuaded a friend from New Jersey, a metal worker, to come over and spend a few nights drinking in selected bars. I was apprehensive as he left, because he would be spending the evening in one of the most disreputable spots in the city. Finally, about three o'clock in the morning, he returned smelling like a gin mill and a bit fuzzy in the head, but otherwise unscathed.

"Hey, what kind of a city you got over here, man? I got invited to four crap games and two card games, and 12 girls propositioned me to sack in with them for a price."

"Get it on tape?"

"It's all there, man, but it darn near got me killed. A big thug type bumped up against me and felt the recorder. He thought I had a gun and was a cop. I drew him aside and told him I was partly deaf and that it was my hearing aid."

We pulled the recorder out of its holster and turned it on. There was nothing but an ear-splitting roar of people yelling and a juke-box screeching. We vaguely heard women's voices several times but could detect nothing they said. The evening was a bust.

Out he went a week later, and again I waited. This time he came in much earlier, and grinning from ear to ear.

"Man, I got her this time. And now I got to get home. Last time I was so tired the next day I almost fell into my forge."

The voices on this tape were loud and clear. "Honey," the prostitute said, "it's $20 and you'll have a great time."

We encountered some frustrations, too. One big man with a booming voice who claimed to know every hood in town took the recorder and never showed up again. He finally sent it back, broken, with a note saying he hadn't been able to get anything. Of course, he'd chickened out.

One pan-faced informant calmly went into a half dozen places, made recordings of bets being placed, and got an astonishing tape of a conversation between two thugs that was enough to turn anyone's hair white. A little woman picked up several bets on tape at various places, but almost all were useless because her voice was so low. Another man got an incredibly incriminating conversation with a local official on tape.

When the fun was over and our evidence was in front of us, we were confronted with the problem of what to do with it. Give it to the police or to the district attorney? I considered ·playing the tapes on my radio program to prove the city was not clean, but the station had changed managers. The new one was vociferous, able and brash, but not very courageous. He talked about libel suits and lawyers and what it might do to his image until I gave up in disgust.

By that time I had run into more problems. Some of my informants were having second thoughts. Several had been quite willing to get information, but were certain their voices would be identified on the tapes. And even if they weren't but someone sued us, we would have to ask the informant to testify. There was also the problem of what would happen if we did play the tapes. Would the district attorney immediately subpoena them and force me to disclose the names of the people who had made them? Our past experience had led us to believe he would do exactly that, because he had always seemed more interested in punishing anyone who dared to show that crime existed than he had in catching the criminals. I don't mean to say that he was dishonest. He was a defensive man who was reluctant to admit there might be corruption anywhere in his jurisdiction. Furthermore, he was up for reelection that year. Although there was never any doubt that in

Republican Westchester he would win, all politicians are nervous and he was more so than most. And then there is the sad fact that many, many politicians today receive money from the Syndicate. If a district attorney puts pressure on gamblers, especially at election time, they shut off funds to local politicians, who blame the D.A. Even if they are not corrupt, local politicians do not appreciate having a D.A. show that crime exists in their backyard.

As a result, I was in exactly the same situation as every other reformer has been in dealing with Organized Crime. I knew it existed, I knew who were involved, and what they were doing. I had evidence, and I couldn't do a doggoned thing about it.

I had a long talk with Pete. He was the best informant I ever had, but he had no stomach for being a witness. "By heaven, Rivrind," he said, "I would be glad to stand on my feet out there in the RKO Theater and tell all I know, but then I wouldn't be able to get any more information for ye."

He had a point, but I have found that, whenever a fight looms and it seems that someone may get hurt, nearly everybody decides that he would be more valuable to the cause in a safe haven somewhere else.

Make no mistake about it, Pete was furious with the hoodlums and anxious for *me* to do something about it, and *quickly*. He had several helpful suggestions, such as taking the tapes to the governor or to the President.

One man who had been with me all the way in gathering the evidence suggested that I call a public meeting and play the tapes. When I pointed out the problem of witnesses refusing to back what they had said on tape in the event of a suit, he was reassuring. Then I suggested that we ask everybody who wanted action taken to contribute to a pool for legal help in the event of a suit. At this he demurred sadly, telling me how bad business had been lately. I also suggested that the entire group of responsible citizens sit with me on the platform as I played the tapes, so that all would be considered partly responsible and the likelihood of a suit would be lessened. He cleared his throat delicately, lit a cigarette, and thought it over. "Well," he said finally, "that is an idea, of course, and I am sure some of the fellows would love it, love to be in the limelight that way. As for me, I couldn't, much as I would like the fame. My company wouldn't like it, and there might be reprisals against my family—besides, I will be in Switzerland skiing that weekend."

I didn't blame him. It's true that as a minister I am less vulnerable to pressures than some. And he was a good man, even though he lacked the gift of courage. It was a shock, however, to find so few men with any courage at all. I have never been able to understand how these very men, now paunchy and lined, were able to stop Hitler's legions when now they shuddered at the thought of a brick through a window or, even worse, the loss of some business. There is little sense in trying to push such persons into doing something that might be dangerous when they resist it so stoutly. What, then, was I to do?

A talk with a good friend, a lawyer, gave me one possible answer. I decided to call agents of the Intelligence Division of the Internal Revenue Service, the men charged with enforcing the federal gambling tax law, legislation clearly designed to give the government a chance to make inroads against nationwide racketeering. I had met two of them during the days of my radio campaign and still had the telephone number in my desk. I dug it out and called it. The agents were in my office that afternoon.

"Mr. Hill, what's this about tapes?"

"Well, a few of us here in town wanted to be sure that we were not just hearing some loose rumors about gambling, so we sent people into these places with tape recorders and made tapes. Some of these people are willing to give testimony—some of them are not."

After outlining the situation and letting them hear our tapes, I said that I intended to make a public statement about the fact that the city officials had not brought about the clean sweep they were claiming. Therefore, I added, the time was short if the T-men intended to make any arrests on our information. They agreed that the information was ours to do with as we wished, and that they could have nothing to do with any political effort one way or the other. On the other hand, they could not turn down evidence offered them of crimes being committed against the federal government.

"What'ya think?" one asked his colleague. "Will the boss let Marv work on this?"

"He's the only guy I know who could make up cases that fast. In fact, after what he did on that Yonkers racetrack thing, he'll probably have half of New Rochelle in jail by the end of the first two weeks."

"Who's Marv?" I asked.

"He's the genius in our office, a senior agent who manages cases," the first agent said.

"He's a genius, all right. Let him get that big brain going on something and you better know that he'll get it figured out. But tell him you'll meet him around the block somewhere and he'll get lost on the way. Put him behind the wheel of a car and he'll have a flat on the way."

"Or have an accident. He's a typical genius, always thinking and never watching what he's doing. His filing cabinet is the pockets in his coat or the lining of his hat. But he is smart."

The agents telephoned their headquarters, an agreement was made, and the next day they brought Marv to see me. He was about five-feet-six, with a belly that hung over his belt, and yet he gave the impression of hardness. His eyes were heavy-lidded and impenetrable, but when he laughed they were marvelously alive. He was a fascinating combination of toughness and compassion, of the serious and the humorous, the dignified and the comical. But his most oustanding trait was his sense of humor. He was a "little Jew boy from the Bronx," as he never tired of calling himself, and he had that wonderful, uniquely Jewish ability to laugh at himself. He had been an accountant before entering government service, but that had been too tame for him. It was more fun to chase bad guys. For all his self-deprecation, he was widely respected by the other agents. I liked him instantly, as I have usually liked most Jews. In fact, there is a strange affinity between Presbyterians and Jews. Both groups put a great deal of emphasis on order, law, reason, education, democracy, and freedom. Both are contentious and forever having internal conflicts. Both form a sort of elite within society and produce far more than their expected share of doctors, lawyers, and scientists. Presbyterians tend to be more stuffy and conservative than their Judaic counterparts, and Jews tend to be more flamboyant, but the similarities are striking. Perhaps this is what made me like Marv so much, or maybe it was the fact that he had grown up in a poor neighborhood, as I had, and was once something of a roughneck, as I had been. Perhaps it was the fact that he had a great interest in ideals and values, as I do, or perhaps it was because he detested bullies and those who exploited the helpless.

That first afternoon we had a long conference at which he tried to educate me on what was needed in order to get warrants for arrest.

"Now look, Reverend—."

"Call me Fay—miserable name that it is, it's mine."

"Right, Fay. The way we do this is different from the way local cops do it. They can get warrants on suspicion and go in and search a place and look for evidence. We can't. We must have a case made before we leave the office. That's the reason we have such a high rate of convictions. Occasionally, we will flub, have a weak case or a witness who loses his nerve or a judge that had a bad night of sleep or is having an attack of sciatica. But we have a case before we ever go for the warrants."

"OK, how do we go about making one of those airtight cases?"

"One of our federal officers must make a bet with the person or clearly observe the bets being placed."

"How can we get them in to make a bet around here? They may be open, but they're not so stupid that they'd just let a federal agent walk in and put down fifty cents on a number or five bucks on a horse."

"There's one alternative, and that is for a citizen of good reputation and character to swear to a federal officer that he has bet with a man and has been betting with him for a period of time. We don't like to do that, but it is a possibility."

"Great! Let's do that! We have lots of citizens of sterling reputation who will give you statements and we even have tape recordings."

"Ah, but one catch. They must be willing to be witnesses in court when the trial comes."

I groaned. "In a couple of cases, that will be all right. Our volunteers have said they are willing to go on the witness stand, but most of my witnesses have become convinced that they will be able to make a more valuable contribution to the war against Organized Crime if they remain anonymous."

"Well, you can't blame them. If they go on the stand, they may sometimes get nasty telephone calls. Or if the guy convicted is a big wheel, sometimes a tire gets slashed or a brick thrown through a window. That's usually all there is to it, but many of these people are neighbors of the hoodlums, or are friends of friends of the bum. So they get frozen out by people who call them 'rat' or 'Judas.' It's understandable."

"And lamentable."

"Look," Marv said, "there are a couple of other things we can do.

We can sometimes force people to testify against a gambler whom they've been betting with."

"Now you're talking. I'll give you a list of bettors in each place."

"But like everything else, this has its problems. You see, this is the way we do it. We must have a good informant who sees these people giving their bets to the guy and who will be willing to give testimony. So we call them in and put them under oath and ask them questions. If they lie, they are guilty of perjury and we get a conviction of them on a felony instead of a mere misdemeanor for the gambler. Then the word gets back that we mean business when people in a town see some poor slob who was just trying to protect his pal, the bookie, go to jail for five years. It is rough, and we don't like to do it if we can avoid it."

"Boy, would that knock the heck out of a bookie's business if it became known that his customers were known and being called to give testimony before a federal grand jury."

"It has been known to have a salutary effect on a hood's business."

"But it leaves us with the same problem of having to have a good informant, one willing to testify that the guy did bet with the bookie."

"Yes, and the cases must be serious enough to go for broke. We don't want to send some poor slob away for five years unless the bookie is a big book."

"But, Marv, this *is* serious business. And if we get soft we'll never get these guys."

"Fay, there's no question about it, but I am just saying that we don't want to be really tough over peanuts."

"OK, you said there are two ways. What is the other?"

"Well, it is a bit dirty, too, but it works and it knocks a hole in their business."

"Let's do it, let's do it!"

Marv shook his head sadly, rolled his eyes in mock surprise. "Wow! I have never seen such a tough minister. My rabbi is always talking about compassion and mercy and forgiveness and looking accusingly at me all the time. You Presbyterians are tough."

"Yeah, what's this other method?"

"Sometimes, when we have a lot of good information on bettors, we can send an agent to get acquainted with a customer and they say, 'Hey, Charlie, know where there's any action around here?' So the poor slob, trying to be nice, says, 'Sure, come with me, I'll introduce you to my bookie. You'll love him.' So our agent gets in there and then begins to complain that he can't conveniently get to see the bookie anymore, so the patsy introduces him to another bookie. We can sometimes keep that up through four or five places."

"But what happens to the poor slob?"

"Sometimes he gets leaned on—you know, dirty names, tires slashed, broken nose. It's a dirty thing to do, but it sure shakes them up. They beat up the guy and the word gets around that some guy who had been betting with them for years was beaten, so all the others decide that they better stay out of there before someone thinks *they* fingered the bum. It has a fine effect on business."

"OK, I'll go to work and see what I can do about a few of these places."

"Right, and give us a ring when you are ready for some introductions or observations or one of those tricks."

For the next two weeks I worked hard. In some cases it was a "pastoral call" to visit a church member who had offered to help. Hazel was no trouble at all. Her eyes twinkled, cheeks dimpled. "So why not? Sounds like fun. Let me know when you want me to take in an agent, but be sure he is tall and handsome. You know I wouldn't be able to take in anyone who wasn't supposed to be my husband, and I wouldn't be married to anyone but a handsome man."

Some of the others presented a slightly different problem. One incredibly good informant who could bet anywhere in Westchester County went through a complete change of heart before my eyes. He had come to me because he knew what beastly people the racketeers were. He had seen men beaten half to death. He had known Johnny Boy Amorosano, and he had seen young kids get hooked on heroin. I had never known him to give me one fact that was not completely accurate. But when I suggested that he testify or introduce an agent into a few places, he pursed his lips, changed color, licked his lips, looked at the floor, bit his lip, stroked his chin, and finally said, "Why, Reverend, I couldn't do a thing like that. I have grown up with these men, they are my best friends. I deplore, I rea'' do, what business they are in, but I wouldn't be able to do a thing like that to them. I couldn't in good honor do that to them."

It was much the same with Pete. There was one big bookie,

a man who we knew did two or three million dollars of business a year, and we had no other informant able to bet with him. Pete could have introduced an agent without being suspected. But he was shocked at the thought.

"Rivrind, we talked about this and you said that I was too valuable as an undercover agint to give testimony. Besides, you have chosen the one man in the whole Syndicate I couldn't do that to."

I pressed him for the reason he couldn't help to bring about the arrest of the gambler known as Big Chin.

"Big Chin is really not a bad sort," Pete said, tears welling up in his eyes. "He was an old-timer here in town before the Syndicate took over and forced him to pay off to them. He's a good family man, a man who sends all his kids to college and is proud of them. Why, I remember the time when his oldest kid, Mikey, played for Notre Dame against Army. Army was ahead and there was only a few minutes left when suddenly the Army fella faded back and threw a perfect, spired pass and Mikey contracepted it and ran for a touchdown. Big Chin wept, he did."

"Now just stop that stuff, Pete. You told me only two days ago that he had taken both his boys into the business with him. If he was such a good family man, he wouldn't do that. He'd want them to go straight. He is a lousy father and you know it."

This time Pete raised his fine old head, his eyes looked off at some distant horizon of memory, his lips quivered with emotion, or at least I thought it was emotion until he spat out a soggy strip of cigar that he had almost swallowed.

"Rivrind, what ye say is true. Big Chin is not the father he used to be, but what a husband he is. What a beautiful love he has for his little wife!"

"Pete, you know perfectly well that bum has kept his wife in her tiny old apartment for years while he keeps his blonde in a brand-new house in Long Island."

"Rivrind, Rivrind. Are ya tryn' to tell me that a man can't love two women? Why, that's just how big his heart is. Rivrind, if you were a Catholic, you'd understand. We Catholics have deep loyalties. You Protestants put laws above people, but for us there is nothing more important than people."

The beginning of my search for witnesses had not been, I feel certain the reader will agree, conspicuous for its success. The next few days were no better. It wasn't that these witnesses were afraid, it's just that they didn't want the "spotlight." They were quiet folk, going their own ways, bothering no one, desiring nothing in the form of recognition. In fact, their modesty was so great that they were surprised I had not seen it earlier and refrained from asking them to step into the limelight. They held such affection for me that they wanted me to have all the glory for bringing these scoundrels to justice. I was able to persuade only two of them to work with us. By that time, the number of possible arrests had shrunk to four.

I began to study the facts about other places and picked out some of their customers for special attention. By several ruses we managed to get an agent acquainted with some of the older bettors. When the agent would ask where the action was, most of them would shrug and say they knew nothing. Few, however, took the bait. I will say nothing more except that, by this means, we managed to have agents bet in several gambling places and were able to bring about 12 arrests. There wasn't time for any more if I was going to prove before election day that New Rochelle's elected and appointed officials were wrong when they contended that their city was cleaned up. The agents wanted to delay and work for more arrests, but I didn't think some of the pious politicians ought to be allowed to fool the public so easily. I insisted on going on the radio to say my piece. The Treasury men gave in. Marv made a date for Thursday night to have all the informants come to the church, where they would be placed in separate rooms to give their statements and arrange last-minute betting by agents.

It was quite a night. There was a church supper going on at the same time. And we had already had problems with secrecy. It was exciting business, and some of the informants couldn't help talking to their friends about it. Treasury agents often visited our home and the children got to know them quite well. The children were told not to say anything about the T-men to other children. But it was a heavy burden to bear. They must have often bitten their lips to keep from boasting that they knew real, bona fide federal agents who had badges, guns, and all the other exciting paraphernalia. My youngest son, Jamie, who was only four, was utterly fascinated, but as the weeks dragged by he said nothing to anyone. Then the Sunday before our meeting, he was in church school when the teacher explained how the children's pennies helped pay the bills of the church:

"We put them in the plate, Louise collects them and gives them to the big boy who comes around with the bag, and he gives them to the treasurer."

"Tweasurer? What's a tweasurer?" Jamie solemnly asked. "I know a Tweasurer agent. Is that a tweasurer?"

Other than this, fortunately, no word leaked out about what we were doing. That night, half of the Sunday school rooms were occupied by informants. It was important that no one know what any other person was doing or even that he or she was working with us. In that way he could never turn against us and inform on another informant, and neither could an inadvertent remark destroy an operation.

Marv was in one room talking to Hazel and her "husband," Oscar, the agent she had calmly introduced to the bookie. As they left the church, he asked if she wanted him to bet any special number, and she laughed and told him to bet 479, the address of the church. Now they were plotting another two bets before the raids.

Another T-man, Tom, was in another room talking to one of our most important informants, who had carried the tape recorder under his jacket and made bets in a couple of parlors. Other agents were writing up their reports in other rooms or meeting informants who would introduce them to bookies. Even Pete dropped by to fill in a few details about one place for the agents and to give advice. Downstairs, meanwhile, the ladies of the church were busily preparing the dinner.

Suddenly the door to my office opened and Jack burst in. Jack, as we called him, was a quiet young man with a long nose, big shoulders, and bushy blond hair. He had been reared in the slums of Mount Vernon and had been told he was an idiot so often that he had come to believe it. He was one of those failures who lurk at every bar and loiter at every bookie joint. Yet, he had been invaluable. He had been scared to death, but had volunteered to carry a tape recorder into half a dozen policy drops and horse rooms. Now he was preparing to introduce a federal agent as his cousin from Cincinnati. Or at least he had been. Now his voice quivered, but a cunning was there, too, and relief.

"Hey, Reverend. Ya hear what happened? The whole show's off."

"What are you talking about, Jack?"

"The commissioner just raided 25 places today. The town's sewed up tighter than a drum. Nobody'll get in a bet tomorrow."

"Preelection raids! I should have known it. Where did you hear it, Jack?"

"It's in the paper. Here, look."

He handed me a copy of *The Standard Star* with a late notice reporting that that very day New Rochelle's police force had sent detectives into 25 of the same places we had been working on, searched them, and warned them not to engage in any gambling activities. One man in his seventies had been arrested with a policy slip in his pocket. He was apparently a customer who had not gotten the word. No other arrests were made. According to the notice, this indicated that gambling was indeed cleaned up in New Rochelle.

"Does this blow it, Marv?"

"Not for the places where we are already in or for the places where you have witnesses ready to testify. It may make things tougher for the places we were planning to get into tomorrow. But I think we ought to go ahead with the show. This may relieve the tension for the bums. They'll think that the raids have been made and now they can go back to work."

"Naw, naw, I don't think so," Jack said. "They'll be looking for trouble now, and if we try to introduce anyone they'll kill us."

The door opened and Tom stuck in his head. "Hey, Marv, my gal just heard that there've been raids and doesn't want to go in tomorrow."

Another Treasury agent, Oscar this time, came in from the other side. "Are we calling off the show? My guy is scared they'll be alert tomorrow."

"I'm telling ya, Reverend, we'll get killed if we try." Jack was trembling badly.

Marv turned to me. "Look, Fay, they're *your* witnesses. I stuck my neck out at the office to go along with this venture. You've got to talk them into going on with things or we'll all be the laughingstock of the office."

"Don't worry, kid," I told Jack. "These agents are pros and there won't anything go wrong. These guys are so smooth that —."

Then came a gentle knocking at my door, gentle but insistent. I hushed everyone and went to it. There stood little Mrs. Snyder, the circle leader who was in charge of the dinner that night. She was dressed in her best maroon suit, a white organdy apron, a lovely hat, and her most comfortable shoes.

"Oh, Mr. Hill, am I interrupting something? A committee meeting?" Her eyes darted nervously but inquisitively over the group.

"Of course, you're not interrupting anything. Can I help you?"

"Wellll. . ." She looked disapprovingly at Pete with his stogie, Jack shaking, Marv, Oscar, Tom, at me perspiring heavily. Her eyes took on a new determination. She is one of those people who are hesitant and whiny until they can disapprove of someone, then confidence rushes back with tidal power. "We are about ready to serve and thought that you should know. You may want to say grace for us old ladies, if you can get away from this. . ." Her eyes swept the room with confident contempt. ". . . committee meeting. I came up three flight of stairs to tell you."

"Thank you so much, Mrs. Snyder. I think the dinner is scheduled to begin at seven-thirty, and I'll be there right on time."

"Welll—will these gentlemen be staying for dinner—you know we asked for reservations and we are a bit short and—."

"Oh, no, they're not staying, Mrs. Snyder. They, er, they, well, they must get home to their wives."

She gave one last, disdainful look, sniffed at the tobacco smoke, and left. I turned to Jack.

"Jack, look, don't let me down now, I'll—."

We heard steps outside as someone started down the stairs. I dashed out and saw it was Mrs. D'Alemandro. She is a lovely person who had come to me months before with much information and had gathered several tapes. She was about five feet tall and weighed about 250 pounds. Her husband was a heavy bettor and a drunk who contributed nothing to support of the household. Mrs. D'Alemandro had had enough and decided to put her bitterness into action by helping us catch the Syndicate gamblers who had made her life so miserable.

"Mrs. D'Alemandro—not going home already, are you? We haven't quite finished yet."

"Mista Hill, escusa me, Father Hill. We try to do the impossible. Nona dese bumsa take action tomorrow. They laya low for awhile."

"Oh, I don't think so, Mrs. D'Alemandro. Some of them may but not that rascal *you* are getting for us. He is so brazen he probably began the moment the cops walked out of his place."

She cocked her little head. "Itsa true—probably took a bet from the cop who came to search the place," she said bitterly. "But maybe they careful and someone get hurt."

"Oh, no, you don't need to worry. This is our chance to give these rats a real kick in the pants. If we back out now the feds will never trust us again."

"Daddy! Mommy told me to tell you that everybody is waiting

for you to come and say grace." My little girl was calling from below.

"I'll be right down, honey. Mrs. D'Alemandro, don't walk out on me now, or we're finished."

"Mr. Hill, escusa me, Father Hill, itsa no use. Nobody ever stop these bums. They won the city, the county, the state, the country. Itsa worse than Sicily."

"No, no, Mrs. D'Alemandro, we *can* do it, but we need your help!"

She thought for a moment, shook her gray head slowly, thought a moment longer. "What the hell, escusa me, Mr. Hill, er, Father Hill, we try anyway, even if it doesn't do any good." She turned and went back up the stairs to meet with the agent again.

The door opened and Jack came out. His voice was loud and with a false bravado. "OK, see you guys again, ha ha. Let me know when you want help. I'll be glad to do it any *other* time." He looked at me with tortured eyes. "See you, too, Reverend. Keep up the good work and sorry it didn't work out this time."

"Jack, don't leave. We can do it, kid. I —."

"Daddy! Mommy says if you don't come right down she'll divorce you, and she isn't kidding. Please come."

As I turned to her, Jack tried to slip past me unobtrusively, grinning sickly.

"Wait! Jack."

"Daddy! Mommy means it! Please come!"

"Jack, don't let me down. You've got to — ."

"Reverend, I can't. I can't. I don't want to die. They'll kill me." Suddenly he began to cry. I knew I couldn't, mustn't force him.

"OK, Jack. Forget it, kid. It isn't worth that kind of trouble. Go home and forget it. You've been great and I appreciate it. Give me a call now and then to let me know how you feel."

"DADDY!"

"I'm coming, I'm coming. Marv, is there anything left with him gone?"

"Well, look, hadn't we better call this thing off for a couple of weeks at least?"

"DADDY!"

"Marv, you *know* that if we lose our momentum we'll never get these witnesses back again. If you guys don't hit sometime next week, I'm going to call a press conference and play those tapes and show our dear city once and for all that nothing has happened to clean up the gambling."

"Yeah, but what have we got?"

The door to another office opened and out came Vinnie, a thin man of about 55 with darting eyes, a stoop to his shoulders, yellowed teeth, and bushy, uncombed hair. He had been a numbers runner years before and knew every bum in town. He could bet any place with no suspicion. For some reason, which he had never told me, he had decided to turn against his pals. He had already introduced an agent into three places and was about to do four more the next day. Now his eye was twitching. The perpetual cigarette wafted smoke into the air around us.

"Zit all off, Rev? They beat us again, huh?" He looked at me hopefully. Marv had his eyes closed, thinking. Tom looked at his shoes. Steps pounded on the stairway and Grace appeared, furious.

"I don't know where you get the idea that you can keep all those people waiting this long, but if you don't come right now—."

Now, I can stand up against threats by the Mafia, roars of outrage by public officials, shrieks of fury by "good people" protesting my blackening the name of our city—but when my skinny little wife with the big eyes makes her will unmistakably known, I have no alternative but utter capitulation.

"Marv, talk to Vinnie and the others and do what you think is wise," I said. "We don't want anybody to get hurt. Forget what I said about a press conference. I'm an idiot." And I left.

Downstairs, people were taking their seats, the ladies were tapping their feet in impatience, and children were screaming as usual. Everyone was tolerant but Mrs. Snyder. "I knew if we sent Mrs. Hill for you, you'd come."

I led the prayer and then watched as our lovely ladies piled my plate with the food they knew I particularly enjoyed. One good friend said, as she served me, "We know how hard you've been working lately, and we want you to have plenty of nourishment." I wanted to crawl under the table and my stomach already had. I was sure it was perforated with at least a half dozen ulcers and it certainly was filled with lead weights. Mrs. Labler, a widow of 60 or so odd years and one of the finest Christians I have ever met, whispered in my ear, "I made your favorite apple pie tonight, and we are saving two pieces for you. We're hiding them so none of those teen-agers gobble them up." Mrs. Clark mocked, as she walked by in a frilly little apron, "You're not eating any of my rolls. I'll never bake them again." My son, sitting beside me, said, "Daddy, will you finish my potatoes? *I'm full*." Mrs. Hansen approached me with a triumphant smile. "You look so tired we saved you seconds on chicken, but don't tell anybody because we don't have enough for others to have seconds." Little Miss Anderson was solicitous. "Oh, Mr. Hill, you look white. You've gone too long without food." She snapped her fingers at one of the waitresses. "Hilda! Bring our pastor some more salad. Look at the poor man, he's so weak he can hardly talk." The president of the woman's society was beaming. "We certainly take care of our pastor, don't we?"

The program was a talk by Norman Stanton about our new worship service. He spoke of the grandeur of God and of how mankind is thirsting after him, whether or not people recognize the source and the cause of their thirst. He reminded us that the real source of peace is to be found only in the worship of God and that the most satisfying kind of worship is corporate, with the whole community of God's people gathered together, sharing their cares and joys and singing God's praises. As I looked at my friends, my parishioners who had put up with so much from me, and as we sang "O God, our help in ages past," I could hardly shake off a feeling of unreality about what I had been doing.

I thought of the tensions my battle against crime had brought onto my congregation, of the pleasant life I could have by just performing my ministry and enjoying the fruits of it. Then the old anger at corruption, at cynical politicians accepting graft, at the police clubbing a Negro kid into unconsciousness because he didn't move fast enough, but accepting money from gamblers not to enforce the law—it all came back. I thought of the headaches I could escape by forgetting the whole thing. I thought of the nice people I could spend my time with—and then I thought of their homes being burglarized by a kid who had become a drug addict because, in a moment of despair over his squalid life, gangsters had lured him into it. I looked at the people before me and thought of all their problems, of the woman who had a bad heart and yet went her way with serenity, knowing that her days would soon end. I thought of the parents whose son had been killed only a few weeks before in an accident. And I questioned my own sanity. The Gospel of Jesus Christ is a healing ministry, not one dedicated to catching bad guys. Then I remembered how our Lord drove the money changers out of the temple because they exploited the poor and profaned the temple. Weren't the gangsters the same? What should I do?

I looked at the door. Several shadows passed. One was unmistakably Marv, another Tom, then Oscar, Mrs. D'Alemandro, Vinnie, Hazel. Well, at least they had stayed awhile to talk it over and hadn't just called everything off out of hand. I felt better.

The next day I tried not to be a pest, but finally I had to call Marv to know if it was off or not. He said Treasury agents had gotten a bet placed that day in one more place and had arranged an observation in another. He was going to the courthouse to consult with the United States Attorney about whether there was enough evidence to justify raids. My stomach dropped and stayed down until the phone rang again. This time Marv said that they thought they would make some arrests, but did not have enough evidence for as many as we had hoped. Nevertheless, the arrests would damage the Syndicate in New Rochelle, and they would serve my own purpose by showing that our city officials had not cleaned out the gamblers as they had insisted.

Later that day I checked with several of my undercover people. They said that some of the betting parlors were not taking action after the police raids, but that some had never stopped. The bookies had cynically waited until the raiders left, spat, swore, and went right back to business. The reaction in town, however, was generally good. Most people sighed with relief. Their city was in apple-pie order. There would be no more humiliations, no more headlines about the Queen City of the Sound being a sinkhole of sin. Only the bettors, the gamblers, and my few informants knew the truth.

The weekend went by quickly and Monday rolled around. I was a mess. My stomach was upset. I paced the floor of my office, drank coffee, and wondered when the raids by the T-men would occur. The agents refused to tell me what day they would move or whom they would hit, but I could guess. Norman Stanton came in for a cup of coffee. He had a speaking engagement that day before a group who, he knew, would ask about gambling. Should he say anything about the city not being clean? I pleaded with him to say nothing until I told him to. He said he had another engagement that evening before some people who were intensely interested, because they lived across the street from a notorious bookie who had operated in New Rochelle with virtual impunity for years.

They would want to know what he as a Reform candidate proposed to do about the problem and they would want to know if he agreed that the gamblers were out of business. Again I begged him to say nothing, but he said that some of the reform people were disgusted with him for not blasting the administration about crime in the city. They were also disappointed in me because I had said nothing. Had I sold out? Lost my nerve? Was I just a blowhard? I asked him to wait. He agreed. I paced some more.

At noon I went home for lunch and stared at my food for a few moments. Still no word about the raids. Maybe they would come the next day, or on Wednesday. Or had they been called off? I decided to make some hospital calls. After that, I drove through the middle of town and past several of the bookie joints I had hoped would be raided. Fat Tony's was closed. Harry's Luncheonette was shut up tight and a few people were looking in the window. Frank's was shuttered.

I drove to the office quickly. The telephone was ringing when I got there. Mrs. Hobbs answered it resentfully, looked at me with disgust, and said, "It's *The New York Times*. Something about a raid. Hmmph." It was a reporter who said that some men had been arrested by agents of the Intelligence Division of the Internal Revenue Service for gambling without having purchased a $50 tax stamp. The United States Attorney, Robert Morgenthau, had announced that the agents acted on information supplied by me.

I had hardly finished with him before our other phone lines began to jangle. The rest of the afternoon was one call after another from newspapers, radio stations, and TV reporters wanting more details. One of the few stations that never called was the local one, the only newspaper that seemed to be uninterested was *The Standard Star*.

By the time I staggered home that night, my cheeks were flaming and my stomach was churning, but I was happy. No one could any longer say that gambling was closed up in New Rochelle; furthermore, if private citizens could gather evidence leading to gambling arrests then the police had no excuse for not doing so. No one could piously weep about how hard it is to find those bookies and get evidence against them.

My wife met me as I walked in the door. Her hands were shaking slightly.

"Boy, did you just get a threat! Some man started yelling at me the moment I picked up the phone. He was so mad he sputtered and shrieked and ranted and raved. When he finally calmed down I asked whom he wanted and when he said you, I said, 'You have the wrong number,' and hung up."

Within minutes the phone rang again, with a request from a television news program for some information. Then it was a radio news agency, and so it went until we took the phone off the hook.

During dinner we carefully instructed the children that something had happened to make some bad people angry at their father and that in order to get at me these people might try to hurt one of them. Kristin, my oldest daughter, said, "Oh, goody! Some excitement! What happened?" My oldest son, David, said, "What have you been up to now, Dad? Did you make one of those radio broadcasts again?" The three younger children got solemn and their eyes widened as I told them what had happened. We asked them to walk to school with other children, to accept no rides from anybody under any circumstances, and not to stay outside after dark. It was a bit frightening, but all in all, they were not unduly disturbed.

I had an appointment that night to meet with a church committee. As I came up the stairs, I heard a buzzing and found several committee members chattering about the rumors that were flying around town. At almost the same moment, Norman Stanton came in with his face contorted and staggered to a chair as we gathered around, trying to decide whether he was laughing or having a heart attack. When he had regained his control, he told us this story:

He had an acquaintance who lived across the street from Harry the Hat. She had noticed that today Harry had not come home at the usual time. She could tell because when Harry was at home he yelled constantly at his wife and teen-age son. He was thoroughly disliked by the entire neighborhood. They all knew that he was a bookie and made enough money in his little fly-specked luncheonette to live better than any of them could afford. This neighbor suddenly saw Harry's wife drive up in her car with Harry beside her. He opened the car door, slammed it with all his might, screaming hysterically at her, and stomped into the house. His wife followed him and for an hour the neighbor heard screams, yells, and the sound of things breaking, and shouts of protest. The teen-age son came home, entered the house, came out with a white face, and drove off in a huff. By this time all the neighbors were hanging out their windows. Harry had gone so long without being arrested and was so arrogant, and they had grown so furious at seeing police cars stop at his house or toot amiably as they drove by, that the scene was enjoyed by all.

Norman was not the only one enjoying the evening. I received a couple of telephone calls from informants who were chortling. Mrs. D'Alemandro was grimly happy but pessimistic about the long-term effects. Vinnie was in his own way elated, quiet, but for his own inscrutable reasons glad.

"Well, Rev, we got 'em, din we?" Vinnie said. "They busted Sam while I was in there. Boy, was he surprised. I thought he was goin' to mess his pants. But the one that gave me the most fun was Fat Tony. To see that little fat bastard being hustled into a cop's car gave me a laugh."

Pete was effusive as usual and took all the credit. As usual he was also the last one suspected. For all his bombast, I had to admit as I listened that he was clever and useful. But he was a bit hard to take.

"Rivrind? I got 'em for ye, didn't I? Ye haveta admit it, now, don't ye? And ye wouldn't believe how mad they are. They'll blow a casket if they're not careful. Fat Tony is going to have a corona if he doesn't calm down—ye know, he's already a heart patient. They're having a big meeting tonight. They know that someone tipped off the feds, but they say they'll get the Arnold Constable."

That night, at about twelve-thirty, I was roused out of my slumbers by the telephone.

"Reverend Hill? I heard on the television tonight that you organized some people up there in New Rochelle and got some guys arrested. That's great going. I know a little about this stuff. I've been fighting the Mafia for 10 years. Of course, I never went for the headlines the way you did, but I was even more effective."

By that time I had managed to get my mind focused and to reassure my wife that it was nothing important, so she could go back to sleep.

"Have you been beaten up yet, Reverend? I have. I used to go into the gin mills and argue with those guys and they'd give me the blitzkrieg—you know a couple of them start pushing me around and then a fight would get going and I got beaten up and arrested by the cops while they went free. The cops hate me because I have shown up so many of them for crumbs. I even went to the commissioner's confidential squad and turned in some of them and when they heard of it they took me out and beat me half to death. But I'm tough and I bounced right back, and they admired me for it. They said, 'John, you're tough, but you don't know when to quit. Give it up. You can't fight City Hall.' "

"Who is this, please?"

"I'm a reporter—used to do the crime column for a paper here in the city."

Fortunately, he did not require much response from me as an incentive for further monologue, and I managed to doze a few minutes between discourses. Even in my state of mind I was able to tell two things about the caller: (1) He knew a lot about his subject, and (2) he was drunk as a skunk. Finally, I got him to promise to call me the next day and collapsed back on my bed.

For about 20 minutes. Again the telephone rang. This time it was a woman in Nyack who had heard the good news on TV. She informed me that she, too, was engaged in a running battle with the Cosa Nostra and was glad to hear I had joined the fight. Her battle was more difficult than mine, however, because she was surrounded. Her neighbor was a high-ranking Mafioso who cleverly put a chemical into his barbecue pit and whose smoke killed all her roses. The mailman was another of their spies. He never delivered a letter without looking at her strangely and trying to look over her shoulder into the house—casing the joint so they could break in and kill her someday. Would I be so good as to "put security" on her? If I did, I would be glad, because she could supply me with an endless amount of information about murders, robberies, and communists. Did I realize that the Mafia and the communists were all the same? Shhhhh! Someone was at her door.

It took half an hour to talk her into calling some other time. Again I slept for a few minutes before my fuzzy brain was goaded by the ringing of the telephone. Grace rolled over, said some unpleasant words, and suggested that I leave it off the hook. Now it was a young woman with an alert, sharp voice and some sharp questions. "Reverend Hill, I heard on the radio tonight that you managed to bring about the arrest through federal agents of some bookies. I wonder if you would mind answering some questions about it. I am a writer for a wire agency." I was so sleepy that I was in agony, but I tried to gather my wits. After suggesting that she might call me at a more decent hour and being told that she had to get the story on the wire before six, I groggily agreed to answer some questions. When she stated them, I woke up with a start!

"Reverend, would you tell just how you did it, and the names of some of your informants so we can interview them? Also, why didn't you go to the local police? Are they all crooked? Could you tell me the names of the ones who are?"

It was my first experience with such interviewing, and I was sure that the woman was calling for the hoodlums, trying to entice me into telling them what they wanted to know. I later learned that it is the practice of some reporters to call a person likely to resist giving information at an ungodly hour, when his brain is fuzzy, in the hope that he will say something indiscreet but exciting, and, threatening to print that, to force him to give still further information. I was wide enough awake from the other calls not to fall into the trap. After she hung up, I did leave the phone off the hook.

The morning *New York Times* article about the raids was on the front page, and everyone in New Rochelle who had missed the news on radio or TV caught it on the commuter train that morning. Naturally, most of the good citizens were incensed at me for having brought the name of their haven from reality into the headlines again. People from Rye and Larchmont snickered at the New Rochellians and asked when they were going to move out of "Sin City."

At the presbytery office, where I had a meeting that morning, I received a call from *The Standard Star* and was asked one question: When was the last time I had gone to see the district attorney? That was all. I also received a call from some good friends who wanted to call a public meeting and have me tell about our work, how we had managed with a handful of untrained amateurs to do what the police had said was impossible. I agreed but asked them also to invite the police commissioner to give his side of the story.

At lunch my wife met me with a nice message. An elderly man had called and identified himself as a Mr. DiGiaccoma of New Rochelle. He said he was all for what we were doing and I could count on him to help. The man had been extremely enthusiastic, Grace said, and would call again to make a date for meeting me. He went on to say that I had done some good work, but that the man who was really in charge had not been arrested, which was certainly true, and that the big man in town was not Joe Tufo but Fats the Baker, also known as Joe the Baker. With that he had hung up.

After a quick lunch I dashed off to the hospital and made some sick calls. Then back to the office, where a call from the IRS Intelligence Division had just come in.

"Marv? What have you guys been doing over here? There are rumors around town that somebody has been very unkind to some of the local books."

"I have never see anything like it, Fay," Marv said. "I go out and work for three years on some *capo* or even *don* in the Mafia and what happens? *The News* carries a little article on page 11 that the FBI arrested a bookmaker. But we come out there and make nine crappy little arrests and *The Times* headlines it on the front page."

"If you think things were hot around here when I was making broadcasts, Marv, you should see them now! The town is so hot the sidewalks are smoking. Just now, in the hospital, people stopped me in the corridors to talk about it. One guy in a sick bed reached out and grabbed me and told me that things are exactly as I said and that he would be willing to help me make more arrests."

"What's the local rag had to say about the thing?"

"It hasn't come out yet, but I imagine they'll say that it was the commissioner who really arrested them."

"Listen, Fay, one other thing. I have never in my entire life seen any crummy bookies so mad as these guys are now. One of our informants in town called and—."

"Who? Pete?"

"No, one of our own informants whom you don't know. And you understand, Fay, I can't tell you who he is because the one thing no agent ever does is to reveal the name of an informant. OK?"

"Yeh, all right, but what'd he say?"

"He said that they are livid, Fay, livid. He says that they're talking about doing something to you. Now, that doesn't mean much, because these guys are always talking big but can't deliver."

"Come on, Marv, I thought they kill guys all the time."

"They do, but not over a crummy gambling arrest. In the first place bookies, policy guys, are nothing—they're just dirt to the Syndicate. Everyone has to take his bounce. They had it good around here for 20 years and now, if they gotta bounce once, that's tough. And bookies themselves are not killers. They're usually the world's greatest chickens. But you gotta watch two things. Some young gun might think he could make a name for himself and take a crack at you, or one of those crazy guys out there might hire somebody to do the job without asking headquarters if it's all right."

"Marv, is this for real?"

"Well, I don't really know. I have never heard of these guys talking so big after a hit. Usually they take their medicine like men and let it go at that. Or they fuss, but after a night's sleep forget it."

"But you want me to be a little careful, stay away from windows, be with other people when I'm outside and that sort of thing?"

"Yeh, and tell all your informants to be a bit careful, too So far as we know, they don't have a clue as to who it was who did it to them, but they're not dumb, they may be able to dope it out, and it is better for some informant not to be around to arouse their ire if they should guess it."

When he hung up my heart was pumping a mite faster than it should. I knew it was highly unlikely that anyone would be so stupid as to take a crack at me, but what of the children? Marv had assured me many times that this was the most unlikely of all, because it would only arouse the public against the racketeers without getting rid of me, the one who was pestering them.

The telephone rang and Mrs. Hobbs buzzed me immediately. "Mrs. Hill, poor thing, on 87. Some sort of trouble, wants you right away. I suppose one of your children has been shot or something."

"Grace! What's the trouble?"

"Honey, remember that nice man who called, that Mr. DiGiaccoma who said that the big man in town is Fats the Baker?"

"Yes, what about it?"

"Well, another man just called, a man who says that he is a friend of his and that the gangsters have surrounded his house and are trying to get at him. He says that he's locked himself in and won't open the door for anyone."

"What are they after him for?"

"The man talked so quickly that I couldn't understand him very well, and he had a heavy Italian accent. As far as I could get it, they think that DiGiaccoma worked for you on those arrests. He didn't, did he?"

"No, I never heard of him before. Did the man call the police?"

"Well, naturally, I suggested that, but he only laughed and said that'd be a lot of help. He said the gangsters would respect your collar, though, and that if you'd go and see DiGiaccoma you could get him out alive and . . . Honey? You won't do it, will you? Can't you call Marv, and have him—."

"Marv just called and said that he was going out into the field and I wouldn't be able to reach him for several hours." My heart was pounding and my hands were moist. "But they wouldn't dare do anything to me in broad daylight."

"Honey! Don't you dare go over there now. Call the police and have them go. I knew something like this would happen and that the children would grow up without a father."

"Oh, honey, nothing'll happen. I'll just run over and see what the story is. I'll call you the moment I get back."

And off I went to the man's house. It was a large home on a well-traveled, well-known road. It seemed perfectly safe, so I stopped the car, got out, and went to the door. If the Mafia had anyone holed up there, the Mafia was certainly not in evidence. Not a soul was to be seen on the street—which seemed a bit odd for that time of day. I went up onto the porch, which was en-closed, and knocked on the door. The corner of the porch was covered with debris, garbage and old clothes and piles of papers and tin cans. I looked through the glass front door and saw old furniture in the front room, trash on the stairs, and a TV set turned on in the living room. I rang—and rang and rang. No answer. My neck began to crawl, and I wondered if I had walked into a trap. Finally, I gave up and left. The street was still empty of people and other cars. I noticed a walk at the side of the house. Because the house was big, it might have an upstairs apartment with an entrance in the rear. As I began to walk around to the back, I caught what might have been a slight movement at the window of the house next door—a curtain rustled in the breeze or someone might have moved behind it. My heart was pounding. It seemed so improbable. Who would shoot a Presbyterian minister in broad daylight on a quiet street in a poor but respectable resi-dential neighborhood? I continued around toward the back, my legs perhaps a bit weak, my heart a trifle noisy. As I approached the back door, the silence, the unnatural silence, was suffocating. I began instinctively to tiptoe. Suddenly the silence was torn apart by a snarl such as I had never heard before. From under the steps of the porch a huge German shepherd hurled himself at me with fangs flashing, jaws dripping saliva. I must have seen him coming before I heard his snarl, because I am sure that I was moving backward by the time he reached the end of his chain. His teeth snapped shut like a medieval portcullis, inches from my face. I have said he was on a chain. That statement is mostly conjecture, based on the fact that he did not reach me, but I never saw the chain. I didn't see much of anything until I was in my car and halfway around the block.

I never went back there, although I did call several times. Days later I finally got someone to answer the phone, a young man who said that he had never called me and neither had his wife nor any of his children. The man who called himself DiGiaccoma never called again, nor did his "friend." I have wondered if I was was sent there in order for the dog to get me, but I doubt it. It is more likely that the dog slept there all the time, on a chain, and that I just stumbled onto it.

A day or two later I discussed the incident with Marv, who roundly lectured me for being a fool—and I had to accept his assessment. He thought the probable cause for the call was that someone had suspected DiGiaccoma of being one of my informants and had made the call to see if I would respond, in which case my amateurish response could have endangered his life. Much later, I met someone who knew the family and discovered that nothing of the kind ever happened to any of them and, indeed, they had been utterly mystified by my telephone call.

I am glad the incident occurred. Although it was a bit startling, it was an easy way to learn an important lesson. From then on I was cautious about answering emergency calls of any kind and leery of any informant who had to meet me in a place that could be a setup. My reluctance, my reticence about such meetings, has been, on occasion, reinforced by my wife's delicate and tactful reminders of what a meathead I was.

Back at the office, *The Standard Star* had just been delivered. "T Men Nab 8 Bet Suspects," the headline read. Under it was another: "Acted on Rev. Hill's Complaints." Most of the article, however, was devoted to a statement by Commissioner Carey saying that evidently the T-men had acted on information they had gotten from his department! His reasoning was that all but one of the men arrested had sometime in the dim past been arrested by local police—some as much as 11 years before—and that the

Treasury agents had merely looked over the local newspapers, noted the arrests, checked to see if the gamblers had purchased the $50 tax stamp, and then arrested them on the evidence provided by the local police in the years-old cases. He did not explain how the apprehension of one young man who had never been arrested by local police was effected.

It is, perhaps, not surprising that the commissioner should have made such a ludicrous statement. After all, his own men had been unable to make arrests, and he had declared the town cleared of gamblers. A few citizens had now shown how wrong he was. It was natural to expect him to come up with a face-saving explanation. The remarkable thing about the story was that the paper should have so embarrassed the commissioner by printing it. Evidently the editors *believed* it, or someone at the paper had reason for thinking the public would believe it. At the end of the long statement was a brief sentence stating that a telephone call to the United States Attorney's office had elicited the information that the agents acted on no information except that supplied by me. But how many people read all the way to the end of a long news story? The majority undoubtedly got the impression that the arrests were the result of the local police department's work. As the commissioner told *The New York Times,* "I'm not the least bit excited about [the raid]. Frankly, I welcome the Federal Government coming in and giving me a hand because my undercover men are all worn out." The thought of his undercover men lying exhausted in hospital beds or being carried home on stretchers because they had suddenly collapsed titillated my fancy.

A telephone call from Stanley Renton, my reformer friend, jarred me out of my reveries. He said that the commissioner would indeed be at a public meeting on Thursday night at the YMCA.

Pete also called. "Rivrind, it's disgraceful, that's what it is," he said. "I have never heard anything so sumptuous in my life. I am absolutely intensed over it. They ought to run the commissioner out of town. The paper says that in order to take this job he took an indefinable leave from his post on the New York City department. He ought to go back there."

The next day's issue of *The New York Times* carried another response by the commissioner. This time he accused me of playing politics in bringing about the raids before the election—but made no comment on the motivation behind his own preelection raids.

On Thursday evening the YMCA was filled, despite an anonymous telephone call reporting that a bomb was planted there. The audience was interesting in its makeup. Most of the women were League of Women Voters types, who try to do something about their city. There were also the social action men, the ones who take the trouble to look into their city's budget, its programs for the poor, and its actions to fight prejudice. They are the people who cannot just live in a city and then, when it gets into trouble, sell their houses to the highest bidder and steal away to the next farther-out suburb. They are also likely to be frustrated people, because it is one of the sad facts of life that voters in American cities always prefer party hacks to idealists. Inevitably the hacks outnumber the idealists and vote them down on every issue of substance. But that night at the Y was a night for the reformers, one brief moment of triumph before they were again buried by the hacks. The hacks were there, too, grinning, handshaking ward-heelers afraid not to be present but wishing the storm would go away. And so were the cops, in plainclothes, with tape recorders to get everything down. There were hoodlums, too, stubby little men with cigars and hard eyes, thin weasel-like men, and soft fat men, all known to my informants. They were there, too. Mrs. D'Alemandro, Pete, Vinnie, and Hazel. It was almost more than I could do to ignore them. Only one person was absent: the police commissioner. He had apparently decided at the last minute not to accept the invitation after all.

I spoke for several minutes, relating much of what I had learned about the city and how wide open it was. Then I played some of our tapes. There were, of course, limits as to how far I could go, because I did not want anything to be traced back to the informants. But I played the tape of the prostitute propositioning my friend from New Jersey, and a tape of a restaurant owner whom the Mob had tried to force to take numbers. The tape of the prostitute was a bit gamy for these chaste surroundings, but on the whole the evening was a success. As the audience guests left, my friends overheard a host of interesting comments. One of them told me that a cop made some juicy remarks about my character, a bookie said discouraging speculations about my future, and a local political hack commented to another that he would like to get his hands on the tapes I had *not* played.

The next days were full of activity as I prepared to report to my congregation about the affair. The evening before I was to deliver the sermon, I received a telephone call from a frightened elderly lady. "Is the church going to be bombed tomorrow during your sermon?" she asked.

I replied without hesitation, "Not at the *eleven o'clock* service."

"But I always come to the nine-thirty service," she said, agitated.

"Well, just to be sure, why don't you come to the eleven o'clock service this one Sunday?"

The election a few days later went about as everyone, including the Reform party leaders, had expected. The Republicans won hands down, electing a warmed-over, crafty old-timer and a young fellow who was rewarded for his splendid inactivity as an assistant corporation counsel by being given the place on the ticket. The reformers had made deep inroads, however, collecting about twice as many votes as in any comparable effort. The overall result was disappointing, yet about what we had expected. New Rochelle is a hard city to wake up, a hard city to alert to danger within. In other words, it is much like other American cities. Most citizens grow panicky, break out in a sweat, as they reach for the lever on the voting machine. They would rather elect someone of known mediocrity and incompetence than take a chance that his opponent might be capable and try something new.

An interesting epilogue to our activities was the reaction of the Organization. The racketeers were furious, far more so than they had been over previous, and much more important, arrests by federal agents. A few days after the election, I was in my study when our dog began to bark loudly. My skin crawled. Someone was standing outside the French door to the study. I jumped as the person knocked. It was Marv and with him was Tom.

"You bums scared me to death. What are you doing out this time of night? I thought you only worked between nine and five, four days a week."

They were in no mood for banter. Marv slapped me on the shoulder and said, "Ats right, kid, tonight we're out for fun, right, Tommy?"

But Marv's eyes glinted, as they always do when he is trying to hide something. Tom made no effort to be funny.

"Why didn't you come to the front door like ordinary people?"

"We didn't want anybody to see us here now. Fay, look, when you got into this thing, you did it on your own, right? I mean, nobody from the Intelligence Division suggested—."

"Marv! Come on, now, what's happened?"

"Well, you know I told you that bookies are great pacifists, right?

That they never hurt anyone. They talk big, but almost never do anything. Well, something is screwy about this town. We've got this good informant in town and he's kept us informed about how things are going. And it seems that some of these bums are being very tough. Now, they have a right to be sore when they get arrested, and nobody cares if they sit around and blow for awhile. You know, 'We'll get that rat Hill and all his dirty finks,' and that kind of stuff."

"But this time they're talking big—this time you think they mean it, that they're really going to make a try at me? Is that it?"

Marv shifted his eyes, glanced at Tom, licked his lips. Tom looked grim. I must have looked sick.

"Well, no, not quite," Marv said. "We think it is nonsense, that it's nothing but loose talk and that they'd never do anything. But we just want to be sure, you understand."

"Now, let's stop all the tact stuff and all the 'let's break it to him easy' stuff and get down to brass tacks," I said. "How bad is it?"

Marv threw up his hands in mock disgust. "Fay, it's not bad at all. It's nothing, but we just want to be double, double careful."

Tom interrupted. "Come on, Marv. Give it to him straight. He's no kid. Tell him."

"Well . . . I don't understand it. This guy, our informant, has never given us any crap before, but now he swears that two of the guys we arrested are going to have you knocked off. It doesn't make any sense. Why be so burned over getting busted? Every bookie gets busted now and then."

"What I don't understand is that they're talking about it," I said. "What about *omerta* [code of silence] and all that? Someone must be awful loose-lipped."

"That's one reason it's hard to take it too seriously," Marv continued. "But then these guys are no Cosa Nostra types. They're nothing. Just bums, bookies, the most expendable guys in the Organization. We arrest them by the dozen and never have any problem like this. Now and then some bookie with good connections with the Cosa Nostra tries to get something going against the guy that pulled the switch on him, but 'the boss' always calls him in and tells him that he had it good for 20 years and now he can just take his medicine like everybody else, without bringing a lot of heat on everybody by knocking off a witness."

"So why all the fuss this time?"

"Tell him your idea, Marv," Tom interrupted.

"Well, I figure it this way," said Marv. "There are three kinds of guys in their world. There are the bad guys, the criminals, and they know it. Then there are the good guys, us, the cops. Now the good guys chase the bad guys, and when they catch them the bad guys are supposed to grin and take it and not cry about it. But there's a third group, too."

"Yeh?"

Marv grinned a bit. "The third group is you, John Q. Public, the sheep. Now, the sheep aren't supposed to turn around and bite the wolves. To their twisted minds that's not kosher. They know that their business is vulnerable. But they can buy off cops and judges and politicians, and there aren't enough of us feds to do much more than harass them. But when the *public* turns against them and reports them and gathers evidence and—well, it's like the ocean suddenly turning against the fish. So they're furious."

I realized that it wasn't only the bookies who were nervous about having civilians involved in the game of catching crooks. Marv and Tom were obviously uneasy, too. They were accustomed to working with professional agents who knew the score, who were tough, thoroughly trained, and ready to defend themselves. And they were used to guarding witnesses. But this was different.

Tom burst into some ungentlemanly oaths. "These dirty rats, if they try anything—."

There was a movement at the door, and we saw Grace. She had heard some of the conversation. Her jaw was set in that funny way of hers and her hands seemed a bit unsteady, but she said nothing.

"The boys say that we're having a little bit of trouble," I said. "It seems a couple of these bookies don't know they're nothing and will have to learn the hard way. But it's nothing to be afraid of."

Marv and Tom looked at each other and then at me in pain. It was bad enough to have *me* know, but to have a *woman* in the mess with us was too much. They clearly wondered how I could have been so dumb as to have told her.

"It's OK," I told them. "We don't hide anything from each other. She knew this could be dangerous when I got into it again. We talked it over and both agreed. You can tell her the whole story."

Grace was superb. But then she always is. We have been married for almost 20 years and I never cease to be surprised at her toughness. She is 110 pounds of barbed wire. My mind went back to the time when the doctor had called me to his office and told me that her cough was not due to bronchitis but rather to nodes of cancer that had spread to her lungs. When we were married we had agreed that if such a day ever came we would be honest with each other. Our faith would be enough to sustain us, or it was false. Not once in the months following that visit to the doctor had she uttered a word of complaint, not once asked, "Why should this happen to me?" To such a woman you do not give lame lies or glib reassurances. You give her the respect of being honest with her.

So Marv and Tom told her all they had told me. When she asked about the danger to the children, the agents told her that only in movies or in exceedingly serious cases, where a top Mafioso has been accused of a murder or a felony carrying a long prison sentence, would the Mob take such an expedient as harming children. Furthermore, they doubted, despite all the big talk, that anything would come of the threats against me.

"Is there anything you can do to protect my husband?" Her chin was firm and her voice level.

"Of course there is, of course there is," Marv said, soothingly. "The United States government is not going to permit anything to happen. But there are limits to what we can do, and we will need your cooperation, too. We want you to warn the children as we told you before, just to be sure. And much more important, Fay, you must be careful when you go out at night. Be with other people at all times, stay away from windows, and just generally be careful. Now, I see you have a big dog. Can you put her in the back room there near the garage so that if some clown gets any funny ideas about tampering with your car she'll bark and scare them away?"

"OK, and since I was a demolitionist in the paratroops during the war, I know something about bombs and I'll check the car each morning. What are you guys going to do?"

"We're going to get the word back to these bums, and to their bosses, that if they try any jokes with you we'll bring in agents from all over the country and bury Westchester County. And they know we can do it."

"Then why don't you do it anyway?"

"Because, in order to do it, we'd have to denude other areas of the country of agents and crime could flourish there. We have only enough men throughout the country to harass the Organization, but in an emergency we can concentrate a lot of men. And by morning they'll know that, if they try anything, we'll have an agent on every street corner; and every time one of them goes to the bathroom we'll arrest him for indecent exposure."

"But when they want someone killed," I persisted, "don't they bring in a pro just for the job, and he does it in such a way that nothing is traceable to them? Why should they fear the government?"

"It might be hard for us to prove who did a murder," Marv conceded, "but the point is that if we sew up the county, they'll lose thousands, even millions, of dollars. Business will be closed down, and yet they'll still have to support all the men and their families. So when the bosses hear of the heat these stupid bookies are about to bring into their county, the word will go out and you'll be safer than the President. Then you'll only have to worry about some nut trying to make a name for himself."

After they left, Grace and I went to bed and lay there talking. She never asked the question that was in both our minds: Was it all worth this? New Rochelle refused to be awakened or cleaned up. Why try when it meant jeopardizing our family? Finally she fell silent, and I thought she was asleep. But then she said quietly, "Well, that's the way you are, and you might as well go ahead and do it or you'll be miserable."

I almost bawled.

CHAPTER SIX

To Tom, this was living. He was seated on a couch with a beautiful woman on either side, adoring him, asking if he was a real, a *really* real Treasury agent. Myron, the other agent sent by Marv, was seated across the room in a deep, cushioned chair. One lovely young woman was handing him a drink, another looking at him with awe. Myron was six feet tall, with shoulders as broad and square as a block of granite. His belly was flat and his arms made of oak. His military service had left him with a neatly clipped moustache and a back as straight as a plumb line.

"What's it like to be a narcotics agent?"

"Well, I'm not with the Bureau of Narcotics now, I'm with the Intelligence Division of the IRS."

The room was overflowing with people, most of them women directing their conversation at the agents.

"Have you ever been shot at?"

Tom tried to look serious as he said, "Many, many times, but seldom hit."

"Can I see your pistol?"

"Do you put people in handcuffs?"

"Have you ever arrested a Mafia man?"

"Does your wife worry about you?"

"When you go on a raid are you afraid?"

"Are addicts dangerous?"

After this had gone on for half an hour, and as soon as everyone had something to drink, I called the girls to order.

"OK, girls, let's get to work. I asked the boys to come over here for a reason. We mustn't take too much of their time."

The talking subsided suddenly, so Tom's voice stood out as he whispered, "Oh, I'm in no hurry."

"Now, I've already told you what we are going to try to do," I continued. "In this last series of arrests, we hurt the Mob, but we want to hurt them badly. We want to get their policy bank. And in order to get it, I intend to unleash my secret weapon—you girls."

"Fay," Tom interrupted, "I feel compelled to go on record here and say that you're nuts. Nice, but nuts. A bunch of amateurs can't get a bank. It is the most closely guarded secret of the Mob."

Anne spoke up in her cool, low-pitched voice. "Why is it such a big secret?" She was the girl who was to head up the project. I had approached her two weeks before with my crazy idea. She was ideal. She had a remarkable mind, excellent organizing ability, and great energy. Most important of all was her ability to get people together, coordinating, coaxing, scolding, leading them till they reached their goal. She was to need all her formidable talents in the months ahead.

"Well, if a bank is hit, their whole organization is thrown into chaos," Tom explained. "They've got to find new collection methods, get new men to do the work, select different places to meet, and just generally reorganize."

"What is a bank, anyway?" Vicki was speaking, beautiful Vicki with the raven hair and the wide eyes and the ethereal skin. She was so beautiful and innocent looking that most men did not even leer at her but treated her with the awe usually reserved for madonnas.

"It's the headquarters for their operations. You see, the local policy joint is only one of several, sometimes hundreds, of places in the Organization. They all send their slips into one central place where they are collated, the sums added up, money allocated to the places that had winners, and bills made up for the controllers."

"That's a bank?"

"Yeh, or an 'office' as it is sometimes called. In Harlem it is smaller; sometimes there's a bank every block. Out here, where the action is run by the Italians, it is probably one big bank for all of Westchester. And believe me, they'll guard that secret with their lives."

"Have you ever found a bank?" Claire was speaking now. She was a strikingly gorgeous redhead with hair that seemed to be afire. She was rich, incredibly, overpoweringly rich. Trips to Puerto Rico or the Riviera, mink coats, and Cadillacs were as natural to her as six-year-old Chevrolets were to the rest of us. She was brassy, trim, confident, a good sport, and surprisingly sensitive. And now her eyes were hot with anger.

"Well, of course, *we've* found a bank. We're professionals," Tom answered.

"You may be professionals," Claire asserted, "but I'll bet we can find one, too."

All the girls began to giggle and murmur in agreement.

"OK, OK," Tom said. "Good luck, but I just want you to know it's hard. And, in fact, it'll be a miracle if you do find it, but it'll be a lot of fun, too—if you don't get yourself hurt."

"Pfoof! They're not going to hurt me, I'll guarantee you that. I'll carry a long hatpin and —."

Myron interrupted. "Well, there's no reason why you should get hurt or even for them to know that any of you are involved in this if you play your cards right. In fact, I have to admit that, even though it sounds kooky, it might just work."

"Yeh," Tom said, "who'd ever suspect that some women with shopping bags are looking for a bank. It's so crazy that something might come of it. That I'll grant you. But in order to get that bank, you'll have to find out who the pickup man is, tail him to a drop, find out who the pickup man is from there, tail him to where he gives off to another guy. They may run it through four or five guys. They may take the work at ten o'clock in the morning, at eleven or twelve or one or even at two, depending on the place. They may walk it out to some car and throw it in, or they may give it to some woman who carries it out, or they may give it to a guy who then drives over to his apartment house and parks the car and leaves it for three or eight hours. What are you going to do about that?"

"Let's take it one step at a time, Tom," I suggested. "Tell the girls first about the way the work moves."

"OK. The number for the day is figured in this area on the so-called Manhattan system from the total earnings on the races at various tracks. Right now the track is Hialeah in Florida, later it will be Tropical and then Aqueduct. They add the total amount won by the horses that win, place, or show for the first three races.

If the amount is something like 469, then the first digit of the winning number for that day is 9. The second digit is computed from the amount the winners pay for the first five races totaled together. The third digit is taken from the total winnings of the first three horses in all seven races. Now, that means the policy work, or the action, the slips, must be in the hands of a trusted employee of the bank by the time the first three races are run. Otherwise, some clown with a shortwave radio could find out the first digit and improve his chances of winning immensely and take the boys for a trimming. That's happened in some places, especially if they are playing bolita, which is on only two numbers."

"You mean that those people are betting ordinarily on three digits? That means they have only one chance in 999 of winning."

"That's right, and yet they don't pay off on those odds. They never pay better than 600 to 1 and often on numbers that are popular they only pay 200 or 300 to 1."

"Why, do some numbers come in more often than others?"

"Oh, no, but if hundreds of people are betting on some number, and it comes in, the banker can be ruined. So he cuts the odds. These guys have to be alert constantly to predict what number people are likely to bet on so they can cut the odds. For example, if the President's grandson is born on Thursday at three forty-five in the morning, there will probably be a tremendous number of bets on number 345 the next day. If it should hit, the banker is in trouble."

"Are people that superstitious?" Jewel found this hard to believe. Jewish, highly intelligent, and vivacious to the point of being almost perpetually in motion, she was also highly skeptical.

"Sure. Most people have some reason for betting a number. A friend is in the hospital in Room 804 or they dreamed an airplane crashed and it was Flight 209, and so forth. They even read these silly little books that give the winning numbers for the last few months and even years. They have articles in them by some astrologer or nut with a name like Uncle Bob or Swami who gives his opinion on what number is likely to 'pop.'

"OK, this means that around here right now the work must be in the hands of that trusted employee by two-thirty at the latest. I suppose that the slips are collected in the drops by two."

"Probably," Myron said. "Some people wait through lunch, and when they have gotten all the bets they are likely to get from the work crowd, they send some slob out with the slips in a paper bag or even in his pocket, and he carries it out to some place designated as a drop. That may be a car parked near several joints or it may be, and this is more likely, another joint where the work is made up in a package or recorded on tapes."

"Then how do we begin to find out all this?" This was Hortense. She was tall, a rough-spoken, homely, but brilliant Jewish woman. A good friend of mine and Norman Stanton's, she was active in a number of community projects. We had persuaded her to work with us, knowing that we could use her energy and intelligence.

"You begin by finding a place where you know, absolutely *know,* that action is being taken," Tom said. "Then you watch it from about twelve-thirty to two-thirty to see if you can figure out who is taking out the work, and where it is going. If he is taking it to another place that is a drop, watch *it* until the pickup man arrives, and you follow him, and his successors, to the bank or at least to the collection depot."

Tom and Myron proceeded to give the girls tips on how to carry out the surveillance without being conspicuous, what to look for, and how to do a "tail job," which, they admitted, was hard without radio cars.

"Well, it does look like a big job, and one that will take a lot of patience. All right, girls, there it is. Do you want to do it or not? It will take a lot of work, but it sounds like fun. What do you say?"

They all agreed eagerly, and Anne began to make up a schedule for watching the place we had chosen to begin with. She told them to show up with pad and pencil and make surreptitious notes. One girl would watch from a coffee shop for 20 minutes while she consumed a jelly roll and, when she left, another girl would go to the bus stop and watch for the next 15 minutes. Then another girl in a car would pull up and call to the girl at the bus stop and the two of them would sit in the car, chatting and watching for another 20 minutes. By this time another girl would have taken up her post in a ten-cent store, pretending to be leafing through paperbacks while she watched.

The schedule was complicated, but we had nine girls altogether, and they were enthusiastic. The agents listened and shook their heads in disbelief. As professionals, they knew it was mad, yet they also had to admit that if the scheme worked it would put a big dent in the Organization. Local and county agencies were obviously unable or unwilling to do much about Organized Crime.

The state police were efficient, but limited in manpower. The federal agents were superbly equipped and trained, but ridiculously short of manpower. They did not have enough men to cover Westchester County alone, yet they had all of our county plus the Bronx, Manhattan, and Staten Island in their jurisdiction. If we could operate effectively, we could gather invaluable information and bring about some important arrests. The plan was perfect. The execution turned out to be another matter. I had to leave the project almost entirely in Anne's hands because I had my hands full with parish duties and receiving and coordinating information from informants and undercover volunteers. As it happened, I was to find my hands more than full with one informant alone.

The girls turned out to be one of the most frustrating, exciting, humorous, and, eventually, effective instruments in our fight against Organized Crime. They worked indefatigably and with imagination. I had strongly suspected that they would. I have come to know women better than most men do. When I make a pastoral call, it is likely that only the woman will be at home, and, because more than half the congregation of any Protestant church will probably be women, it follows that more than half the counseling and committee meetings involve women. I have come to see just how miserable and bored many of them are. They have minds as highly tuned and as capacious as their husbands', but what do they do with their talents? Wash dishes and dust and wipe babies' bottoms and ferry kids around in their station wagons. Then, when the husband comes home from the office in the evening and his wife tries to start a conversation, he falls asleep from exhaustion. If she joins groups and tries to forge a life of her own, he objects strenuously to her being out in the evening when he is home. He finds it difficult to fall asleep in front of the television set in the den unless she is somewhere in the house. He is likely to give her a lecture about the importance of the home and how he wants her to be a mother and wife above all else. She is trapped. Increasingly, the club work that absorbed Westchester County matrons in the past leaves younger women bored stiff. These graduates of the best universities and, in many cases, of our business and our industry are rarely interested in rolling bandages or hearing a woman author talk about her racy book on a trip through Europe. So they sit at home and steam, gossip and grouse with friends, or, in some sad cases, drink. The hardest of the insults and indignities they endure, however, is the condescending manner of their husbands, who assume they could never understand the arcane mysteries of Wall Street or Madison Avenue. Rarely did I ask a woman to work on the crime project and get turned down. They were looking for something headier than the PTA or the Mother's Club.

I must admit that throughout the project I chose them with care. I looked for women who were good sports and had a love of adventure. I have always liked salty women who are competent and willing to talk back to their men. The recent rash of articles claiming that the American woman doesn't know as much about how to treat a man as does a French or Italian or Japanese woman leaves me cold. I am less interested in a woman who is an ornament, or who is helplessly lacking in independence, than in a woman who will argue with her husband and have her own opinions on many subjects. I don't mean that I like those female tanks who drive their cringing husbands before them through supermarkets, women with voices like bullhorns. I do like to see women with clear eyes and firm chins and straight backs, women who swat their kids when they are naughty, who deflate their husbands when they become pompous, and who run their modern, complicated American households with aplomb. That is the kind of woman I went looking for, and found.

It had started the night I called the first meeting of the Citizens Against Organized Crime. Anne and Vicki came at my special invitation. We organized, elected the usual complement of secretaries, treasurers, and vice-presidents, and then proceeded to work secretly with the members who were *really* willing to pitch in and do something. In this case it meant these two. Anne is the wife of a young executive and the mother of two boys and a girl, Rachel. She is strikingly attractive, with a fine carriage and the poise one finds in professional models, which she had been before her marriage. Anne is the daughter of a fundamentalist minister and has always been troubled by religion. Unable to accept much of what she learned from her father, she nevertheless has the highest respect for him and an instinctive religious nature. But the old-style fundamentalist would be shocked by her. Anne bleaches her hair, is carefully made up at all times, and smokes constantly. I can think of no one else who could have headed up our operation. She has level green eyes that smoke with indignation when she is crossed, and I have seen her shrivel tough Treasury agents with the fury of her criticism. Only those of us who worked most closely with her have seen that very feminine chin quiver and tears come to her eyes when she made a mistake or when all seemed lost.

Vicki, a close friend of Anne, was very different. After high school, she had worked for a few years as a secretary before she married and moved to New Rochelle. She was a wonderful girl, not only to look at but to know. Not as brilliant as Anne, she was still keenly intelligent and capable. The most amazing thing about Vicki was her soul. She was one of the few truly innocent people I have known. This meant, of course, that at times she was naïve, childlike, and vulnerable to the cruelties of life. But she had her tough side, too. She worked feverishly on our project.

I asked Anne and Vicki if they would stay for a few minutes after the first meeting of the committee. It was then that I broached my plan. Their eyes almost popped out of their faces and I could see their throats pounding. But they agreed calmly and without hesitation. I suggested that they might want to talk it over with their husbands. They both denied it was necessary, saying that, if their husbands could make decisions without consulting *them*, they could do the same. I sighed, and then presented my second request. I wanted them to hold onto my notebooks, containing all the information I had accumulated about hoodlums and public figures, and to add to them whatever they learned and the new information I would periodically receive. When they agreed again, I got the books out of the safe and handed them over, with suitable warnings to be careful with them and not to gossip about the contents because much of it was only rumors. Anne's hands trembled as she took the books, and I am not sure to this day whether it was from trepidation or eagerness. At any rate, they soon left and I locked up and went home.

Not until much later did I learn how terrified they were when they went to their car. They kept to the shadows and looked carefully to be sure nobody saw them as they got in. Then they started the motor and gunned the car into traffic. They felt so self-conscious with the explosive notebooks in their car that they were sure every shadow hid a man watching them. As they headed into traffic, the motor died, and there they sat in the middle of the road trying to start the motor, while other motorists honked and swore. Anne panicked and flooded the engine. Finally, a policeman came by and asked if they needed help. By this time their hearts were pounding, their cheeks were flaming, and they were close to tears. Anne assured the officer that nothing was seriously wrong with the car and Vicki elaborately tried to cover the note-books with an old raincoat—only calling his attention to them. Blinking in puzzlement, he was about to ask what the devil was going on when the motor roared. The girls flashed their best smiles and started off again. Again Anne let out the clutch too fast and the car jerked, rocked, and shot off at high speed. They could see the policeman scratching his head behind them.

At Vicki's apartment, they made a pot of coffee, locked the door and put on the chain, and sat down to read the notebooks. Cigarette butts piled up in the ashtrays, the coffee cups were drained again and again, and Vicki's husband called grouchily a half dozen times for her to come to bed. They read the books from cover to cover, squealing excitedly when they came to adverse information on someone they disliked and oohing over tidbits about someone else. Occasionally they caught their breath at a reference to a friend or acquaintance. Once a door slammed in the apartment next door just as the girls were reading the entry, "Said by informant number one and three to be the Mafia *capo* who killed Johnny Boy." They jumped up so quickly that the books and ashtrays crashed to the floor. It was one-thirty before they finished, and for a moment or two sat staring at each other.

"I don't know whether to be scared or excited," Vicki said.

"What gets me is that it is all so obvious when you see it gathered together like this," Anne declared. "And to think that I have lived here so long and never knew."

"You hear about it happening other places but you don't think it could be in your own backyard."

Eventually Anne gathered up her things, slipped out to her car, and went home to her angry husband and to the beginning of an experience she would never forget.

The next day I was at my desk going through mail and getting ready to go to a meeting at presbytery headquarters when Mrs. Hobbs rang me on the intercom and said, "There's a young man here who wants to see you—says it's personal." That usually means some itinerant looking for a handout. They invariably say that they want to see the minister on something "personal," come in with an amazing, "stranger-than-truth" story tightly woven, full of rich details and corroborative facts to give it an air of authenticity. I am a perennial sucker for such stories and Mrs. Hobbs knew it. She shooed them away when she could, but apparently she had not been successful this time. In all candor, she was probably more realistic than I, because I have never yet had one of them come back and repay me, as they all solemnly promised they would. But then, even bums, even professional moochers, are human beings, and because they have chosen such a strange way to make a living they are probably neurotic and in need of friendship. So I told her to send the visitor in, and met for the first time the young man whom I'll call here Bob MacPherson. I was to get better acquainted with him.

Bob, as I said, was young, in his mid to late twenties, broad shouldered but thin chested, with the tucked-in hips and small bottom, the grace and posture of an athlete. When I offered him my hand, his eyes slid away and his hand was limp. I immediately suspected him of being a double agent sent by the hoodlums. I should have known that they would never have sent anyone so improbable, although the double agent they finally did send was just as improbable. Bob's voice was so low that I could hardly hear him, and he spoke through ruined teeth and sluggish lips. He had the crewcut of a college athlete and was obviously intelligent, but his clothes showed he was in deep financial trouble.

"I've read about your work and I want to help," he began. "I know a little bit about this town and I said to myself when I read your article, 'Yep, he's right, and I ought to help him.' So here I am."

He grinned crookedly and self-consciously, trying to hide his brown, dying stumps of teeth and swollen gums. I invited him to sit down and began to pump him for information. He listed some of the best-known betting places in the downtown section of the city, but had bet in none of them and did not know any of the bookies by name. He had heard of some of the more sinister gangsters in town and had rubbed elbows with several of them in bars, but he had no connections that made him immediately valuable. However, he seemed sincere, and I uneasily decided to use him. I say uneasily, because it was apparent that he was a disturbed young man. Nothing about him made sense. His conversation disclosed that he was indeed an athlete, that he had held some swimming records at high school and at college, but that he had dropped out of the latter after completing only two years. Since then, I gathered from his evasive answers, he had drifted from one place to another and from one job to another.

Generally, we had found it better not to become involved with unstable people who might cave in at a crucial moment, or give in to the pressures and tell all they knew to the hoodlums. Or get drunk and let something slip.

Most of the time, it was fairly easy to guard against that sort of thing. I purposely sent each informant out only on his own project and never let him know what anyone else was doing. That way, there was little he could tell except what he was doing. Anyone who came to ask a lot of questions instead of giving information was assumed to have been sent to find out something.

Another reason for not dealing with an unstable person was the danger to the person himself. Stable people are less likely to get themselves into trouble. On the other hand, stable, respectable people seldom frequent the places on which I needed information and were seldom willing to do the things we needed done. Stable, solid citizens were at home with their children, happily ignoring what was happening to their city. Throughout our adventure, I had to work either with unstable people who were acting from special motives or with truly remarkable people who were stable but also idealistic and determined. If I had depended only on the stable ones, however, I could never have gathered enough information to be of much good, because we could seldom use them in any capacity except surveillance. Their very poise and personalities marked them as respectable and, therefore, strange people to be spending time in bars and bookie joints. There were a few exciting exceptions, and by far the *best* volunteer undercover agents were stable and perceptive, but they were hard to find.

I decided to work with Bob despite the red flags of warning flying in my subconscious. Before long, the red flags would be flying in my conscious mind.

"Look, you know Ike and Tony's place?" I asked. "Well, go in there and hang around and have coffee and look at the racing sheet and listen. Don't try to make a bet right away, because they are too jittery, but observe and let me know what you hear. If you know of any other place where you feel more at home, spend time in there, too, and keep me posted. If something develops, I'll give you a new assignment."

Bob smiled crookedly, sadly, his dull eyes lighting up a bit. "Yeah—OK—uh—Reverend. I'll call ya."

As he left, the red flags were waving more urgently and alarm bells were also ringing, but I shrugged them off.

Nine out of ten of the persons who came to me offering to help did not work out. One man was intensely interested, but when I outlined what was necessary he disappeared and didn't even answer my telephone calls. Another came because he obviously wanted to sic me onto his enemy and put him out of business. A third had political aspirations and was trying to worm his way into my esteem so that I would affirm his candidacy at a later date. Still another was an incredibly brilliant man who would have been invaluable except for one thing: he was as nutty as a fruitcake. He did some splendid work and then vanished with his young male lover, only to return, chastened and anxious to work but unable to stick consistently at anything. One woman who telephoned me with excellent information and whom I met to plan further work seemed highly promising. I was sure she was determined to work. She called one more time, with good information about an organization dealing in narcotics, and then did not call again when she had promised. I called her, again and again, but no one answered. Finally I called her office and was told that she had quit and vanished. I never heard from her again.

There were dozens of others, old women and young women, men of all types, sizes, and stations in life. Few were of any value. As one seasoned investigator told me, "Mr. Hill, you take your informants where you can find them." So I took Bob MacPherson— and lived to regret it.

Yet, in another sense, I did not regret it. All the aggravation, vexation, and troubles of my long battle with the Syndicate did not add up to one-half the trouble that one young man caused me, but I have to concede that I liked, and still like, him. He was intelligent and idealistic, never really vicious, and quite charming in his own way. It is just that he was so difficult, so very, very difficult.

After he left, I grabbed my briefcase and set out for the presbytery. The meeting was under way when I entered, and one of the ministers sang out, "Well, hello, glamor boy."

Someone else said, "Fay, something must be wrong. One day last week your name did *not* appear in the paper. You're slipping."

"Getting rid of sin in New Rochelle, Fay? Har, har, har."

"I suppose that church attendance is increasing in at least one of the churches of our presbytery."

"I know what Fay is up to," said still another of my friends. "He wants to move to a bigger church and needs to catch their attention."

"Well, being on the front page of *The New York Times* shouldn't hurt any."

They were only trying to be funny, with no intent to hurt my feelings, even if there was an edge in some of the voices. But one of the burdens I had to bear was that virtually nobody, including my brother ministers, believed that my sole purpose was to do something for the community. They were quite sure that I had ulterior motives. I was constantly asked if my campaign and all the publicity it was receiving had not brought me dozens of calls to important, rich churches and if it had not increased the membership in my own church.

In fact, it did neither, and I had never expected that it would. People who ask such questions do not understand the church. Only an exceedingly small fraction of churchgoers attend to be stimulated, to learn, to be challenged. Most persons go for exactly the opposite reasons. Life is difficult, full of hideous dangers, ultimately lethal. The place of man in the universe is ridiculous! He exists for a few years on this blighted planet and then vanishes forever. He knows this and dreads it. The sheer absurdity threatens his sanity. So he wants to forget it. He wants his church to be a haven from reality for awhile. Fill the sanctuary with organ music (full tremolo), turn down the lights, and when it is suitably quiet the minister is supposed to stand up and reassure him that all is well, that life is not the trial it seems to be, that he has no hard ethical choices to make, that he should continue to live his life pretty much as he always has, but with a bit more vigor. The minister must never mention the problem of mortality without covering it with tons of those flowers in which we bury caskets at funerals. No note of reality must jar the already ragged consciousness of the people. All must be bland and pleasant. And then, if the minister really wants to make a hit, he will play all the familiar tunes, repeat cleverly all the familiar and well-loved platitudes. He will adorn his address with some interesting statistics and stories about individuals who overcame handicaps by prayer and hard work, and conclude with an appeal to the Great American Idea.

This idea is that, if we only *believe* a thing to be true, it will *become* true. If we think that we are the world's best salesmen, then we will become so. If we are sick but think positive thoughts, we will recover our health. The important thing is not to be morbid, not to dwell on our failures and the cold facts of reality, because that is being negative.

This is the formula that has worked successfully in religion in America for decades, and it still works today. Truth, genuine Christianity—reality—is not popular. The Word of God is sharper than any two-edged sword, cutting to the marrow of the bone. It is a hammer that breaks stones apart. It is a blinding light that sends men reeling backward into the comfort of dim twilight. Indeed, one of the reasons the church has been so sluggish in responding to challenges such as the civil rights crisis is that it is so fat, so puffy with members, that it cannot move. If it does, all the fat puts a strain on the heart—that is, the core of dedicated members—and the church collapses in exhaustion after having moved an inch.

I want to be courageous enough to remain true to the Gospel I am sworn to preach and to live. Yet I know that few things will so quickly ruin a promising career in the church as preaching Christianity. Like other men, I am ambitious and would love to be in a "prestigious church," with a thousand or two adoring parishioners gathering weekly to receive from my lips pearls of wisdom. In my breast, as in the breast of every pastor, these two desires fight. I have never been completely able to resolve the conflict. I knew when I became involved in the fight against Organized Crime that I was probably destroying my "career" as a minister, because few churches want a pugnacious prophet in the pulpit.

I did not realize all this when I entered the ministry. I had come out of World War II determined to speak the Truth that alone can bring "healing to the nations" and show the way to peace *among* men and *within* them. The Christian Gospel is exciting; it is Truth in action. It completely captivated me, and I will serve it as long as there is breath in me and the church will have me. In seminary I believed that the church was a kind of "center of maximum conflict" with the evil in life, the place where God's warriors gathered to whet their swords on the Bible, gird their loins, and plan their next battles. In short, I thought that it was where the action was. It is not—or at least it seldom is. The church has changed a small band of lean, tough, honest men who were a sort of guerrilla band into a big, flabby, mushy army of volunteers who mill about listlessly, ready to desert at the first shot.

Many of my illusions have been burned away, but I have found that the church does still have a core of heroes who make all the majestic biblical descriptions strangely true. These few have seen in the Living Word something better than themselves that leaves them forever dissatisfied. And when their yearning and unhappiness are sincere, they have produced wondrous things.

We all want fame and comfort and wealth, want desperately to be able to serve God *and* Mammon, to speak the truth, but also to live in such a way that the truth is not too bitter and does not stimulate persecution. We all want to save our souls, but not by losing our lives. By the time I entered the fight against crime, I had matured enough to know that, if I did, my church would suffer in membership and financially, and I would compile a poor record and damage my "career." The fun, the teasing of my fellow ministers that day, was therefore more bitter than they knew. Some members had already left our church. One man said that he did not want to sit under a policeman every Sunday. Another who refused to pledge said he was not paying my salary to have me play Junior G-man. Most of those who just stopped coming to church said nothing, indeed they may not have arrived at a rational reason for their defection. The church for them had ceased to be a restful retreat from life. My very presence, however tactful I might be, reminded them of the reality they were trying to escape.

"Tell me, Fay, what did you accomplish? After all the publicity and the furor, what did you accomplish? Did you get any of the big bosses or did you stop that 'wicked' gambling in New Rochelle?"

"No, we didn't get any big ones," I answered my fellow clergymen. "But in wars the generals seldom are captured. And we didn't stop the gambling, but we did diminish it. They are afraid to accept new customers now, and yet their old customers are moving out of town or dying or losing interest. So they have less money with which to corrupt officials, import narcotics, and take over legitimate businesses. We only stung them, but that is something, anyway."

"But isn't it hopeless? Aren't the gambling laws impossible to enforce? Won't there always be gambling?"

"Traffic laws are hard to enforce, too. There will always be speeders and there will always be bank robbers, but that is no excuse for not trying to enforce the laws."

"But isn't it better to work to remove the causes of crime than to punish the criminals?"

"Organized Crime *is* one of the causes of poverty and corruption, and for that matter of unorganized crime. One of the reasons our cities and states are so unable to meet their problems today is that the politicians were in so many cases elected by money provided by the Mob because those politicians agreed to do nothing."

"But, Fay, aren't you likely to get yourself killed? And what about your children?"

"Well, there was a rumor of some clowns plotting to have me knocked off, but—."

"Oh, come on, now, no gangster would touch *you*. To murder a minister would create too big a furor. They're not so stupid that they don't know that. They'll never touch you."

I, too, doubted that they would hurt me, but for a different reason. The IRS agents had let them know that if they killed me the government would get even by closing down their business for good. But, as for public reaction, the hoods knew perfectly well that it would probably be mixed. There would be relief, for if *I* were killed some persons would feel justified in not having done anything themselves. There would be satisfaction, too. Many people pay us "religious types" respect, but deep down they hate us because we represent, officially at least, the voice of their consciences. Then, the Great American Public has a strange love of gangsters. All of us live frustrated lives, wishing we had the nerve to throw off restraints and steal the money we can't seem to earn in sufficient quantity. Or we want to carry guns and "plug" anyone who gives us a hard time. Or we want to be feared so that we need only glare at somebody to have him cringe. As a result, we have an affection for gangsters who live uninhibited lives. One has only to read his local newspaper to see the truth of what I say. A gangster's daughter is married and the mayor attends. County bigwigs go to funerals of gangsters, and who cares? The hoods knew that if they killed me there might be an uproar for awhile, but it would quickly subside. But how could I explain such thoughts? So I said, "They haven't killed me because I haven't hurt them enough to make such drastic steps necessary."

"Boy, have you become a cynic!"

I gave up trying to explain. I'm not cynical or I wouldn't be trying to be realistic.

CHAPTER SEVEN

I was exhausted after the meeting at the presbytery. When I got home that night I could hardly get out of the car. Grace met me with news of several telephone calls from informants, and during our evening meal they all called again. She suggested again and again that I just ask them to call back, but I didn't dare. They were sensitive people and would be insulted. As it was, they felt important, the "insiders" trying to "wise up" the innocent minister. After the meal, I had a meeting at the church, and by the time I dragged myself home again I was gray with fatigue. Bed felt good.

When the telephone rang, I dreamed that it was the school bell in the little California town where I had grown up. The pleasant dream was shattered by the second ring. My wife groped for the phone and handed it to me wordlessly.

"Reverend Hill? This is Dr. Mullins, the mad genius, tee hee."

The caller went into a long description of the bar he had entered in an attempt to get information "for me" and about how hard he was trying to help. The next thing I knew Grace was prodding me awake and he was saying, "Hello, hello, are you there?" I muttered something about the connection being bad and said he had better call me on the office phone because my home phone might be tapped. He caught his breath with fear, agreed, and hung up.

It must have been an hour or so before the phone rang again. It was agony to come out of sleep and pick up the receiver. I knew it would be Pete with some drunken advice, or a reporter. It wasn't either. The voice was pleasant, fairly literate. In fact, if I had been fully awake I would probably have called it silky.

"Reverend Hill? This is a friend. You don't need to know my name—I don't want to get involved. But I thought you should know."

"Know what?"

"Well, I'm in a restaurant here in the Bronx and there are a couple of guys sitting behind me, and I couldn't help but overhear them. It seems that they're cops from New Rochelle and they say that you caused them to lose their jobs and they're going to bomb your place tonight."

"Cops? You must be mistaken."

"Well, all I know is what they said, but they sounded really mad and they sure seemed to know about how to rig up a bomb. I just thought you should know."

The caller hung up and my tenseness told Grace that this was no ordinary call.

"What is it, honey?"

"Oh, a nut who says some cop is going to bomb the house tonight. It's just some bum calling to try and frighten us."

With that I collapsed again. But I didn't sleep. What if it were true? The chances were one in a trillion, but the children slept on the street side of the house, and if a bomb should be thrown from a speeding car. . . . But no mad bomber would be so stupid as to plan such a thing in a public restaurant.

"They wouldn't *really* do it, would they?" Her voice was firm and had only a slight edge.

"Well, they *might* be stupid enough to do it, but they wouldn't be stupid enough to warn us ahead of time."

Grace turned over and lay still. I was wide-awake, staring out the window. It was three in the morning, but someone was walking outside on the sidewalk. I got up and looked out. It was a young man apparently returning from a date. He continued up the street.

"You don't suppose they *would* plant a bomb, not meaning to hurt us, but then call us to warn us before it were to go off, so we would discover it and really be scared and—."

"That's rather devious logic and, while they're devils, they're not noted for intelligence—guile maybe, but not intelligence."

"But what if they did?"

We discussed what we could do. If we called the local police, we would be the laughingstock of New Rochelle; the incident would inevitably end up in the newspaper, and the hoodlums would know we had taken their bait. If we didn't? Should I call Marv? What could he do? Should I call the fire department? They would also have to make a report, and it would get in the papers. And they would almost certainly call the police—so we were right back where we began. The thought of the local police searching my house for a bomb left me with a distinctly uneasy feeling. The only thing I could think to do was to call the state police. That didn't make much sense either, but at least they had jurisdiction—if anything did happen, they would have a record of the call.

I called a sergeant at the state police barracks in Hawthorne. That was stupid of me, because all he did was to call the local police and ask them to check out the threat. Within minutes a policeman from New Rochelle called to say that they had been informed of the threat and wanted to send some men to search the house. The police came. So did two fire trucks and heaven knows how many squad cars. They all turned their lights on the house so that it seemed as bright as day, and their red lights blinked and flashed. Detectives and uniformed officers tramped through the bushes around the house and then through the basement and first floor. Some of them looked at me with hatred, but they were courteous or silent, if obviously amused. Up and down the street, lights went on in homes as neighbors were awakened.

We got a few hours of sleep before the children had to be sent off to school. We told them about the search. None of them had awakened, but now they gasped. Kristin, my oldest daughter, turned white as a ghost.

"Daddy, why do you do it? Why don't you give up?" she said with anguish in her voice. "Nobody else cares. At school the teachers laugh at you. The kids think you're a nut. Why don't you just be a minister and a daddy? You'll get us all killed."

David scoffed, but she was serious. The little ones merely sat there with big eyes and white faces. Grace consoled them, and told them to be on their way to school and not to accept any rides from strangers. The telephone rang. It was a reporter from *The Standard Star*. Could I give details? Why had I called the state police instead of the local police? My stupidity was bitter in my mouth. After some evasive remarks I returned to the breakfast table. Kristin was pounding her fists on the table, her face contorted in pain.

"It's starting all over again! In the papers every day and people making cracks and teachers smirking at us and us being afraid of every car that drives past the house."

"Kristin! Your father is doing what is right. If nobody else in this town cares what happens—."

"Well, I don't care either. I just want to be let alone."

By the time I got to the office, I was sick with renewed doubts about the fight. *Was* it worth it?

The telephone ring in my secretary's office, then the intercom.

"Yes, Mrs. Hobbs?"

Her voice dripped sarcasm. "There's an 'Agent 009' on the wire for you, Mr. Bond."

"Agent what? Oh, yes, I'll take it."

I had long ago taken the precaution of giving all my undercover agents code names to use when they called the office. Then, if Mrs. Hobbs *did* gossip about them, no one would know whom she meant. Moreover, if a nosy operator should listen in on the line, or in the rather farfetched eventuality that it might be tapped, none of the names used could implicate anybody. The day before I had said that we must find a code name for Bob MacPherson. He had soberly suggested calling himself 007. I had jocularly suggested 009, but we had parted without arriving at a decision. He had apparently taken the 009 designation seriously, and from that time forward he was known as 009. I picked up the receiver, surprised at his calling so soon.

"Is this 009?"

"Yeh. Well, it's the bit."

"It's the *bit?*"

"Yep."

He paused to let that valuable piece of information take full effect. I hadn't the remotest idea what he was talking about.

"Maybe you had better tell me about it."

"It was really hot, very hot. Wow!"

"Ummmm?"

"Yeah, that was really something. I'll let you know if I run onto something else important."

With that he hung up. I sat for five full minutes staring at the receiver.

I got in an hour or two of work before the phone rang again. This time it was Pete.

"Rivrind, is it true that you framed that kid who was arrested with those other hoods?"

"Frame? Don't be absurd, Pete. You know perfectly well I wouldn't frame anybody."

"Well, the word is goin' around town that the feds didn't have anybody betting with the kid and that you ruined a nice kid who didn't do anything but carry a bet from a customer to a bookie, that he wasn't actually in the action himself."

"That's nonsense. Wait until the trial comes up, they'll find out. We had an informant betting regularly and watching the pickup man come in every day. The agent also bet there—."

"You're sure? The boys say that the feds didn't even have a warranty for his arrest."

Shortly after the federal arrests, a statement I had made about the young man who was rounded up with the bookies appeared in the newspapers and I had received a telegram demanding that I say nothing more about him before the trial. Apparently the Mob had decided to use his arrest to discredit me. A high-ranking city official went so far as to twit me about ruining the life of a young boy who had done nothing more serious than transport a bet to a bookie. The talk subsided when the case came to trial. A Treasury agent testified to making bets with the young man. He was promptly convicted and sentenced. That stopped the rumors.

I was amazed, however, to find how agitated I got when accusations and attacks were made against me. It is wearing to be berated and attacked even if one knows he is innocent. When I was told that someone was saying nasty things about me, my heart would pound and my stomach go sour. There is something unsettling about being shouted at or slyly accused of a nefarious deed. My determination would be shaken and again doubts would arise.

That day I was unusually blue. My daughter almost hysterical, the newspaper about to come out with the story on the bomb scare, my idiotic mistake in calling the police, the strange behavior of MacPherson—was it insane? Stupid? Was I becoming a crime buff, like those men who hang around the police station all the time? Was I like the fans who follow a football team, slapping all the players on the back and making pests of themselves? Was I like an old grad who grows up, returning every year to the campus to play Joe College? Had it become some immature, juvenile game? I was so tired and upset that I could no longer analyze my motivations.

The afternoon was topped off by a call from Anne to report on the first afternoon of spying. It had gone with clocklike precision. The girls hadn't seen anything, but they had been in position on time, had been able to watch the betting parlor, a luncheonette, and had taken copious notes that would be typed up for me to read. The day had had its less auspicious aspects, too. Vicki, who had gone into a five-and-dime store to look at paperbacks, had noticed a man who worked in the store watching her. She had continued to leaf coolly through the books, surreptitiously watching the policy joint and priding herself on her poise. Finally the man had walked up to her and said, "Lady, are you sick? You're as white as a ghost. I'll get you some water if you'd like."

On the whole, the operation had gone smoothly. Anne had coordinated from her car, giving one girl a nod when it was time for her to leave, and blowing her nose when it was time for another to take up her position. She had been so preoccupied with the timing that she hadn't noticed a man watching her until she had heard him say to another man, "What do you suppose all those women in the trench coats are doing, nodding and waving at each other?" She looked for the first time at the girls' clothes. Every one was wearing a trench coat. On top of that, the son of the elderly lady Anne had hired as a baby-sitter, she had discovered, was listed in our books as being tied in with the rackets. Anne had carefully hidden the books in a closet and explained her trip that day by saying she was going out shopping. She returned home with an armload of boxes that she had the foresight to ask another girl to bring for her, threw them down on the couch, and said, "Oh! Are my feet tired! I've been in every store in town, but I got what I wanted." She paid the sitter and went to get the woman's coat from the closet when she noticed that the sitter was staring at her daughter. Rachel had opened three of the boxes and was saying, "Mommy, there's nothing in these boxes. I thought you got something." Anne stammered something about the rest of the purchases being delivered later and quickly ushered the mystified sitter into the hall.

The next few days were filled with telephone reports from the girls as they gathered information and experience. They were soon relaxed about the work and found no difficulty in melting into the background. Unfortunately, all we learned was that we wouldn't get what we wanted to know out of that place. It either was not a drop or the owner or somebody he appointed took a walk each day to another place with the work under his jacket. So we moved operations to another luncheonette, taking notes on everybody who went in and out of the place from eleven-thirty in the morning until two-thirty in the afternoon.

Meanwhile, Bob MacPherson had turned into quite an agent. He was the kind of fellow who could slide into a booth at a luncheonette or onto a stool at a counter and never be noticed. He could sit, read a newspaper, listen, and come back with fantastic information.

"Hi," he said to me over the phone one day. "They did it, and you were involved."

"Oh?"

"Yeh. It's not that they're going to do anything *now*. But they were. Boy, *were they!*"

"What were they going to do?"

My ears perked up at Bob's words. He had been at the crummy little fly-specked luncheonette whose two seedy owners had, according to the Treasury agents' informant, been planning to have me "done in."

"But good, that's what, but good," Bob went on. "And were they mad. At least until this guy came in, and then they cooled it, I'll tell you. I don't know much of what happened then, because of the thing they did."

"Oh."

"You shoulda seen it when this classy dressed guy came in. Boy! He musta been Frank Costello or somethin'."

"I don't want to seem unduly self-centered, but would you mind telling me what they were saying about me?"

"About that bit. You know, the thing like they were going to do but the feds put on the heat."

"You mean they were actually going to have me hit?"

"Oh, ho, ho, *were they!* I heard them tell the one guy with the moustache about the guy they had all lined up to do the bit with your car. You must be feeling great to know they thought you deserved the best. The guy comes from the big city and they say he never misses."

My hands were sweating and my mouth was dry, but I tried to chuckle. It sounded more like a death rattle. "What made them change their minds?"

"The bit with the feds, you know, with the lawyer and the boss man."

"The boss man?"

"Yeh, through this lawyer the feds let the bums around know that if they like busted you but good the feds would sew up the whole county and business would be bad like for indefinitely. So apparently some boss guy sent down the word to these clowns like drop dead and stop making like Mafia types."

"Well, that's comforting, but who was the classy dressed guy you mentioned? Was he the boss man?"

"He musta been some boss, because of them closing the place."

"Closing what place?"

Bob was sincerely wounded that I had failed to get the full meaning out of his cryptic phrases. "Yeh. Ike and Tony's place, where I been all this time. Suddenly the place gets quiet as if somebody were praying or something." He paused to snicker. "An' two guys come in with their hands in their topcoat pockets and look around. They got faces like a disaster area and they talk with gravel in their throats. Ike and Tony both come out of the back room and turn white. So then *he* comes in, dressed in a camel's hair coat and manicured fingernails and a thin moustache and dark glasses and looking just like a successful gangster. His eyes were as black as hell itself and he nods to the big guys and they say, 'OK, boys, the place is closed. Beat it.' And Ike and Tony hustle around and say, 'Yeah, yeah, the place is closed. Come back to-night,' an' we all left."

"Did you wait and get the license number of the guy when he left?"

"Oh, ho, ho, no! I started to wait around but one of them big guys came out of the place and stared at me as if he were trying to decide whether to beat me to death with brass knuckles or cut out my heart. So I left and stood a block away. After an hour or so, I went back, but the bit was over. The place was open and the guys gone."

I questioned him about the man they had tried to hire to murder me, why they should go to such extremes, and if these men had had anything to do with the bomb scare. After half an hour of obscure syntax, I managed to make out that the hoods had enjoyed a good laugh over the scare but didn't seem to know who had tele-phoned. They had, Bob said, been so unusually furious over the arrests because a *civilian* had brought them about. "Why, we're an old and established place," Ike had said. "If this can happen to *us,* it can happen to anybody!"

Bob casually mentioned that he really shouldn't be working on Ike and Tony's place because he was much better known in another place—the J and J stationery and luncheonette. That was the drop to which the girls had turned their attention. I already had two persons who could enter it and wager, or sit and gather information, but a third might be helpful, and it was obvious that Bob had the courage and was a good observer. I suggested that he hang around there to see if he could get in a bet, or just listen.

Bob was very verbose during this conversation, and I also found out why he had so much time to spend on the streets. He was unemployed. He was married, had a child, and was on the verge of starvation. I occasionally gave him money and that kept him from starving, but if I had known what I was in for I would have tried to get him a job and refused to let him work with us. A few days after our conversation he did get a night job that permitted him to help us during the day. He was obviously hooked on it. Hardly a day or, for that matter, a night went by without a long, obscure call from him. He got terribly excited over the slightest detail of new information and drew the wildest conclusions from it. But his observations, we were later able to establish, were always meticulously accurate.

Meanwhile, the girls were accumulating information on the J and J. They watched the owner as he went next door to deliver coffee orders and when he made trips up the street and around the corner. Everyone who went in or out of the place was logged to see if any pattern would develop. My only contact with them was daily calls from Anne.

There were days when nobody went "spying," as the girls called it. The day the Mother's Club met, for example, they were all out of action. Or they would have someone lined up to go but her son would develop a cold and she would have to stay home.

They had a few problems along the way, too. Men stared at them and whistled when they stood outside. If they sat in their cars, the children in their snowsuits got too hot and cried. They tried using binoculars from a distance, until they noticed that some construction workers nearby had become suspicious. Once they thought they had found just the right place, a block down the street in front of a little stationery store. But the woman proprietor came outside and looked them over, seeming to take their license number. They drove away quickly, and that evening, studying the notebooks again, they came across a note identifying that store as a bookie joint. The city was so peppered with gambling establishments that it was almost impossible to park anywhere in the business district and not be more than half a block from one.

I did not tell Bob about the girls, or about the other two informants who occasionally dropped in to the J and J, although he dutifully reported their entrance, as did the girls from outside. Eventually, he became so accepted in the place that he was able to bring out invaluable information about the owner and his customers. The owner was something of a fool who lived in Bronxville, one of Westchester's most exclusive suburbs, where no Jew or Negro was permitted to buy or rent a home. I was wryly amused to think that a bookie could live in such a chaste community but that the Negro and Jewish Treasury agents who later arrested him could not.

The girls had wondered about one man who went into the store at the same time every day. Bob managed to find out his name and address and that he was, as a matter of fact, not a pickup man but was bringing in work from another place. In time we identified several stores that were feeding work into the J and J, and we eliminated the men who brought it from our list of suspects. The girls tailed all of them as they left the store but found no pattern in their movements. One day a man would go to his boarding house, the next to a delicatessen. None of it made any sense until we realized that he was finished with his part of the operation when he left the J and J. We were still unable to identify the pickup man. It was frustrating. Marv called periodically and couldn't understand why a pattern hadn't become obvious.

I finally told the girls that I had an undercover man in the place much of the time and also decided to let him know about the girls so we could coordinate our operations. A conference was called at my house one evening when Grace would be at choir. It was somewhat dangerous to have Bob come, but he agreed to do so and said that he would park his car around the corner, hoping no one would spot his license number and suspect he was spying for us. The girls slaved for days over their notes and even constructed a large chart of the comings and goings at the J and J.

I shooed the kids off to bed, even though they were dying to meet the mysterious 009 who had left so many cryptic messages for me. Anne and Vicki arrived first, and then the doorbell rang and I watched their eyes grow big. They were at last to meet one of my undercover agents. When Bob came in—slunk in is more accurate—they were fascinated. He could walk into a room and leave you uncertain afterward as to whether anyone had actually come in. He had a way of sitting and acting that made you forget his presence. This time, however, he was more conspicuous. In fact, in his strange way he was highly excited. His dull gray eyes flickered with lights and his voice had an edge to it.

We sat around the table pooling information and scratching out names and descriptions on the chart. One man, we discovered, was an employee of a work gang who came in for pastry and coffee each day at the same time. Another tended the counter when the owner delivered coffee to the office next door. A prime suspect was one of my undercover agents, and I suggested they drop him from the list.

The coffee pot was drained and the ashtrays filled as we grew increasingly frustrated. The pattern *had* to be there. We sat in sulky silence.

"Wait a minute," Anne said, "could it be the milkman? He spends so much time in there and comes two or three times a day. He leaves at the same time each day and I have seen him parked at half the bookie joints in town. What does he do when he is in the J and J?"

"Patsy? Why, he just comes in and sits there and talks to Big John. They yack and yack and finally Big John goes into his little room and comes out and hands an envelope to Patsy with the order in it."

"You don't suppose—." Vicki was excited.

"Well, it's possible, but it is more likely that he's giving his milk order for the next day."

Anne was hurriedly scanning the chart. "Monday, Tuesday, Wednesday, Thursday, Friday—even Saturday! Here he is every day leaving at the same time—at the right time!" Her voice rose with excitement. "What a perfect front! I'll bet he takes out half the work from New Rochelle." Her green eyes were burning and her fingers flew over the charts pointing out the times the milkman was there. "We'll just begin tailing him around town—and then we'll follow him when he leaves."

I was still skeptical. "No tailing yet. We don't want to alert him, and if he is on the route he'll be jumpy. Bob thinks the bank is right here in New Rochelle, on the west side. Let's get a map and see if we can find every entrance to that area and plant a few girls there in cars. If he appears, follow him from there. He'd be cool by then and never suspect anything."

We got out a map and plotted strategy. It was agreed that we would have girls posted near telephones all around town and that Bob would call me if it seemed that Patsy did have the work. Then one of the girls and I would telephone the others to alert them.

A heavy snow had begun to fall while we worked. Bob went out to get his car so that he could follow the girls and see them safely home. We waited and waited. Finally he came back with a sheepish grin to say that his old Volkswagen was hopelessly stuck. We all went around the corner to Bob's car, he got in and we began to push. The car only slipped deeper and deeper into the ditch. We were nearly exhausted when an automobile came slowly around the corner and stopped. It was a police patrol car. A cop stuck his head out of the window and said cheerfully, "Hi, Reverend Hill. Having some trouble?" With that the cop jumped out, came around to us, and began to push. With his added strength, the little car came free immediately and Bob thanked us. When he saw the cop, who might, after all, be curious about my visitor and take down his license number, his face tightened. He grinned slyly, mumbled something, and jumped back in the car. The girls did the same and they drove off in tandem as the friendly cop and I stood chatting in the snow. So far as we knew, he never checked on my visitor.

The next day Anne began getting her troops lined up for the stakeout. She got Hazel and several new girls and eventually had enough signed up to cover seven locations. Meanwhile, Bob was observing from the inside and called to say that, although there was a good chance that the pickup man was Patsy the milkman, it might be someone else on some days. He had seen Big John, the owner, take out a package at the right time and noticed that he was terribly nervous, but was relaxed and even cheerful when he returned. That was unusual because he was highly nervous most of the time. He owed thousands of dollars and never got out of debt, despite his brisk business in the numbers and horses. He sold traveler's checks to make extra money, and one day we read in the newspaper that he had been arraigned on a charge of not having turned in the money for the checks he sold. Creditors pestered him constantly, threatening to take away his car and his restaurant equipment. Big John did everything he could to pick up extra money. One day some men came into his shop, whispered with him for awhile, left, and returned with several cartons of what must have been bootleg cigarettes. On another occasion, he bought some merchandise that had been hijacked from a truck in New Jersey. None of these expedients seemed to help; he was still in financial trouble. Probably one reason was an apartment down near Long Island Sound to which he occasionally repaired. His friends said he had a mistress there who absorbed most of his funds. And then, like many of the less successful bookies, he himself gambled, occasionally playing a number or a horse but rarely winning. At any rate, he was seldom in a good mood, and his cheerfulness upon returning from this short errand had aroused Bob's suspicions. We later became convinced that on some days Big John did take the work to a messenger. He ran similar errands many times and was always nervous when he did.

Finally, everything was arranged. The girls were stationed at strategic spots where they might spot someone taking the work from the J and J to the west side. Each was standing beside a pay telephone waiting for a call from me. I, with one girl, was waiting at the office for Bob's call. We had sent my secretary, Mrs. Hobbs, on an errand that would take care of her for some time.

At last, the telephone rang. It was Bob.

"Yeh, hi. It's the bit." He started to hang up.

"Bob! Wait, what do you mean? Who took out the work? John or Patsy?"

"Our boy did!" His voice was dripping disgust at my obtuseness.

"Which boy?" I was screaming in frustration. We had seven cars full of women waiting to tail the man if he appeared and I couldn't get it out of Bob which man it was.

"Patsy took it." The receiver clicked. I dialed Hazel. She answered almost immediately.

"The milkman took it," I said and started to hang up, when Hazel said, "So?"

"So? Well, if he comes that way, follow him! That is the whole point of being there."

"Oh, I never did quite know what I was doing here."

By the time I got the next girl my hands were shaking. "Hello, Jewel. The milkman has the work, so keep your eyes peeled."

"What do we do if he comes this way?"

"Do? Follow him, of course, what do you think you are out there for?"

"How? Hortense had to go pick up her little boy at school and I don't have any car."

I gritted my teeth, blinked back hot tears. "Well, at least let me know if you see him come."

I was frantic with rage. I called Anne, who was waiting at the most likely corner. She at least was sane. "For heaven's sake, Anne, I thought you had all the girls instructed. They hardly know what is going on. It is the milkman."

"You must have been talking to Hazel and Jewel. I had Alice and Gail, but Alice's husband heard about her going out and blew a fuse and Gail forgot that she had an appointment at the hairdresser and—well, I had to get Hazel and Jewel and Hortense at the last minute and they missed the briefing session and . . ."

I settled down to wait for the girls to return and give me the news. Finally Anne and Vicki came trudging up the stairs, dragging their children behind them. Their faces told me that they had had no success.

"Nothing happened, nothing. Nobody ever came, neither the milkman or John or anybody we recognized."

We were disappointed. We had eliminated the possibility of the bank being on the west side, but otherwise had made no real progress. We agreed that even though the next day was Saturday a few of the girls would go out again and try to tail the man. After six fruitless telephone calls, I got Bob. He agreed to be inside the place and to nod to a girl who would be there, drinking coffee, if he saw the milkman had the work. She in turn would go out and nod once to another girl in a car down the block and then walk off in the opposite direction. The girls in the car would follow the milkman. That way neither Bob nor the girl would be suspected.

As usual, nothing worked out. Bob simply didn't show up, and the girl inside was so nonplussed that she drank three cups of Big John's black, poisonous coffee out of worry that something had happened to him. The milkman came in, chatted with the owner, and after some legerdemain with envelopes went out and drove away. Shirley and Jean were watching and decided to follow him, even without the signal. He got on the Thruway, drove to the Zerega Street exit, then to the milk plant! When the girls told me, I joined in their dejection. One good theory was shot down. He wasn't carrying any work.

It wasn't until several days later that we found out what had happened to Bob. He had been sulking over the fact that I hadn't been appreciative enough of his undercover efforts and had decided not to go to the luncheonette that day. I had called him in the afternoon to find out where he was but his wife said that he refused to come to the phone. In a few days he called me as if nothing had happened. He said he had a job, nights, but would continue to work on the case. In fact, he had already been watching for three more days and was absolutely certain that the milkman had the work. He had heard the owner tell Patsy, "Get going! When you've got the work, don't stop for nothing."

I was beginning to get skeptical about the accuracy of Bob's observations and expressed some doubt. The next day he decided to tail the milkman himself. He called me ecstatically to say that he had seen Patsy pull up alongside a car half a block before the plant entrance and throw out a small package. He had actually seen the pass! I decided to play it cool and have some of the girls check it out before I got too excited.

The next day he was back on the telephone in great excitement. "Yeh, hi. We really chose the right place. The big boss came in today."

"The big boss?"

"Yeh. Boy, did he throw the fear of God into John. He said, 'The meetin's at nine, and you better be there and on time.' John turned white. I guess this is Mr. Big himself."

As I questioned him more closely, it became evident that the "boss" was only a big-mouthed errand boy who passed on instructions from the boss man. We had picked him up going from one place to another and had the girls tail him long enough to find out where he lived and who he was. By checking with other informants we had definitely established that he was a small fry in the Syndicate who liked to throw his weight around. He would glare malevolently and talk out of the side of his mouth, all the while keeping his hand menacingly in his jacket or topcoat pocket as if fingering a revolver and trying to make up his mind whether to liquidate the victim there and then or wait for a more opportune moment. Pat Ladrone, as I'll call him here, was unemployed, yet always had enough money to get along on. We ran across his trail often. One of the most interesting times was at a political function when he and a local candidate for the city council slobbered over each other declaring their mutual undying affection and loyalty.

From the Ladrone incident we also learned something about

Bob. In fact, we were always learning something new about him. This latest revelation was that he had a tendency to "sew a vest on a button." He was so excited by his undercover work that, although he was accurate in his reporting, he put too much emphasis on what he saw. Every peanut in the Organization was to him a muscleman or high Mafioso. And the project he was working on was the only one that counted. We had other undercover people out, too, all the time. During the period we were working on the J and J, we had other operations going that brought about a series of important arrests, but, to Bob, his work was the key to breaking the Mafia along the entire eastern seacoast. He became deeply wounded if we did not give him adequate recognition or did not immediately respond to a telephone call or check out his information. He wore us all out with his incessant demands for attention.

There was, however, no doubt about the accuracy of his report on the milkman. A couple of girls "walked their children" in the Bronx and, on two occasions, watched the milkman toss a package of the right size to a man in a car who immediately drove away. The girls got the license number and we finally called Marv. He suggested a conference in his apartment that night.

Marv had agents Myron and Tom with him. We spent the evening planning the next operation. At first Marv admitted that he found it hard to believe a milkman was actually carrying the work. He wanted to know how we knew that he wasn't simply handing someone the record of his day's sales. That made us see just how dependent we were on Bob for facts. It was clear that we had to get solid confirmation. It was agreed that Marv would approach his superiors at the Internal Revenue Service for permission to have Myron, in an undercover capacity, enter the restaurant to see if he could observe bets being made and the work being passed. The girls would continue to watch and tail whenever possible. It was also agreed that, if Marv's superior would permit it, other agents would be assigned to the case to take over the girls' surveillance duties. We were happy. Our work was coming to a conclusion.

A few days later, Tom and Myron met with Anne and me in my office for further planning. The IRS had approved the project and it was ready to roll. From the attitude of the agents, however, it was obvious that the approval had been accompanied by skepticism and that they had taken quite a razzing from the other agents.

"Are you girls ready for the action today?" Tom asked.

"Well, I hope so," Anne said. "It has been quite a day."

"What do you mean?"

"I had to get the kids off to school this morning, the baby to a nursery, and my darned husband hung around the apartment working on some papers so I couldn't make my telephone calls."

"Telephone calls?"

"Yes, I have to call each of the girls who have agreed to go out to see if they're still able to, and I hate to do it when Art is around. He says that I spend more time on crime than on my home."

"Sounds like my wife," said Tom.

"And then at nine-thirty a new girl came to the apartment to get instructions on how to do her part. I could've killed her for coming so early, but she had appointments all the rest of the morning. I hadn't even made the beds, and she looked at me as if I were a pig or something. She really turned out to be quite nice. While she was there, I got two telephone calls, from Bernice and Louise. Bernice's two-year-old is sick and she won't be able to go, and Louise broke a tooth last night and has to see a dentist. So I spent a half hour on the phone pleading with some more girls to forget about the Mother's Club lecture on child rearing and go out for us instead."

Myron looked at Tom out of the corner of his eye. Tom took a long drag on his cigarette, and the misgivings he felt were hardly noticeable in his voice as he said, "Got it all arranged now?"

"Oh, sure. This is nothing, it happens all the time. We're all set. I flew around the house like a tornado getting the beds made before lunch. I needed to do the laundry, but didn't have time, so I didn't know what to do. If Art found the laundry in the cart ready to go to the basement one more lunch time he'd murder me. So I dumped it into the bathtub and closed the shower curtain. I'll get it done when I get home."

"Do the kids come home for lunch?"

"I'll say they do. I had to go get Rachel from the nursery school and get a full lunch for the kids—they're beginning to complain about peanut butter sandwiches."

"Where's Rachel now?"

"Vicki has her downstairs. She's playing in the Sunday school room with Johnny."

By this time Tom's face showed dismay at what he had gotten himself into, and Anne saw it.

"Oh, don't worry. Rachel is good as gold on our spy trips. I just put her down on the back seat with her panda bear and she goes right to sleep—or at least she does if I can get her to go to the bathroom before we go. But sometimes she's stubborn and won't go and then wants me to stop in the middle of my work."

Even imperturbable Myron was beginning to look sick, so I steered the conversation around to that day's operations.

"Now, let's see, Anne, do we have this straight, what you girls are going to do?"

"Well, because we are less conspicuous than the agents, we'll stay outside and across the street in my car. When Patsy leaves, we'll radio down the street to the boys to let them know which way Patsy is going. We'll let him get ahead of us and then try to follow at a distance."

"And Vicki?"

"She and Jewel will be in the other car and just watch the road to be sure he doesn't get away."

"They don't have a radio?"

"No, Rosalind and I have a portable—and Tom and Myron have one in their car."

"Which reminds me, we'd better show you girls how to run these little portables." Myron bent over the radios and showed both girls how to operate the two channels and the telephone-style microphone and earpiece. Then, for better or worse, it was time to go.

I had to make hospital calls that afternoon but went down to the cars to see them off. We stopped at the Sunday school rooms to pick up the other girls and their children. Johnny was crying because Rachel had clouted him, the baby was shrieking for her bottle, and all of them were smeared from ear to ear with cookie crumbs.

"OK, let's go, everybody." Anne was as cheerful and matter-of-fact as if she were going on a family picnic. She gathered up the panda bear, a blanket, the snowsuits, a coloring book and crayons, and her own coat. "Here, Tom, carry these." The T-man was so dazed he hardly noticed she had handed him a box of cookies, a baby's bottle, and Johnny's favorite pillow.

"Have you kids all been to the bathroom? How about you girls? All right, then, Vicki, give everybody a tranquilizer."

"Bathroom?" Tom was baffled.

"Tranquilizers?" Myron was mumbling to himself.

"Oh, sure," Anne said cheerfully. "We get so excited when we go out and it's dangerous if we don't go to the bathroom first. And we all take tranquilizers to help us keep cool."

I took the agents gently by the arm and led them downstairs to the parking lot. Their powerful Pontiac was parked at the curb, but the girls' cars were not in sight.

"Where's your car? I'll get it for you, Anne." Tom had recovered his gallantry if not his confidence.

"Oh, thank you, Tom. That's my car over there, behind the truck." She handed him the keys.

He stood stock-still, staring, his face gray. "But that car is pink, pink and cream—pink and cream. You go tailing in a pink and cream car?"

"Isn't it cute? We call it the 'Pink Poodle.' I used to have a black car, and I was so happy when my husband sold it and got me this one."

Tom started for the car.

"Be careful not to sit on the urine sample."

The agent stopped dead in his tracks. He turned to Anne. "The urine sample?"

"It's Rachel's. I have to drop it by the doctor's."

Tom got in the car as if he thought it were going to explode. He fussed with the ignition for a minute, while Vicki and Jewel went to their car. "It won't start," he said with deliberation. "The pink and cream car won't start."

"Why, I never have any trouble with it." Anne was mystified. "Oh, of course. Did you turn on the heater?"

"The heater?"

For a moment I thought Tom was going to cry, but he leaned forward and instantly the ancient Plymouth roared into action. He drove over to us and wordlessly got out and into the Pontiac with Myron. For one moment he looked at me accusingly, and then drove away quickly. The girls followed.

When I got back from the hospital, I found Tom and Myron waiting to give me the story of the day's adventures, and I want to make it clear that at no time did either of them say one word of disapproval or anger. Tom did most of the talking.

"We got down there and the girls parked across the street in an excellent position to see the action and we parked down the block as agreed. The girls knew the layout, all the guys who would be bringing in the work from other places and this Ladrone and so forth. Well, we decided to test the radios and tried to call them, but couldn't raise them. We didn't know what to do. If we walked back to find out what was going on, some hood might be watching and the day would be blown. But we had to get them on the radio, so we drove by and we could see Rosalind working over it. We figured that they hadn't turned on the switch, so I rolled down the window and took a chance and yelled out, 'Hey! Turn on the radio switch!' And damned if she doesn't look up and start bawling, she was so frustrated. So we said to hell with it and stopped, and I went over and she had it on B channel when it should have been on A.

"So we took up position again and hoped that the day wasn't dead. I called her and said, 'Sixty-three to portable, come in, portable.' And do you know what she said? She says over the government channel, mind you, with other agents able to listen in, even FBI agents, who love to get something to razz us about, she says, she says, 'Hi, sixty-three, this is the Pink Poodle.'" He shook his head.

Myron took up the story. "So we sat there awhile and then Anne comes on the air and says, and I quote, 'Two-vee-six-four-one-one just drove up!' I thought she was using some sort of code, so I asked her what gives. And she explains that a guy that brings in the work from another place just drove up and went inside. And I says, 'You mean that blue Chevy that just pulled up in the parking lot next to the place?' And she says, she says, get this now, she says, quote, 'Oh, is that a Chevy? I don't know one car from another, so I just memorize their license numbers. It's so much easier than trying to remember the different kinds of cars!'"

Myron lit a cigarette. His hands shook. "So all afternoon this Anne keeps coming on the air and squealing and screeching, 'Oh, boy! Everybody is here today! There goes 6WW5809 and here comes WHK2666.' Then she finally says, 'OK, boys, here comes YSA7549.' And I didn't know what the hell she was talking about till I see this milk truck."

Tom took up the narration again. "So, anyway, this milk truck driver comes like you say he will, and he is looking all around as if he is nervous and we figure that is good. So we tail him, playing it loose and easy, dropping back with five or six cars between us when we can. He goes around in a perfect circle, around the block, as if he is doing his check, and then onto the parkway. We're still playing it loose when suddenly the radio comes on. 'You're going to lose him if you don't stay closer,' this Anne says.

And in the background I can hear some kid saying, 'Mommy, I have to go to the bathroom.' So I tell her to take care of her kid and I'll take care of the tail job. But then, before we know it, that damn pink car comes sailing by us like a bat out of hell and gets right up behind the truck."

Myron was mopping his forehead. "So Tom yells at them to get the hell out of there before she alerts the bum. And this Rosalind comes over the air and says, as calm as a cucumber, 'We've done tailing before. He'll never suspect us.' Then we see Zerega Avenue coming up and we yell at them to drop back and they do. So we turn off behind the guy and they follow us. Then I radioed to them to go home, and Rosalind comes on the air again, with the whole world listening, and she says, and she is sobbing, 'But *we* want to see the pass, too.'"

Tom talked in a low voice, his eyes glazed. "We didn't know what to say, so we just kept driving, and finally they dropped back. Sure enough, this milk truck guy slows up beside a parked car and tosses a nice little package right through the window of the car, which takes off right away, like he should if he is a pickup man, and we begin to tail him carefully. And those women were tailing us. But I have got to hand it to them, they hung back a long way then and the guy never saw them. He went to an apartment house and got out. We got his number, of course, and are having it checked. What a day!"

"Where are the girls?" I asked.

Myron looked helplessly at Tom. "Tell him, Tommy."

"They went to the school to pick up one kid, and to the dentist to drop off another, and then they're doing some quick shopping at the supermarket so they will have something for dinner. Then they're picking up some dry cleaning for a neighbor and dropping off some laundry and they'll be here in a few minutes."

I had hardly had a chance to speak before we heard the girls and their children coming up the stairs. Anne was exuberant and Rosalind was dancing with excitement.

"Oh, Fay! Was it exciting! Everybody was there today. YSA7549 and WHK2666 and—."

"Anne, the boys told me they appeared and that the milkman ran a routine that looked good."

"Oh, did he! Boy, down the Thruway like a bat and off on Zerega and then we couldn't see much because these guys made us fall back, but we did see that there was a car there."

We finally got the girls settled down. They told their story of what happened at the luncheonette and the boys took it all down. Myron, who had cheered up as the story unfolded and the setup unquestionably began to look like a real numbers operation, said, "Say, you girls must use a lot of gas and make a lot of phone calls, so let me have a little list of your expenses and I'll give you some dough."

The girls objected to that, but at last they withdrew into a corner, engaged in solemn conversation, and made some notes on a slip of paper while Tom and Myron reported to headquarters. Then the girls rather timidly handed Myron the slip of paper.

"If you're sure it's all right, here it is," Anne said.

Myron took it and reached for his wallet. As he read the list, with his hand still on his wallet, he looked first at me and then at Tom.

The girls froze in fright, their eyes widened. "Is something wrong? Is it too much? Look, why don't you—."

Myron read slowly:

" 'Two boxes of Oreo cookies to keep the kids quiet, because they get hungry while we are out—39 cents a box, 78 cents total, but some are left in one box and we won't need any more for awhile.

" 'One box of Sugar Pops for same reason, 38 cents.

" 'Five Cokes for kids while we plan our next day's adventures—.' "

Anne interrupted. "One for Rachel, one for Johnny, and one for each of Sue's little boys. They usually don't go out, but they did that time because Sue couldn't get a baby-sitter and her cleaning woman had too much to do that day to be bothered with the children."

Myron completed his sentence as if he hadn't heard her:

" 'Fifty cents. One lipstick, brand new, which apparently dropped out of the car when we got out in a hurry to follow Big John on foot when we thought he was walking the work out himself (but he wasn't), $1.49.' "

"You can forget that," Anne said. "There's a chance we lost it here at the church—although I asked Jake the sexton and he didn't find it.

Myron went on as if he hadn't heard her:

" 'One pair of nylons, snagged on the broken piece of chrome that sticks out on the left side of the Pink Poodle, 49 cents.' "

"I asked Art to fix that piece of chrome. I should charge *him* instead of the government for those nylons. Mark that out."

Myron went on:

" 'Two packages of Compoz to calm us down before we go out, 98 cents a package, and we have used most of two packages and one more day like today and we will use all of them! $1.96.

" 'Six gallons of gas, regular, 34 cents per gallon, and one-half quart of oil, cheap, 30 cents, total $2.34.

" 'One teddy bear thrown out the window by Johnny when he was mad at Rachel for stealing the Oreo cookies, $1.02.

" 'Twenty-seven cents for a coloring book for Rachel when she wouldn't be quiet and we had to do something or she would give the whole thing away. And 25 cents for crayolas, too. Total, 52 cents.' "

The girls didn't know whether to be furious or to cry. They bit their lips and shifted from one foot to the other.

" 'One-half bottle of Bromo Seltzer to calm down our stomachs after having some of the pie in Big John's place the day we went in to see if we could see the pass. We had to buy something and we thought pie was safe, boy were we wrong. Nineteen cents (we got the smallest bottle we could).' "

Myron stopped reading and looked at Tom. I thought they were going to call off the entire operation right there.

"Girls," Tom tried to explain gently, "we have got to turn in the list to the office to get reimbursed, and—."

Anne was close to tears. "Well, I'm sorry. I didn't mean to do anything wrong. I am perfectly happy to pay for the stuff myself. Give it back."

"You don't understand at all," Tom said. "It isn't that it's too much. It's just that if we turn in that list we'll be the laughing-stock of the office. Teddy bears, nylons, Bromo Seltzer! We thought you'd put down something like a dozen ham sandwiches and coffees and a couple of tanks of gas."

They all looked at each other. Rosalind began to giggle, Tom snickered, Myron chuckled, and the rest of us held our sides and roared. That helped to dispel the tensions and get us back on the track. The agents were learning that they couldn't expect the girls to be like hardened Treasury men, and the girls vowed to try harder to be professional.

The ensuing days were busy. Pictures were taken with a tele-photo lens from various locations, observations of significance were made, and we began to function like a team—if a wobbly one. Myron put on work clothes and went into the luncheonette in an undercover capacity. "Ooh, Tom," our T-men heard over the radio one day, "have you seen Myron dressed like that? He's just darling."

Myron had some spare time on his hands and asked if he couldn't try to get in a bet or two at some other places around town. I suggested the Blue Room, which was in action again, although Rispole was no longer running the show. Myron casually sauntered in and in no time was placing a bet.

We had our troubles, however. Security was a constant problem, because the children sometimes knew what was going on and wanted to tell their chums. The girls had trouble keeping quiet, too. Jewel spent a few days in Florida and fell into a conversation with another young Jewish matron who spent some time telling Jewel about her work on several community projects. She then asked patronizingly, "And what do you do in *your* spare time?" Jewel airily replied, "Oh, I go spying for a Presbyterian minister," and walked away, leaving the woman with her mouth hanging open.

Relations with the agents improved steadily, and they came to have a certain respect for the girls. Even when the girls did something dumb, the agents had to admit that working with them beat working with the seedy informants they usually had to deal with. In fact, the operation became legend in the IRS office, where it had at first elicited laughter. One veteran T-man, a good friend of Marv's, began to treat him coldly and even to sulk. When Marv asked him what the trouble was, he answered, "You say you're my friend, but you never send *me* out to work with Anne and Vicki and Sue and Rosalind and them other girls."

Our biggest problem during this time was Bob MacPherson. He had become so excited about his work that he looked with contempt on everything else in his life, including his job, which he soon lost. That threw me into despair, because I felt somewhat responsible for his welfare, even though he was a volunteer, like the rest of us, and his petty expenses, too, were being paid by the government. Obsessed, he would call in the middle of the night from a bar to say that he had just seen one notorious thug talking to another, or he would appear at my office in the midst of a meeting and expect me to drop everything to talk to him. He often appeared at one or another of the girls' apartments, talking half the night while her husband fumed. He even called the agents several times to report that he and his wife were having a fight and would they come over and settle it. I spent more than one early morning hour trying to patch up his marriage.

Shortly after he lost his job, Bob called jubilantly. Big John had hired him! He was to be a counterman in the luncheonette and would probably be taking bets in no time! We were thrilled. Marv was wary. Myron and Tom were sure they could handle Bob until after the raid, but Marv was leery of working closely on a sensitive project with someone as obviously disturbed as he was. But we were able to placate Marv, and he secured approval for Bob to take the job.

Immediately he began to bring in terrific information, once about a big Mafia hoodlum from Yonkers who dropped by the store, another time about weekly meetings the hoods held. A "big shot politician," an employee of the business next door, used to come in to bet and chew the rag with the owner of the J and J, but he turned out to be one of those little men who talk constantly of running for councilman or mayor but never quite get up the nerve.

Within a few days after taking the job, Bob was taking bets. Then one day his wife called in a panic. Bob had gone out for a few drinks and had not returned. I called Marv immediately, but he thought we should wait awhile. Bob finally appeared, unshaven and sleepless. He had not been on a toot, but was a mess. He had gone to his usual bar for a drink. Some men there were talking about cops arresting somebody and about somebody else having "ratted," and they kept eyeing Bob. He waited a few minutes and then went into the men's room, where he was followed by a couple of short, gangster-looking types who were either Cuban or Puerto Rican. They accused him of having talked to the police and began to shove him around and slap him. Bob denied their charges, and the men finally warned him to keep away from cops and left.

I believed him, but Marv doubted the story. In the first place, why Puerto Ricans or Cubans? There was no report of the Mob in Westchester using anybody but Italians and a few Negroes. And if he had been that terrified, why was he still willing to go ahead with the operation, as he insisted he was? We never learned whether Bob's story was true. When he returned to the J and J he upbraided Big John for his "test." The bookie, he said, colored but said nothing. Patsy the milkman heard the exchange and told

Bob, so Bob also said, that he had received the same treatment when he first "entered the rackets."

Back at work, Bob immediately ran into more trouble. Big John was such a wretched businessman and owed so much money that he never had enough to pay Bob's full wages. That presented a problem. If we wanted Bob to stay there, he had to have enough to live on. We had virtually no money. The Treasury Department had no funds for such an emergency, or so the agents said. I always suspected they were reluctant to spend money on someone so unstable as Bob.

Poor Bob was in desperate straits. Marv coldly suggested that he quit his job and give up the project, but he could no more have done that than he could have flown to the moon. He struggled along, while I begged from one businessman after another and reached down into my own pocket, never too full to begin with, to keep Bob and his wife, now pregnant, from starving.

Big John had his own solution to Bob's financial woes. He suggested that Bob should borrow $400 from Fats the Baker and give it to him so that he could pay Bob. He neglected to mention that Bob would have to pay back $500 dollars for the $400—and within six months. Nor that, if he didn't pay it back, some of Fat's musclemen might just mosey over and break his legs. Fortunately, Bob had sense enough to decline the offer.

This was not my first experience with one of Organized Crime's most vicious monsters, the loan shark, the Shylocker—or Sherlocker, as Pete called them. One man who came to see me told a typical tale of his problems with a shark. He had borrowed $400 two years before, fallen behind in his payments, been threatened, run away, returned, been threatened again, and had a "fine" levied against him for having run away. At the time I saw him, he had paid back more than $2,000 and still owed $1,000 more. He gave half of every paycheck to the loan shark's collector, got drunk on the rest, and let his aging mother support him.

I heard more from Pete, who hated loan sharks more than any other kind of gangster, including the detestable narcotics pusher. He told me about a man named Dino, a simple soul who was forever on the bottle, gambled endlessly, and had gotten so far in debt that the Mob was going to have him killed. Pete demanded that I put a guard on Dino day and night to "alert this tragedy." Where I was to get such a guard, he never said. Dino wasn't killed, but the next we heard of him he was driving a pickup car from Heavy Eddie's place, gathering the work at Dimps' and several other places and delivering it to another man. Apparently he was working off his debt.

Meanwhile, every few days Myron and Tom would tail the milkman and, when they could, his contact. The latter would disappear into an apartment house, where he could either go out the back to another car, or into an apartment. The agents didn't dare follow him, for fear of heating up the place.

The girls went out daily and tried to establish the rest of the pickup pattern. With every day of experience, they got better. They started to watch other places, to find out which were on the same circuit of pickups. Myron continued for awhile to bet at the Blue Room, and then one day the T-men raided it and arrested the owners on a charge of not having a $50 gambling tax stamp.

Meanwhile, a problem developed from another source than the J and J. Two fantastically good informants had been bringing us information from a neighboring city. Neither knew the other, but both worked the same circle of gangsters. One, an old man, was the confidant of a loose-mouthed gambler high in the Syndicate. The other was a young man who penetrated into the inner circle of the gangsters; indeed, he was peripherally related to some of them. I have said nothing about these men until now because, although they were the best informants we ever had, their work was so dangerous that they would have been murdered instantly if they had become known. Both have since left this area and are now relatively safe. Suffice it to say that they brought us names of men high in Westchester affairs and, for that matter, in New York City affairs, who were involved in the rackets. Their information led to several arrests so important that the part they played was never announced because such an announcement might have led back to the informants.

One of them called one night and breathlessly informed me that I was going to be killed. Then he hung up. A few minutes later he called again to say that someone had come to the door of the phone booth and he hadn't dared to continue the conversation. He went on to say that he had heard the hoods calmly discussing the fact that I was to be killed. They had never quite gotten over the outrage of a civilian mixing in with law enforcement. Business was down badly, the public still angry, patrons frightened. The hoods didn't dare take new customers because they feared it might be someone working with me. There was only one solution: have me eliminated. They had carefully weighed the heat that would follow and the fact that business would languish for awhile because people were frightened, but felt they had to teach ordinary citizens to stay out of their business. It would restore a healthy sense of terror in the community if it were known that not even a minister was immune to their violence. They had voted on it. Although some had voted against, the majority had decided to go ahead with my execution.

Naturally I called Marv, and we had a meeting with the informant the next day. The story seemed too fantastic to be taken seriously, and yet this informant had never before given any false information. Marv checked with the second informant and got the same story. That clinched it. The second man not only confirmed it, but added that the night before he had heard a discussion of which "hit men" to use for the job. He had tried to call Marv, but had been unable to reach him. He had not called me because he knew the attempt was not imminent and he hadn't wanted to frighten me.

"I can't understand it," Marv said. "I've been fighting the hoods for years now, and I have put some big ones behind bars, and never encountered anything like this."

That night I spoke to every informant I could reach to ask what they had heard around New Rochelle. Not one had picked up any whiff of a plan against me. Was it all a mistake? Only loose talk? The next night the first informant called again, and again there was urgency in his voice.

"I'm up at you-know-where and they're talking again. I can't get it all, but I know they mean business. You tell Marv it's not loose talk. They've even settled on the guys to do the job. For God's sake, be careful. I'll call you again."

He did, an hour or so later, to say that he could hardly believe what he saw. The hoods were sitting in a corner table near the bar, talking over their plan in the presence of a politician and a local businessman.

Marv and Tom came to see me the following day with a subpoena to appear in federal court. That made me a federal witness and put me under the protection of the government. Then Marv gently suggested that I take all the precautions I had taken before. He also said he would have to go to the local police and ask them to give me a guard. I was not overwhelmingly thrilled by that prospect, but what could I say? He had alerted federal law enforcement personnel to be on the watch through their informants for any sign of known "hit men" and to send back to the Mob the message that my demise would be looked upon with extreme disfavor.

The police commissioner readily agreed to see that our house was guarded and that the word was also passed through his informants that I was to be left alone. When I arrived home for dinner that evening, a police car was sitting across the street with the motor running and a uniformed officer was in it, watching our house. It gave me a creepy feeling—but it gave me a still creepier feeling when he was not there. And he was not there all the time. He would watch for several minutes and drive away. Within a few minutes he or another policeman would return for a short while. Sometimes they would stay half an hour, at other times they would simply drive slowly by. We kept the drapes and shades drawn. The children were again warned, and Kristin especially felt the tension. However, David, my oldest son, said with at twinkle and no noticeable concern, "Dad, doesn't it make you feel important to know that someone wants to kill you?"

It was not a pleasant experience. When I left meetings at night I had to be sure to leave with others, and when I arrived home, if the police car was not around, had to exercise caution about getting out of the car and into the house.

One night the dog began to bark and wouldn't stop. Grace woke immediately and we lay there in the darkness wondering. I got up and crept around the house in my bare feet without turning on the lights, but didn't see anything. After I got back into bed the dog began to bark again, furiously. This time we could hear someone walking outside, apparently on the driveway. I looked out. No police car was there. Were the steps on our driveway or on the one next door, behind the high hedge? I couldn't tell. Grace and I padded silently about, looking. There was no doubt that someone was outside our house, walking around. Suddenly headlights swept around the corner and the police sentry arrived. He sat there for some time with his motor idling. The dog continued to bark ferociously. Then I heard the steps again, but still couldn't see anything. Finally the steps were gone, the dog only whined, and the police car continued to sit there with its engine idling.

The next day the younger of the two informants reported that he had been in one of the key joints the night before and heard several hoodlums making sly remarks about my approaching demise. One of them had asked the head hoodlum, "Hey, Joe, are those the guys that are going to take care of Hill?" He pointed to two strangers sitting in a corner. Joe had angrily hushed him up.

That day I was unusually fond of the indoors. Dinner was grim. Worst of all was the fact that I had to go out to a church meeting. I walked to my car, which was parked in front of the house. Another car was sitting half a block away with its motor running and the parking lights on. Could it be the police car, parked in a different place? I got into my old wreck and started the motor, breathing a little easier when the engine started without setting off a bomb. I let out the clutch and started to move, but heard a loud scraping noise and realized that a branch was caught underneath. I pulled over and got out to remove it. Suddenly tires screeched, blinding lights flared around me, and the car I had seen sitting down the road with its motor running was hurtling, roaring toward me. In the split second I had to think anything, I thought that being crushed between two cars was a miserable way to die. The car slammed to a stop and out stepped a friendly Irish cop. "Is something wrong, Mr. Hill?" It apparently never dawned on him that what made be turn white was his driving. He offered to help and to follow me down to the church, but I was so embarrassed that all I wanted him to do was beat it.

The meeting was a long one and I knew Grace would be worried, but there was nothing I could do about it. Finally, it ended and I dragged myself home. I hadn't realized how much it was taking out of me to know that I had to be on guard everywhere, and I was exhausted. When I arrived home there was no police car waiting, but there were a couple of male dogs looking mournfully at the house. I put the car away, got inside without getting shot, and found Grace waiting for me.

"Will you put Gretchen out and see to it that none of her admirers enjoys her favors while she is out?"

"Enjoys? You mean she is in heat?"

"That's exactly what I mean. That's all we need, isn't it?"

"Say, have you seen that cop's car around lately? It isn't there now."

"No, I haven't seen it for some time. I suppose there is an emergency somewhere."

I put the dog out, fought off her suitors, dragged her back into the house, and went upstairs to bed. But not for long. A dog began to howl outside the window, then another, then a third, all calling to their female companion. She began to bark back. It was bedlam, yet I was afraid to go out to throw tin cans at them as I usually do for fear some crazy hood might be lying in wait for me with a carbine—a rather improbable possibility, but, then, the whole thing was improbable.

"Well," Grace said, "you should feel safe tonight. If some poor gangster came here tonight to shoot you, he would think you had a whole K-9 Corps guarding you."

We heard no more about the threats and to this day are uncertain whether the hoodlums were just gassing or really meant it. Gangsters are great loudmouths who love to pretend that they know everything and can push a button and cause someone to die. But it is seldom really that way, particularly in Westchester, where they are not as well organized as in areas such as Brooklyn or the Bronx. Musclemen in our county are rarely very tough. One, in fact, is forever getting beaten up. When two or three of them are together, with no witnesses around, and particularly if the victim is afraid, it's another story—they're vicious. But individually they are not half as tough as they try to make the public think.

Bob, meanwhile, had been driving us all so crazy with phone calls demanding action, and Marv was afraid he wouldn't be able to keep control of himself long enough for us to track down the bank. The T-men decided to raid the J and J and arrest Big John and maybe the milkman. The raid occurred, fittingly, on Friday the 13th. The girls hadn't been told when it would happen but were at their posts that day, with great excitement at first. Then they fell to thinking about their operation being over. Big John would go to jail, if only long enough to be booked. They suddenly decided it wasn't fun at all—indeed, they had become quite fond of Big John. He was *their* bookie. They actually sniffled at the thought of his being arrested.

Patsy the milkman parked his truck and strolled into the luncheonette. He was out in a flash and drove away to the sound of screeching tires.

Inside, Big John whispered to Bob, "Get the work, and burn it. It's in the file cabinet under 'I.'" Bob managed to pass this word to the agents, but they misunderstood it to mean an old file in the J and J. In fact, Big John hid his work next door. The superpatriot who had pretensions to political ambitions overheard Big John, rushed next door, and destroyed the evidence.

Bob was not arrested. He stayed in the shop for a few days to see if the raid would stir up some interesting activity. It did. The next day Fats the Baker came in to pledge his undying support of Big John, who was, of course, taking bets again. The superpatriot was there to boast about his exploits. And in a few days this 100 percent American, the owner of the business next door, and his son were sitting in the office of an assistant United States attorney waiting to be questioned and to appear before a grand jury. Bob was there, too. The three agreed to "know nothing" and warned Bob not to talk either.

When Bob was called in for questioning, he was told that the others had not cracked. Would he be willing to be identified as an undercover man? That might, of course, subject him to some harassment or danger, but we were prepared for that. After he had told his story, we planned to send him to the Midwest, where he could work part-time and reenter college. Friends of mine had offered to help him get a job and a place to stay. NBC, which was doing a three-and-a-half-hour report on Organized Crime, had asked Bob if he would consent to be interviewed, and the money he got for that would enable him to go back to college. Bob, therefore, was more than willing to give testimony to the grand jury. The other three were then called back for questioning, one by one, and informed, with Bob's consent, that he had been a special undercover agent for the United States government for four months. All three cracked when faced with charges of giving perjured statements.

Later that day, Bob went to a hotel room in New York and gave a long taped interview for the NBC television crew. When he finished, the TV people paid him. I gave him a considerable amount of cash that I had scrounged around for, we got his car out of the garage where it was being repaired, and he packed to go. I was never in my life so happy to see anybody go, like him though I did. He left behind an expensive, smashed tape recorder —obviously thrown against a wall during one of his rages—but I felt a wave of relief come over me. Bob would start a new life and perhaps things would be better for him now.

CHAPTER EIGHT

The girls and I had to admit that the operation had been good experience, but largely a bust. Out of our months of work, we had brought about the arrest of one small-potatoes bookie, and we were told that a warrant had been sworn out for the milkman. Hundreds of dollars, more than we had spent on all the other arrests together, and more hours than anybody could count had gone into the project and we had gotten two arrests. The policy bank seemed as safe and as remote as ever.

It was very discouraging, but we were determined to try again. We tentatively chose another spot—Heavy Eddie's—for surveillance. Anne got out her notebook and began to draw sketches for the girls' assignments and to make schedules.

"It would be so much easier if we had somebody inside, like Bob," Rosalind said pensively, thinking of all the fruitless hours of watching before Bob had identified the milkman.

The next day Anne and a couple of her girls were at their stations to watch Heavy Eddie's luncheonette, trying to pick up the routine. In some ways it was a difficult place to watch, because heavy traffic often blocked it from sight for prolonged periods. There were also many loiterers nearby who whistled at the women or ogled them, so that they didn't dare stay too long in one place for fear of being found out. It was hot by this time, too, and much of the time the girls were standing in the sun.

They watched a long time that first day and saw nothing of significance. There were the usual hangers-on, as there seem to be at every bookie joint. One old man sat there most of the day, leaving only to go down the street to another bookie joint and back, once or twice. We surmised that he was probably collecting work for Eddie from the other place. And a forlorn, skinny truck driver spent several hours there, apparently waiting until it was time for him to go to work. On the whole, the first day was difficult and tedious. We weren't sanguine about the future.

"I just hope you know what you're doing," Grace, obviously disturbed, warned me. "I know it's the girls who actually do the work, but I know how much of your attention it takes up, how much time you put in just talking to your informants. I hope that you're being fair to your church, that you're not spending too much time on this thing."

She had pricked me at the one point where I was the most sensitive, and I became irritated. I had tried to be exceedingly careful about the time I put in on my job. A minister's job, however, is one that does not consist of regular hours, nine to five, five days a week. He may go to the office at nine, but he may also have a meeting that lasts until midnight and then get a call from some troubled soul in the middle of the night. It is almost impossible to get a day off during much of the year. That is the reason most churches give their ministers two weeks off each year in addition to their vacations. My church is generous. Besides the summer month of vacation, it gives its ministers two extra weeks of vacation and, in accordance with presbytery requirements, it also makes available a two-week study leave that the minister can spend, working independently or in a seminary, to refresh his thinking and his soul. Only once had I taken the two-week winter vacation, and many times I had gone weeks and weeks without a single day off. Only once did I take my two-week study leave. I have always maintained, and I think justly, that it is my family I robbed of attention in order to carry on my anticrime activity. In fact, I instituted so many changes and new programs that persons in my congregation complained, not about the lack of progress, but at the rapid rate of change.

Needless to say, however, I was always nervous about the time I spent on the campaign against Organized Crime, so I was sensitive to Grace's criticism. Then she dropped a real bombshell, the thing that had made her so concerned about the energy I had already put into the project and the energy she feared would soon be demanded of me.

"Oh, by the way, you got a telephone call just before dinner. Bob's wife Dolores called."

My throat turned dry. I could hardly speak. "*Dolores?*"

"Yes, Dolores. Mrs. Robert MacPherson. Had you forgotten her so quickly?"

"Stop it, Grace. For heaven's sake, what is it this time? They haven't returned to New Rochelle, have they?"

She took her time about answering. "No, not at all. She just wanted to tell you that something went wrong with their car. It's a total loss. They're broken down in West Virginia and staying in a motel at the rate of $15 a night. They want you to call Marv and have him call the nearest office of the Internal Revenue Service and have them send out a special agent to tow them to the next town to a garage."

I wanted to cry. "Do they want me to call them?"

"Oh, no, she said she'll call back, collect, of course. I am sure she will. We had a delightful chat the last time, for about half an hour."

When her call came, I realized that I had good reason to be apprehensive.

"Dolores, will you put Bob on the line? I want to talk to him, personally."

"Well, frankly, Reverend, he won't talk to you. He's mad at you because he says you must have taken his car to a poor mechanic for it to fall apart so quickly. He said you must have been trying to save money because you're so tight and—."

"Put him on the line!"

"Oh, no, Reverend, he won't talk to you. He's really mad. But he wants me to ask you where the agent is who is coming to haul us to the next town—."

All in all, it was not an edifying conversation. After a sleepless night of worry, I arrived at the office to find Pete had just rung up. He was in one of his less pleasant moods. Things, he said, were just the same as they had been for the last 30 years: the bookies were running wide open. Furthermore, he wanted me to get busy and do something about it. I had talked big and not delivered. After the news of the evening before, Pete's half-drunken rantings were hard to take.

"What difference has it all made? Nothin', Rivrind, nothin'!" he shouted at me. "These bums are all in action and all laughing *at you*. Are you going to take that? *Do something!*"

I hung up and took another call that was waiting. It was from a public official who shall be unnamed here. He wanted a conference with me immediately. I dropped everything and walked over to his office. I found him with several other "distinguished citizens." They had heard that NBC wanted me to be on its program about Organized Crime. They were, of course, proud of me and delighted with my work. Although they did not always agree with my methods, they certainly wanted to see our beloved city rid of these vermin—not that they knew anything about gambling, naturally. They wouldn't know a bookie joint if they saw one. And, of course, they were eager to clean out any corruption that might possibly exist in the administration. Still, they had some hesitations about my appearing on NBC. What would be accomplished? As my friends, they thought I should know that there were people in our fair city who thought I was something of a Joe McCarthy who waved lists but wasn't able to produce any results. Furthermore, people were also saying that I was a publicity hound. The gravest rumor was that I was anti-Italian, which they said they knew to be untrue. They had also heard that some of the more affluent members of my church were preparing to cease supporting it with their gifts. But perhaps the most alarming of all was the remark that New Rochelle was becoming known as a "sin city" among other residents of Westchester, families were moving out, and property values were falling. If I appeared on TV and if I continued my drive, the situation could become worse.

I was moved by their candor and sincere concern. Perhaps somewhat ungraciously, I suggested that, if the city were getting a bad name for its high crime rate, the answer would be to get rid of the criminals instead of the person who was proving they existed. That did, indeed, prove to be an unkind remark, because it provoked a brisk dissent. I was assured vehemently that I was absolutely right, that the criminals had to go, that these citizens wanted them to go as much as I did and more, because they had lived here longer than I had, that, in fact, they had endured this corruption and infestation by criminals for 30 years.

Why, if they had known about it for so long, hadn't they done something about it? I remember with regret the silence that followed my question. One man licked his lips, another studied his fingernails, another scratched his head. One prominent citizen finally spoke. They had done something about it, he declared, and without making headlines. They had worked quietly, behind the scenes, not attracting attention to themselves.

I lost my composure. If they had known about crime in the Queen City for decades, I pointed out, their methods could hardly be said to have been successful.

Another pained silence followed. At last one businessman broke it. After all, he said, was it so important? People *will* gamble, the stock market is a gamble, life itself is a gamble. Why should we bother?

To say that I was on familiar ground is to understate the matter. I went through all the arguments I could muster. "Have you ever known a cop to take a payoff from a robber or a burglar or a narcotics peddler? Rarely, if at all, right? But it is well known that not only cops, but politicians, judges, and other officials also take payoffs from gamblers. And once they are indebted in that way, they perform their jobs improperly. Once 'on the take,' they want 'ice' for everything they do. If they get money from a gambler for doing nothing, they soon expect payoffs to approve an application to build a house, electrical work, or to grant zoning adjustments."

"Well, Reverend, just what is it you *want*, what are you *after?*"

I was dumbfounded by the question, but none of the distinguished citizens seemed to be.

"What do you mean? Isn't it obvious? I want our city to be rid of these men who are ruining it, and I want our public officials to do the jobs they are paid to do, honestly and efficiently."

The man who had asked the question, a public official, smiled indulgently. "Well, we *all* want that, Reverend, but what *else* do you want, I mean, what do *you* want?"

"You ask what I want," I said angrily. "I ask what it is *you* want."

At that, one businessman screamed, "Want? My God, man! We only want to get this damn thing settled before you ruin our whole city! *We just want to get it settled and have some peace!*"

There was nothing more to say. I walked back to the church, leaving the city leaders to swear despairingly at their *enfant terrible.*

Two phone messages were awaiting me. Anne had said to tell me that they had had not a smidgen of luck that day, and that a woman by the name of Dolores had called, collect. I dashed out to make pastoral calls, partly motivated by wanting to be out of the office if Dolores called again.

The next few days were fruitless for the girls, except for one thing. They found that an old man came and stood at the same spot every day on the corner near Heavy Eddie's and went through the same peculiar routine. He would arrive, stare at Heavy Eddie's luncheonette for a few minutes, turn and chat with the policeman on the corner, cross the street, peer into a liquor store, turn around, and walk back toward the spot he had come from. An informant thought he might be a certain person, semiretired, who did odd errands for hoodlums on occasion. We conjectured that he was a lookout posted to see that no police were around when the work was moving.

The girls began to follow him. Within a few days they had reconstructed his routine. It looked interesting. He would sit in front of a store until about the "right time." Somebody would drive by and honk (or at least the girls witnessed this on two occasions). Afterwards he would stroll down to the corner where the girls had first seen him, stopping at certain shops every day to speak briefly to people or simply to stare.

Anne and John Peterson, my other assistant, managed to stroll along behind him one time without arousing his suspicions. He went to the train station, which excited Anne and John because we had heard that some bookies delivered their work to lockers in the station where the pickup man got it. They casually strolled in after him and sat down across the room. The old man sat down and looked around. He sat and sat and sat. Anne and John were afraid he was becoming suspicious. Trains came and went, but still neither he nor they moved. Finally, a young man came in with a small gym bag in his hand. Was he the pickup man? Anne and John tried desperately to think of something they could do to avert suspicion and give them an excuse to stay longer. The old man was staring at them steadily now. Anne was so nervous that she dropped her handbag and the hundreds of items in it spilled all over the floor.

"Beautiful, Anne, beautiful, a brilliant idea," said John as he bent to help her pick up the trivia, keeping his eye on the suspect.

The old man did nothing except continue to look around curiously. The young man walked out to the platform and caught the next train. Eventually the old man walked back toward town.

A few days later I found an informant who knew the old man.

He was not an employee of the Mob, only an old man, somewhat senile, who whiled away the hours chatting with acquaintances and had unconsciously fallen into the habit of doing the same things at the same time every day.

After hearing that frustrating news, I went home to hear from Grace that Bob MacPherson himself had called. He and his child were still in the motel in West Virginia. Dolores was in the hospital, where she had given birth, prematurely, to a boy who was an Rh baby and in critical condition. Bob was insane with worry and almost out of money.

I called the assistant United States attorney who had handled the case on which Bob had testified, and he agreed to try to get some money to him. We managed to scrape some together and wired it to Bob, but it was only a drop in the bucket compared to what he needed. He was carrying his older son on his back five miles each day to walk to the hospital. The situation was nightmarish, and he used it to make us all miserable. He called the agents one by one, day and night, collect, then the United States attorney, me, and the girls, bitterly telling each one how he had been abandoned by all, how we had used him and then forgotten him in his time of need. I asked so many people for money that they began to dodge when they saw me coming. I sent money out of my own pocket, although I was hundreds of dollars in debt already because of Grace's illness and the anticrime work.

The surveillance of Heavy Eddie's store was showing a dismal lack of success. One day the girls noticed a young man emerge from somewhere near the entrance to the luncheonette, walk from there to a stationery store we knew to be another bookie joint, and then disappear downtown. We considered the possibility that the work was not being carried out through the front door. At the rear of Eddie's place was a window that overlooked a maze of hallways in a basement. We speculated that the pickup man might come through the basement and stand under the window while Eddie dropped the work to him. The man could then emerge from a doorway in the apartment house next door and proceed to other bookie joints for his pickup. If so, that skinny young man might be the one we were after.

The girls tailed him, using elaborate strategies. He would walk down Huguenot Street, followed by two girls pushing baby carriages. A block or so farther, a woman walking a dog would pick him up and follow him until another girl in a car would take over.

He was tailed to the same bar each day. He always carried a gym bag, which aroused our suspicions to a fever pitch. Several hoodlums lived in the immediate vicinity. He might be taking the action to the home of one of them who would hold it and later drive to the Bronx or wherever the bank was.

We couldn't find anybody who knew the man. Finally, we got a movie camera and had a friend sit hidden in a car and film him as he left the bar. We had another man inside trying to see what he did with the bag—and were disappointed to find that he did nothing with it except set it on the counter while he had a beer. We showed the films to some of our informants. One laughed when he recognized the fellow, a lonely man who lived in the apartment house and worked an afternoon shift near the bar. He would walk down to the bar after buying a newspaper, have a beer or two, and go to work. Again we were bitterly disappointed.

I decided to approach some of the men who owned businesses across the street from Heavy Eddie's to ask if the girls could stand inside their places to watch for the pickup man. We thought that perhaps the cars and trucks that obstructed our view had made us miss the routine.

The first man assured me how much he admired what I was doing and how eager he was to help, but—he didn't want any trouble. He knew the boys played rough, and he didn't want a brick through the window or the tires of his truck slashed. The second man wouldn't think of it because he didn't want to get killed; besides, what was wrong with a little gambling, and didn't I know that they were harmless fellows who weren't hurting anybody? I gave up asking for help.

I tried one other trick. I parked my car in a lot that looked out on the back window of Heavy Eddie's luncheonette. I could see if Eddie dropped the work out to someone in the hallway below. I watched all of a blistering hot Saturday, dressed in old clothes and pretending to be working on my auto. Nothing happened.

Then I thought of a friend of the MacPherson's, a sad, disheveled creature called Mary, who had served time in prison for prostitution. I called her and asked if she knew Eddie. She did. Could she wander in there during the time when the work moved, see the pass, and let me know who did it? She agreed. The next day I called her. She had forgotten to go in. The day after that she had to see a friend. The third day she went but didn't see a thing. The fourth day she also went in, but never saw anybody do anything to suggest that he was the pickup man. The only thing to do was to send in somebody intelligent and alert enough to see what was going on. I asked a handsome and intelligent friend of mine, who had a job with unusual hours that left him free much of the day, to go in as her "boyfriend" to see if he could place a bet—and also see the work move.

Mary was delighted when she met him. He was delighted until he met her. It was an improbable match, but he was a good sport and began to go around town with her, being seen in various cruddy bars and bookie joints. The word got out that Mary had found a boyfriend. It was a sacrifice for Dick but Mary loved every minute of it—so much so that one night she even washed her face and dressed in her best clothes. She fell in love with Dick, disregarding the fact that he was happily married to a pretty wife and had three lovely daughters.

It got a trifle sticky for Dick for awhile, so we decided to make our pitch before the "affair" developed too far and caused Mary to turn against him. The next day she was to take him in to Heavy Eddie's while she bet a number.

They sashayed in as arranged, ordered sandwiches and coffee, which took courage because the food was notoriously bad, and she shoved a quarter at Heavy Eddie and cheerfully said, "Here's a quarter on number 538." With admirable aplomb, Dick whipped out a dollar bill and said, "That's a good number. Put this on it for me." Heavy Eddie erupted. He roared, he screamed, he cursed, he ranted, he frothed. A number? Heavens to Betsy, he wouldn't think of doing such a thing in his nice place. Mary should know better. He stomped back into his little back room and his counterman appeared and asked Mary to join him. Mary, the cool con, the rough-spoken, confident mistress of all occasions, began to shake all over. She hesitated before making her way obediently to the back room. Dick told me later that he heard snatches of conversation, for the most part obscene but also including such phrases as "Bring a cop in here," "How much did you get paid?" and "You'd better get him out of here before I kill him."

They left. Mary hardly spoke until they got to her hovel. Then she looked at him reproachfully and said it was all his fault for not being more cautious. She said goodbye and vanished. Dick returned many times to look for her, but she was gone.

He tried to brazen it out by going back into the joint to show how "innocent" he was. The coffee came with salt in it, and the sandwich had sugar on it. As he sat there, during the period when we knew the pickup man was due, Heavy Eddie became increasingly furious. Finally, he came over to Dick's table and began to scream, "You dirty S. O. B., why don't you get out of here? We know who you are, and if you don't stay out of places like this someone is going to break your neck. Coming in here just at this time! Now get out of here before you get killed."

Dick, tough little guy that he was, looked him in the eye and said, "Go to hell."

The thought that some ordinary citizen, some young, obviously middle-class citizen, was not terrified by the threats of a man in the rackets was so appalling that Eddie slinked off like a little boy who had been scolded. In time, Dick left. Standing outside waiting was a notorious petty hoodlum, whom I'll call here Tommy Cassone. As Dick walked away, Cassone entered the luncheonette and in a few minutes came out with a paper bag in his pocket. It was the first time any of our people had ever seen the pickup. But Dick couldn't risk following him, and we never again saw Cassone there, and don't know why he was that day.

We were completely frustrated. We had tried everything and knew no more than we had to begin with. Anne left on a trip with her husband and children, and most of the other girls knocked off for the remainder of the summer. A few of them tried haphazardly to pick up the routine at another known place, but soon found that they had misunderstood my instructions and were carrying on a surveillance of a perfectly honest delicatessen.

The calls from Bob began to come in again. He had gotten some help and had arrived in Columbus, Ohio, at the home of my wife's cousin, where he, his wife, and two children were now comfortably ensconced. I had asked Rodge and Ruth to be on the lookout for an apartment and a job for Bob, and they had cheerfully agreed. I should have known better. Rodge and Ruth were on a brief vacation and had left the house to Bob and Dolores. The calls to me were lengthier, more frequent, and no longer collect. But eventually Rodge and Ruth returned and nudged him out of the house into an apartment and a job. At last Bob was settled!

One day during this time I went to visit an informant who had had a tragic life and needed help. While we were chatting, her mother came in. "Why, you're the crime fighter," she said. "I have heard about you." Her next words woke me up. "I want you to know you are absolutely right. I used to bet every day with Heavy

Eddie over there in the midtown area until I realized that he was part of the rackets." I muttered pious platitudes about the evils of crime and gambling and tried desperately to think of some wily way to induce her to work for me. I finally asked her outright. She objected violently that she could never betray a friend. She had known Heavy Eddie for years. She wouldn't think of it! I talked of how every bookie was part of an organization that also imported narcotics, corrupted officials, and so forth, but she still shook her head in stubborn refusal. I took another tack. "You know, we *pay* for the bets our informants make, they keep any winnings, and we also pay every time an arrest is made." Her head stopped shaking, her eyes lit up. "Oh, well, I wouldn't do it for the money," she said, "but if you're sure that he is part of the rackets . . ."

So I had another informant, even if it meant that I had to prod and cajole my friends into making more contributions. Within a few days she was in Heavy Eddie's getting me valuable information. She noticed that Eddie went into the back and made up a ham sandwich that he put in a paper bag and handed to a skinny, bad-toothed man who came in and went out every day at the same time. My ears perked up. The girls had never reported a word about this man, but at last it sounded like the real thing. I decided to goad Pete into doing some work. He hated to go into Heavy Eddie's, but he agreed. He called me within minutes of the time the work was moved.

"Rivrind, d'yo remember the man I told you was going to get murdered by the loan sharks for not paying them? Dino? Well, he's taking out the work! I hear that Heavy Eddie helped him out of his troubles and he's paying off the debt by moving the action. He's driving an old blue Ford station wagon with a dent in the front door. He's a truck driver and goes to work after he delivers the action."

The truck driver! Dino! We had known he spent a great deal of time in there, but he had never left at the right time. We were getting closer.

Anne was back from vacation by now and I called with the news. She was grimly excited. She had been so frustrated by those fruitless weeks that she was determined to get going again, but she needed new girls. Many of them had moved away or lost interest. We went through the list of the Woman's Association and began calling some of the members. We also had some prospects who were friends but were not members of the church. We looked for girls who had ability and would like a dash of adventure.

Most accepted with alacrity. When they arrived at Anne's apartment for their briefing, it was obvious that we had assembled quite a team. In fact, they were the best Ladies Aid I have ever seen in a church. Anne, Vicki, Rosalind, Sue, and Alice remained from the team that had worked on the J and J. We still had Claire, the brassy, bold beauty who was the wife of a millionaire. She was so brash that she often seemed insulting, but she was really a big softy. Her chief feature was her touching sensitivity, and her feelings were easily hurt, although she would never admit it. She was one of our best spies, although sometimes a bit too bold.

Helen was a widow whose houseful of wonderful children were mostly grown up now, leaving her lonely and at odds with herself. She smoked constantly and lines of suffering had grooved her face. Sometimes she was a little too tenderhearted to be a good spy, but nobody worked harder than she or was a better sport.

Honey was a raven-haired beauty in her early thirties who was quiet and cultured, a wonderful mother of two cute little ones, and the wife of a successful executive.

Maureen was our Irish rose. She was tall and striking, with a glowing complexion and the bearing of a woman of distinction. Her mind was sharp, with a tongue to match. A great gal. She often insisted that she was not going to work on the project any more because she was frightened, or because she had doubts about its effectiveness, but she could never stay away when we called her.

Belle was a sleeper. She was short, rather quiet, and seemed dull to many people, but she turned out to be one of the best. Not only was she adventurous and extremely intelligent, but also she had a sense of humor that kept us in stitches much of the time.

Barbara was a recently widowed young matron, soft-eyed and gentle. Perhaps too cautious to be as effective as some of the others, but always willing to work. She suffered terribly from her husband's death but was too courageous and proud to burden others with her grief.

I looked them over that night and realized that they were an unusual group of women. If we were going to get the bank, this crew would do it. We told them who was the pickup man and how we intended to follow him. We believed he left Heavy Eddie's at about ten after two and went to a rendezvous with another pickup man who took the work from him. We knew he didn't take it to the bank himself, because he always returned too soon.

Anne put girls in one car on Main Street, another car on Huguenot, and a third on Grove Street, so that whatever way he went they could follow. The operation now had the feel of reality.

The very first day they spotted Dino leave in his old car and head for the west side. They tailed him. Two cars were lost immediately at a red light, but the third car followed him easily. He drove directly to Dimps' place. Anne saw him get out and go in as she drove past. By the time she circled the block he was coming back out to his car. This time she was even more cautious and tailed him for a distance. He headed right back toward Heavy Eddie's. She stuck with him, noticing, as she came around the corner, that both of the other girls' cars were gone. They had given up and gone home when they lost Dino.

This time, Dino made a U-turn and parked across the street. As Anne drove past, he got out and went into Eddie's. Anne was bewildered, but she went down the street a block, turned around, and came back again in time to see Dino walk out of the luncheonette and get into his car again. She was at an ideal distance for a tail and thought she would be able to follow him easily, when he did another U-turn in the middle of the street and shot past her. We learned a lot from that series of maneuvers, but it was exasperating.

Anne had four cars out the following day. She told them to wait until Dino returned from his run to Dimps', which we had decided was a last-minute pickup of more policy work. Apparently we were right, because again Dino came out of Eddie's, drove to Dimps', and returned. This time there was no series of U-turns. They must have been running behind schedule, because Eddie walked out of the lunch shop and handed Dino a paper bag right through the car window.

The girls, as excited as children with a new lollipop, shot off after him down the street toward Long Island Sound. The light changed, and three cars sat with engines throbbing out their drivers' disappointment as Dino disappeared. They shot off in the same direction the minute the light changed, fanning out in hopes of picking him up again.

Within seconds, one of the girls saw him driving nonchalantly back toward Eddie's. She turned around and drove back past the luncheonette. Dino was there casually sipping coffee, obviously with no more duties to perform that day. He must have dumped the work within minutes of leaving, we decided, and we knew approximately where. He might have left it in another luncheonette or a house, although we doubted it, because the hour was late and the work had to get to the bank quickly. We decided that Dino must have tossed it to another car. He had gone in the same direction as the day before, when he got away from Anne, so we believed that the meeting place must be in the area from which he had come.

The next day, Anne had seven cars spotted in the general area into which he had disappeared. She reasoned that one of them could pick him up "on the fly," as it were, when he was relaxed and sure he was not being followed. He never appeared. The day after that the girls watched the restaurant again and saw Dino appear at the "right time," get the work, do a U-turn back toward Huguenot, and turn west. We had a lookout in a car on Huguenot, headed west but on the wrong side of the light. She scurried after Dino as soon as she could get free—and met him returning after only a few blocks. It was Anne's car again, and she speculated that he might have just had time to get to the parking lot of the Thruway Diner. She drove past and scanned it carefully but didn't see any car or person she knew to be associated with the rackets.

The days dragged on without any further results, yet by the end of two weeks we realized that we had accumulated a good deal of information. It was obvious that Dino was our man. He would go from one bookie joint to another, coming out again almost immediately. The checks he ran in and out of little alleys, the series of U-turns were also standard procedure for pickup men. We knew that he was not going far, that he did not always go to the same meeting place, that he followed no set pattern. We became convinced that he was meeting his man in an area near the Sound, that he was probably using the Thruway Diner parking lot, and that he had at least two other locations.

One day the next week Anne was short of girls, even though she now had a larger squad. It was Mother's Club day. Most of them were members and felt an obligation to attend, although only a few were very much interested. When Anne mentioned needing another girl and a car, I suggested that she ask Grace. Grace had by now completed her therapy and was slowly edging back to a more normal life and diet. She could use some excitement. I also had an ulterior motive. I have always felt that the way to win over a critic to any good cause is to get him involved in it, so he can see at firsthand what is going on. Grace was not a critic in the sense of questioning the rightness of what I was doing, but she did think I put in too much time on it.

Anne did ask her, and when I went home for lunch that day Grace's eyes were glowing. "I am going out with your girls," she said. "I'm probably a dope to get involved, but I'm so tired of sitting around the house I want to do something different." She hastily put my lunch on the table and dashed out to meet Anne for a briefing.

Grace went with Belle, using our old wreck of a second car. Our station wagon would have been certain to be recognized: bookies are alert to license numbers. Grace and Belle parked a block away from Heavy Eddie's and waited. Sure enough, around the corner came our quarry. They followed Dino with ease, and Anne and Claire followed them. When Dino made a quick turn, they followed. He made another. This time they didn't dare go after him, for fear of alerting him. They kept straight on, hoping that Anne would see the pattern of the check Dino was running and pick him up at the next block. They drove around awhile but didn't see Dino again.

"Wowee, is that exciting," Grace told me afterwards. "Anne said we should wait there and, if he were going that way, a blue station wagon with a man driving who hangs his arm out the window would come along at two-oh-four, and at two-oh-three down the street he comes! Oh, was I excited!"

Belle added, "This was the first time in two weeks that I've ever seen the guy except at a great distance. The other girls have always been in the right position, but I've missed it until today. Boy, was that fun. I could see him as clearly as—."

"Wait a minute, girls. You're not supposed to get too close to the bum."

"Oh, but he drove right by us and—."

"Did you do anything to attract his attention? Did he notice you?"

Grace was scornful. "Ho! He was looking all around, but he looked right through us."

Belle was still breathless with excitement. "If only we could have stuck with him a little longer."

"Maybe some day we can get radios to communicate between cars and then it'll be much easier. When you think you're burned, you can radio to another car to pick up the chase, and you can drop back and then take over again later."

Belle wasn't listening. She was having the time of her life. "Boy! What a day! Does this beat the PTA."

Anne came in, and I could tell from her expression that she had something good to report. Claire was with her, looking disgustingly smug.

"Well, Mr. Dino wasn't quite clever enough," she said. "We got him all the way to the pass."

"You saw the pass?"

"Well, not entirely, but . . . you tell him, Anne."

"When Grace and Belle dropped back, we knew they did it because they were afraid of alerting him, so we took a chance that he was going to come out on Lockwood. Sure enough he did and turned right in front of us. He had no way of knowing that we were on him. And when he came to Warren, he turned and we followed him. But then he turned into the Medical Building parking lot. So Claire let me off and I ran into the building and up the steps and looked out the window. He couldn't see me."

"But what did you see?"

"I saw him parked next to a green taxi, WDD1351, and I think they had been talking, but it had taken me a little too long to get there, and our guy was pulling out. He pulled back, and then watched as the cab backed out and drove away."

"You didn't actually see the pass?"

"No, but I'm sure the green cab had the work."

"Did you get the name of the cab? Could you see the driver?"

"It was a La Rochelle cab and it was driven by a Negro."

"Did you try to follow the cab?"

"No, not really, because by the time I got out to the car and we got turned around he was gone. But we did look around and just now we drove past Lincoln where the cab company is located and the car was just pulling up, so we know he didn't go far."

I was thrilled. At last we were really getting somewhere. I asked Anne to call a strategy conference the next morning. As they were leaving, I heard Belle say, "After this, ironing is going to be hard to go home to."

The next morning eleven girls turned up in my office, including my wife. No longer were there any words of criticism. Her eyes were bright and she leaned forward as I began to speak.

"Girls, yesterday was a big day, as you've heard. It's fairly certain that we have identified the number two man. It is a Negro driving a green cab, license WDD1351. Now the action for today, and for a few more days until we learn more about this man, is for some of you to try to pick up Dino again and for some of you to sit up there at the top of the hill. When you see the cab leave, at about two or two-five, you try to tail him to where he meets the blue car. Then all of you who haven't been left behind stay on the cab as he leaves."

"Anne, shall I take the hill? Dino has seen me around a lot lately. I don't think he recognizes me or even notices me, but it might be better not to let him see me too often."

"OK, Claire," Anne agreed. "Grace, will you take Dino again? If you'll drive, I'll go with you."

They chattered on for a few minutes, arranging their day. I sternly warned them not to get too close and not to take chances. Then Anne took over, to arrange the schedule for the rest of the week.

"I can make it today, but tomorrow I have to take my poodle to the clipping salon," Claire said. "I have to stay with him because he gets nervous while he's being clipped unless I hold his head."

"How about Thursday?"

"Yes, but I can't have my white car. Andy says that if I don't get it to the garage for a lube and tuneup he's going to take it away from me."

"I can be here today, too," Belle interjected, "but tomorrow I'm going to the eye doctor to get my glasses adjusted and Thursday I'm going to a PTA tea—I don't want to, but I'm supposed to pour."

"Friday?"

"I'll be here Friday, and I can have my husband's black car. We haven't used it yet. Only don't tell him because he's afraid they'll find out what we're doing and slash our tires some night."

"Grace? When can you go?"

"Today, of course, and Wednesday. But on Thursday I have a conference with Cydney's teacher about her reading and—."

"Friday?"

"Mmmm, yes! I can trade with Sue about picking up the kids and be here for that day, but Monday I'll have to take her place and—."

"Oh, that's all right, Grace, I'll pick up the kids both days, since I can't go out either day anyway. Then you can take them and pick them up both days the next week."

Before long, they were all talking at once. "I'll pick up your groceries that day if you'll get Rachel from the nursery when you come back from spying, and don't be late because she gets scared if she . . ."

"Rachel, too? Jimmy used to be frightened if I were a minute late and . . ."

"You owe me 38 cents for the Kleenex I got for you yesterday, but I owe you $1.19 for the lipstick you got me last Friday and . . ."

"But I never did pay you for that cake mix you picked up . . ."

"I can't be here on Thursday because I have to work in the thrift shop, but tomorrow I have the car . . ."

"I'll be here today, but I may be a little late because after going to the dressmaker's I have to take that towel rack to the tile place and . . ."

"If you'll go with me to the antique shop where they're repairing my rattan chair, I'll go with you to the curtain shop, and then it won't take much time because one of us can wait in the car while the other runs in and we won't have to find a parking space and . . ."

I broke out in a sweat. It clearly would be impossible to untangle these schedules and mount an offensive. The planning for the invasion of Normandy, the preparations for the massive airdrop at Nijmegen, Holland, the intricacies of the Berlin airlift were child's play compared to this. Anne saw my despair and asked what was wrong. I said, "It's impossible, the hoods have us licked."

"Why?" All the girls spoke at once, in alarm.

"Because none of us have the time to work on this problem. It was too much to imagine that you girls could. I don't want any of you to feel guilty about the project collapsing."

"No time?" Anne was aghast. Grace gave me a bewildered look. "Why, we have it scheduled all through the next two weeks already, with at least three cars every day."

"What? All I heard was people saying they had to get their ski pants repaired or visit their aged aunt in Montclair."

They all burst out in pitying giggles except for Grace, who gave me a withering look. "You just don't understand women," she said. "This is their life, one detail after another. But you can be sure that, if you just get out of the way and leave us alone, we'll get the job done and find that bank."

There was no denying that my best contribution was to keep out of the way, so I sank meekly into the recesses of my chair while they chattered on, arranging schedules and budgets. I had the distinct feeling that the male world has passed up a great advantage in not having women plan the construction of dams and the scheduling of railroad trains.

CHAPTER NINE

Thanks to the girls, the pieces slowly began to fall into place. They tailed the cab driver as he left his Lincoln Avenue headquarters and saw him meet the blue station wagon almost every day. Once or twice they saw a black cab from the same company take the work, and once or twice a gray Thunderbird. They often lost the cab and the station wagon, but were able to follow one or both enough times to get a full picture.

The hoods were using at least five different places to pass the work: the Thruway Diner parking lot, an open road in the Rochelle Heights district, the Medical Center parking lot, a stretch on Church Street, and some place near the end of North Avenue. We found out in a few days where that place was.

Jean, my new secretary, was chauffering me one day to a Bible class I taught. As we came longside the Daitch Shopwell on North Avenue, a green cab rudely passed and turned into the parking lot in front of us. It was the pickup man. We pulled over and, sure enough, along came the blue station wagon. I am certain that I spoke to my class that afternoon on the subject of the prophet Amos' demand for justice with special glee and forcefulness.

The surveillance efforts continued, effectively and with their comic moments. Grace is intelligent, fearless, virtuous, disciplined, sensitive, and tender, but my wife's long list of virtues does not include foresight as to the amount of fuel required to keep an automobile running. One day she and Anne were headed for their post near Heavy Eddie's when suddenly the engine stopped. She coasted toward the curb and stopped, double-parked. Anne volunteered to walk to the nearest gas station. Before long cars were honking and people swearing. Grace sat there in a cold sweat. Where in the world was Anne? Soon a man came over and said, "Lady, I don't want to frighten you, but do you know who is parked behind you looking very annoyed?" She was too scared to say anything, but she shook her head. He said, "Commissioner Carey." Fortunately, just then Anne arrived with a can of gas.

As they pulled away and headed back for the church, Anne said, "Guess where I had to go to get gas. Right across from the joint! Dino had his car parked there and he came out of Eddie's and got into his car at the very minute the man was pouring gas into the can. Was Dino nervous! He was looking in every direction. I turned my head so he wouldn't notice me, but Heavy Eddie came out to talk to him for a minute. He looked me over as Dino drove off. I'm hoping it was just because I'm a woman and not because he was suspicious."

The project was becoming increasingly difficult. It was cumbersome to try to coordinate so many cars without some sort of communication. The girls were "flying blind," never quite knowing what was going on, and we had to have many more cars and people than we really needed. Clearly we needed two-way radios. We tried small walkie-talkies with long antennas, but their range was too limited. We needed good radios, the kind that required a license and cost $650 apiece, and we needed at least three of them.

I asked a friend who did law enforcement work outside New Rochelle if he could lend us some radios. He was able to borrow two for us. They were powerful little walkie-talkies of the type that the police use. They could broadcast from automobiles for a distance of up to two miles, and because they were portable, they gave us the advantage of being able to change automobiles daily.

The first time the girls went out with the radios they tailed the blue station wagon to Church Street, where they saw him hand over something to another man and head for the west side. They continued to tail him, trading positions occasionally. It was duck soup. The girls followed him all the way into Pelham before they got caught at a red light.

The next time out, two cars managed to tail Dino to the Thruway Diner. This time one of them drove into the lot and watched from a short distance away. Anne was in the other car, sitting in the street and ready to pick up the second car, when she heard Claire say over the radio, "Here comes the green cab. It's parking next to the blue station wagon. Dino is talking to the driver of the cab. Now he's handing a bag of something through the window to the cab driver. Now the driver of the cab is pulling out and heading for the entrance to the lot. There he goes past you. Dino is watching to see if the cab is being followed, so we'll have to wait until he leaves—which is just as well because I'm so excited I might wet my pants if I had to move now."

Anne and Alice picked up the cab and followed it easily. The driver was asleep at the wheel. They tailed him closely this time as he headed for Pelham again. They were right behind him when he pulled to the curb in front of a notorious bar in North Pelham. North Pelham was notorious enough in its own right, crawling with bookie joints as it was. A state policeman had once asked me if I didn't have some good gambling leads for him to follow. Because I didn't want him to heat up the situation in New Rochelle just when we were close to beating the bank, I had mentioned a bar in North Pelham where a man called Freddy Two Fingers was said to be handling a lot of action. Freddy and his sons, incidentally, were said to be in charge of all the action in Pelham. This was the bar where Freddy sat and sipped his drinks and took his bets. When the girls told me, I knew we had hit pay dirt. But it would be just our luck to have the state police hit Freddy just when we had found that this was where the New Rochelle work went.

The girls did no tailing for the next few days because we had to give back the radios. Nevertheless, they sat in cars to watch the bar, pushed baby carriages past it, or strolled back and forth in front walking their dogs. A couple of them shopped in a store nearby and watched from the doorway with groceries in their arms. Soon we saw that either the cab driver or Dino would come every day and meet with Freddy Two Fingers or other men we identified as hoods from North Pelham. One day the girls saw Dino walking with a man who looked vaguely familiar. He turned out to be Tommy Cassone, the man we knew was in charge of all pickups from New Rochelle. Our informants said that he rarely did the pickups himself, but that he supervised them. We knew we were close.

That night the telephone lines hummed as the girls chattered and made plans for more surveillance. They decided that the bank must be right there, above the bar! It was a heady thought. We were finished, and soon we would call Marv and say, "Hi, Marv, kid. Howzit going? Got a pencil, kid? Take down this address. It's the address of the bank." Then we would wait for the startled gasp, snicker to ourselves, and, when he and the other agents grasped what we had done, put on our best cool and sophisticated act. It was true that we had expected the bank to be in Yonkers, but this might be a good place, too. We had heard rumors that the Mob had decentralized operations and broken up the bank into several smaller ones. How things had changed since the frustrating days with Bob MacPherson!

Things had also changed with Grace. No longer were there stern looks of accusation about the amount of time I was spending on the project. When I got home, the table wouldn't even be set for dinner. I would expect to be scolded for being late, but instead would find Grace just hanging up the telephone.

"Hi. I got Belle to go with me tomorrow," she'd begin, all aglow. "We're not even going to follow Dino from the joint—his checks might burn one of us and we'd have to fade or bury the car. We'll wait for the bum at the diner. We're sure he'll come, since he hasn't been there yet this week. When the cab or blue wagon leaves, there he'll be wearing a tail three or four cars long. The other girls will have a fix on the bar, and if Cassone turns up they'll try to tail him when he leaves. I just hope that they're not alerted and have some muscle around to take care of us."

Burn? Checks? Fade? Bum? Tail? What had happened to my gentle, ladylike wife?

"What makes you think they might be alerted and have some, uh, muscle out?"

"Well, there's always the chance they burned one of us or that some canary sang. And then the cops are out all the time. We saw a cop talking to Freddy Two Fingers and a couple of the hoods yesterday, and today we saw a cop's car come up and almost immediately a hood came out of the bar and handed an envelope to the cop, who burned rubber out of there fast."

I didn't know whether to tease her about the deterioration of her language, reprimand her for not having dinner ready, or question her about the "canary" and the "cops." I decided on the last as the better part of valor. By "canary," she explained, she meant that she still wondered if someday Bob MacPherson wouldn't sell out to the other side and tell them about the women watching them. I told her she was crazy, but within a few hours she was suggesting that I eat my words. I also said that if there were any chance the girls were known they should not go out for a few weeks.

"Not on your life," Grace said determinedly. "Not when we're this close to busting the bank. Why, with what we've found out, the feds could hit the joint in a matter of days."

"Well, whatever you say," I sighed. "Are we going to eat soon?"

"Sure, the TV dinners are almost hot."

"TV dinners? But I thought you despised them."

"Well, I haven't had time to worry about food today. I had to call some of the girls to get the action ready for tomorrow."

We ate dinner in silence. The children were cowed by their "new" mother, cringing before her crisp assurance and authoritative manner. She chattered like a magpie, every sentence crackling with the argot of the hoodlums. Once Jamie interrupted to say, "Mommy, I don't know what you're talking about." But she swept on. When she mentioned Dino, Kristin said, "Dino? That's a funny name. I heard it today for the first time. One of my friends, Joanne, says her father is named that."

I stared at her.

"Where does she live?"

"Remember, you met her at my slumber party last week. She lives across town."

Grace froze and my heart turned to stone. The skinny truck driver with the bad teeth was Joanne's father. Grace looked at me in helpless agony. I tried to keep my voice calm.

"You say Joanne's father brought her to the slumber party here? What kind of car did he drive?"

"I don't know—oh, yes, I do remember, because he had had some kind of accident in it and Joanne was apologizing for it. It is an old blue station wagon."

After the kids were in bed, we discussed the matter. Grace's excitement was gone and she had tears in her eyes.

"I know all about that man," she said. "I had never connected him with Dino. But his wife is one of the nicest women in the world. She works to support the family because her husband is a dolt who drinks and gambles away his salary. I even knew that he was a truck driver, but it never occurred to me that he and Dino were the same."

At first she wanted to stop the entire operation, and also to warn Dino that if he didn't stop he would be arrested. She soon realized that was impossible. There was nothing to do but move ahead, and weep a little when the arrests came. All the fun, however, was gone out of it for my wife, who soon became her old self again.

It was about three o'clock in the morning when the call came. I groggily picked up the phone expecting to hear from Pete, who had a proclivity for calling in the middle of the night. I had even learned to talk to him without quite waking up. I woke up that night. It was the old, familiar, soft, slow voice.

"Yeh, hi."

"Why, it's Bob MacPherson. How are you, Bob? How's the new job going?"

"Well, that's partly why I called you. I quit. I had to, because I found them cheating on the milk they delivered and then I didn't like the work. We had to get up early and work late and there wasn't money in it. I'm broke and have a month's rent to pay tomorrow."

"Gee, that's, that's awful. Have you tried to borrow it from the bank?"

"I already owe the bank from the last time I was out of work."

"The last time?"

"Yeh, you see this is not the other milk company I been working for. I quit them right away. The boss was an idiot who treated me as if I were a fool."

"So you borrowed from the bank then?"

"Yeh. And when Dolores left me, she—."

"Dolores left you?"

"Yeh. And she took what money I had."

"Oh."

"I hate to bother you, but Ruth and Rodge have given me all they can."

"Ruth and Rodge have given you—you borrowed from them?"

"Yeh, but they don't have any more and I—."

By this time Grace was sitting up, her eyes smoking. I could hear her muttering to herself, "He borrowed from *my* cousins. Think of all *his* relatives we could have offended instead."

"Now, look, Bob. I can't go on indefinitely supporting you—."

"Once I do the job you wanted me to do, you drop me, huh?"

"You were a volunteer like all the rest of us. And I paid out more money to you than to all my other informants together. You'll just have to—."

"Sometimes when I see the way I been treated by you and the government, when I risked my life and limb for law and order, I just think I've been a fool, that the only thing to do is to join the other side, you know, and make some dough."

"Don't be a fool, Bob. You know you couldn't do that."

"I think the only thing to do is to blow the whole bit."

"Blow the whole bit?"

"Yeh, about the girls and everything."

I could hear the blood pounding in my ears. "Bob, you couldn't be a fink and you know it. How much money do you need?"

"I ain't going to beg. Just forget it." He hung up.

Grace and I spent several hours discussing the conversation. It was to be many a month before we would hear from him again, although Dolores was to call in a few weeks to say that she had gone back to him and that he had received a telephone call from someone who said "they" knew where he was and "they" were going to do something to him. He had gone to the federal agents and for awhile they had given him a guard as he made his rounds on the milk truck. The reason for the threatening call, we later came to believe, was that Mary, Dolores' ex-convict friend, had told the hoods where Bob was. Nothing ever came of the threat, of course. Threats are made *instead* of action, not as precursors of violence. Bob's action in going to the agents for protection, I believed, was not so much out of fear as from a desire for attention.

But we did not know this the night he said he was going to "blow the whole bit." Again we contemplated calling off the entire operation, but after some discussion we decided that, however frustrated Bob might be, he couldn't go that far.

We still had no radios. Nevertheless, we knew that we had to trace every step of the action from Heavy Eddie's to the bar in Pelham to be sure we had something definite. Accordingly, we stationed four cars of girls at the Thruway Diner and one car at the bar in Pelham. The first bad break was that Alice couldn't get a sitter for Chucky, her precocious four-year-old. We should have known that meant trouble, for the child knew what was going on and was intensely interested. Once before he had come home with his mother from a day of tailing and had calmly started to walk toward police headquarters. His mother watched him dumbfounded and then said, "Where are you going, Chucky?" He called over his shoulder, "I am going to tell the policements how much I am helping them. I'm a de'tive, too." And once in Sunday school the teacher had caught him reciting the Lord's Prayer, "Forgive us our bets as we forgive our bettors."

One by one the girls arrived at the diner, certain Dino would meet his contact there that day. The lot was so crowded, however, that they had to park close to the spot where he usually met the cab driver. Some of the children got cranky and began to cry. Even the ubiquitous Oreo cookies couldn't calm them. Right on schedule, Dino drove up and parked two cars away from Alice and Sue. The cab was late, and Dino began to gaze around at the other people in the lot. He showed a surprising interest in Alice. He may have suddenly realized that he had seen her around a lot, or maybe he recognized her distinctive car, which was bright red and white. He couldn't keep his eyes off that car, and when the cab drove up he nodded toward it to point it out to the cab driver. At that moment Chucky became really cantankerous, and Alice decided that the only way to allay Dino's suspicions was to walk away from her car. She took Chucky by the hand and said loudly, "Come along, dear, let's go to the bathroom." "But, Mommy," he screamed, "you made me go just before we came." Then, to make a complete shambles, Chucky saw my wife and said, "Mommy, there's Mrs. Hill in somebody else's car. Hi, Mrs. Hill."

Alice was never certain that Dino had heard Chucky, but something happened. The cab driver gave a package to Dino, who took off. The cabbie watched to see if anybody followed. Alice sat still and let him go, knowing that Anne was in position a few cars away. Anne was driving the famous Pink Poodle, which promoted some cause for worry that he might have noticed it, too, on former occasions and was beginning to put two and two together.

Dino drove over Kings Highway. When he came to the turnoff toward Pelham, he suddenly slowed to a crawl and was obviously looking in his rear-view mirror. Without hesitation, Anne shot right past him and drove on to Pelham, where she parked out of sight and walked to a position from which she could observe the bar.

Alice and Sue had seen the incident and decided to take a chance and follow from a distance, because the other two cars had been stalled in traffic and were lost. Dino did not look back, so far as they could tell. But he did not go to Pelham. Instead, he drove into a little street leading to the truck depot where he worked. They followed, not noticing that he had pulled over and stopped. When they did notice, they had to keep going in order not to turn his already flaming suspicions into a bonfire. The street was a dead end.

They had fallen for the classic trap, the standard maneuver of men who think they are being tailed. Alice stopped her car at the end of the street, backed up—and got stuck in the mud. She panicked, stepped on the gas, and spun her tires hideously. The engine whined and screeched, and she almost wept with mortification. Several truck drivers came out of the depot and pushed the car out of the mud. Then the girls had to drive past Dino, who peered intently at them. It was utterly humiliating. Their one consolation came later, when we told the Internal Revenue agents about the incident and they admitted that the same thing had happened to them.

Alice and Sue were not ready to give up yet, however. They drove to the top of the hill, out of sight of the truck depot but with a good view of the exit from the one-way street. Several cars left, but not the blue station wagon. They waited for more than an hour and left. They were on their way back to the church when Alice said, with terror in her voice, "Oh, my heavens, don't look now, but we're being followed. It's Dino, and he looks mad." In a near panic, they drove onto Main Street and then to North Avenue. The blue station wagon stuck with them. They speeded up and wove through traffic, but they were no match for him. They came to a yellow light and shot through; he ran the red light. By this time they were close to hysteria. They spotted a policeman near the high school and slowed down to tell him about the tail, but changed their minds and turned up Forest Avenue. This time Dino did not follow. They drove for blocks to be sure he was gone before they went home, two shaken women, to have coffee and bite their lips to keep them from trembling.

Meanwhile, Anne and Vicki were watching the bar in North Pelham. They had almost given up their vigil when Dino turned up, but not in his blue station wagon. He was driving a green sedan the girls had never seen before. He went into the bar and came out almost immediately with Cassone. The two had a long chat, and shortly they were joined by several other hoods. Obviously something was up. Their faces were strained and, when they finally parted, they all drove off with a burst of speed. Anne and Vicki, in their car, and Helen and Claire, who were watching the bar from another position, tried to follow Cassone, but he drove like a madman and both cars lost him immediately.

It was a somber meeting we had that afternoon. There could be little doubt that one of our cars was "burned." We would never be able to use it again for surveillance, and we also decided to give up the beloved Pink Poodle. From then on, we used nondescript, average-looking cars that did not call attention to themselves. We decided, too, to drop all attempts to tail Dino for two weeks at least. It was quite possible that we had completely blown the operation, that the hoods would change the routine and we would have to start all over again, this time knowing that the hoods would be on the lookout for women following them. We finally decided that we could at least keep watching the bar in Pelham, because the hoods had no reason to believe that we knew it existed.

We were all nervous about the next day's surveillance and I sat near the telephone all the time the girls were out. Not that they were in any real danger. What could the hoods do? Walk up to a woman they suspected and belt her in the teeth? Risk the social opprobium of hitting housewives in front of their children? That would possibly arouse even Westchester from its civic slumbers. I had tried to persuade the women to call it off for awhile, but they had the scent of blood in their nostrils and wanted to close in for the kill. And they were furious. So out they went.

They had been sitting at their posts for about 15 minutes when I got a telephone call from the captain in charge of the state police. He cheerfully reported that my information about Freddy Two Fingers had been correct.

"Our undercover man did a lot of investigating there and found that he was taking bets," he said. "This noon we raided the bar and caught him."

I thanked him weakly and hung up. The girls were out watching a bar where an arrest had been made that very noon. The entire area would be hot and, after what happened the day before, the hoods might be especially on the alert for the girls, might even think that they had caused the arrest. Fortunately, within minutes, the girls came in and reported that nothing had happened. Dino had not appeared, Cassone was absent, and the other hoods who usually hung around were nowhere to be seen.

Again we considered calling off the surveillance, and again the girls insisted that nothing could happen to them, that there was no reason to believe North Pelham was too hot for them. Anne remembered having once seen Dino come out of a different bar with Cassone and thought that this might be a new meeting place. She tried to get some cars to go there. I was terribly busy the next day and didn't know about the plans until lunchtime. Grace and Rosalind were handling the surveillance.

They returned white as ghosts. They had parked a block away from the bar and had seen the action there. The usual thugs appeared and as usual policemen chatted amiably with them. Then the hoods looked toward the girls and said something to one cop, and he looked, too. It seemed fantastic to think that he was one of their errand boys, but in a few minutes the cop drove past and looked Grace and Rosalind over carefully. They didn't know what to do except to converse as the cop drove past. He slowed down, and so did their hearts. To their horror, he stopped, got out of his car, and walked over to them.

"What are you women doing here?" he asked in a rough voice.

Rosalind was the first to find her voice, and it wasn't worth finding. Her usual deep-throated, sexy voice sounded more like a child's squeak. "Why, uh, we, uh, we're meeting somebody."

"Yeh? Who? What's his name?"

"*His* name? Teehee, why, uh, teehee, ha-ha, you, uh, thought we were meeting a man? I mean two men? I mean, what kind of women do you think we are?" That involved blurt was from my wife.

"Well, we've been having complaints about a white car around here, and I just wanted to know who you are."

"We're just meeting a friend," said Rosalind. With that the cop seemed satisfied, got in his car, and drove off.

The poor girls waited a few minutes and then sped away in a great hurry. They had reason to be worried. They were driving my big white station wagon. All the cop had to do to find out who they were was to make a telephone call about the license number.

We called to tell Anne about the incident, and she replied that Helen had just told her something that explained our story. The day before, Helen had been driving through Pelham on an errand that had nothing to do with our surveillance at the same time as the girls were keeping their futile vigil at the raided bar. She had suddenly come upon Tommy Cassone in his black car waiting at a stop sign. She followed him a block and, when he turned, she went after him. He looked in his rear-view mirror, saw her, and did a screaming turn into a side street. She realized instantly that he was worried and gave up the chase. But in order to get back to the main street, she, too, made a turn at the next intersection, and there she met Cassone head-on. She said that sheer terror convulsed his homely, pockmarked features. He stepped on the gas, shot past her, and disappeared in a cloud of exhaust fumes. At the thought of this tough gangster being in such a panic over her, she had begun to giggle hysterically and pulled over to the curb to regain control of herself. As she was wiping her eyes, around the corner came Cassone again, as if pursued by a demon. When he saw her still there, he almost went off the road. This time, instead of careening past her, he slammed on the brakes, gunned his car into reverse, rocketed into a driveway, and screamed away again. Helen was helpless with laughter. She finally managed to get her errands done and staggered home, and now we knew what sort of "complaint" there had been about a white car!

It had been quite a week. We had let Dino know he was being tailed by women, and the hoods would certainly know that the women were working with me. We had also terrified the tough Tommy Cassone and had gotten one of the North Pelham cops lined up against us. We had no choice now but to do what we should have done the moment we knew Dino was suspicious—cool it for a few weeks. It was clear, too, that if we were ever to do any more tailing, we had to have radios that would permit some coordination between cars. We decided to try to raise enough money from friends to purchase some.

We hadn't, however, heard the end of that week's tribulations. A few days later, I received a telephone call from Mary, Dolores' ex-convict friend.

"Hi, Revren Hill, how ya been?"

"Fine, thank you, how have you been? I have missed you."

"I been out of town. My mother died and my brother got out of the can and then got into some more trouble, and I been busy."

"Sorry to hear about your mother."

"Revren, could I see you? Can you come over for awhile?"

It was obvious that Mary was going to play "double agent" and come in ostensibly to give me some information but in reality to gain some. On the other hand, if I played it right, I might get her to play triple agent. If she were to talk even a little, I might be able to get a line on what the Mob was thinking. So I said, "I couldn't possibly get away, but if you could come over here, I could see you."

"You couldn't come over here? I hate to go into the church."

"I couldn't make it at all, but if you don't mind coming over here, I could see you."

"OK," she said, "but it would be better if you'd come over here."

She eventually agreed to meet me at the church. I wouldn't have gone to her room for all the tea in China, and I had my doubts about the wisdom of meeting her anywhere, but my curiosity got the better of me. It was already dark, and my secretary and the sextons had gone home. Mary might be bringing a couple of gunmen along. I went into a room from which I could observe the doorway and waited with considerable trepidation. Finally, a cab pulled up and out stepped Mary. She was alone, but still I watched to see if anyone followed her in. There was no guarantee that a couple of bums might creep up the stairs while we talked and take a potshot at me, but, then, it was impossible to be sure of anything in life. I finally went to greet her and we sat down. My eyes slid constantly to the door where an intruder would have to enter.

Her first words were, "Revren, ya better tell those two women of yours in that big white car that the next time the cop stops them he'll arrest them for molesting a citizen."

"Women? Cops?" I stammered. "Molesting a citizen?"

She snickered and said, "Yeh, for following some of the boys around."

I feigned surprise and ignorance, but if she had an ounce of intelligence she would have known I was bluffing. Fortunately for me, her quota was more like half an ounce. Soon she was telling me that the hoods knew I was using women to follow them. They also knew that I had undercover women trying to entice some of the hoods into talking! It seems that one night in a bar Tommy Cassone had been offered a drink by a woman who said, when he hesitated, "Oh, come on, enjoy it. It doesn't cost me anything. The Reverend Hill is paying me to get you drunk." Tommy had recoiled in horror from such an immoral proposition and hurried home. It was, of course, utter nonsense. I never had a woman try to get a hoodlum drunk, and surely no woman in her right mind would say she was working for me if she weren't. It is doubly certain that no woman would say so if she *had* been. Had Cassone dreamt up the story? Was it, as I found so often, a hoodlum's way of maintaining he knows about everything that's going on? Friends who know big-time hoodlums tell me that they have mentioned my work and been told that the Mob knows all about me and that I was being given exactly what they wanted me to have.

Cassone's fears went further. He had confided to Mary that I had a big blond woman tailing him in a school bus. His misguided calculation gave me a splendid idea on how I might be able to turn our setback into a victory. I leaned forward and said confidentially, "Mary, if I tell you something, will you promise *never to tell a soul?*" After she had crossed her heart and hoped to die, I said, "To tell you the truth, I *do have* women out tailing the hoods."

She was stunned at my candor. Her probing was proving successful beyond her wildest dreams. "Really?"

"Yep, I do. I have gotten all the women of this and two other churches organized. I had 36 cars out yesterday. I have Cassone being watched every minute. Tufo doesn't make a move that I don't know about. And each of my women is getting two others. Soon we'll be able to keep a 24-hour watch on every hoodlum in town. I guess it was inevitable that one of them was identified. But they haven't seen the dozens of others yet."

Her eyes were popping out of her head. "You're putting me on!"

I feigned indignation. "I am not! You know I wouldn't lie to you! I can trust *you*. I've had every one of these girls deputized by the United States government as a deputy federal marshal."

"My God!"

"And, furthermore, I have girls in every bar in town, and even working as bar girls, and waitresses. Cassone identified one, but you ought to hear some of the *other* things he has said to my *other agents*."

"You're putting me on."

"I am not! You remember that meeting at the Y when I played those tapes and told about the arrests? Well, remember all those women there? About 200?"

"Yeh."

"Well, they're *all* working with me now except those still taking training in Washington."

"My God."

"Neat, huh?"

"No wonder the boys are so shook up."

"Are they pretty shook up?"

"I'll say they are. That's the reason Cassone sent me in to see you. He knew I knew you."

"He sent you?"

"Yeh. He asked me if I could set you up and said I could name my price if I would."

"Set me up? You mean with a nude woman and hidden cameras and all that jazz?"

"Oh, no, they wanted you set up for good—you know, my apartment and then, bam! Ten thousand bucks for me."

The poor thing. She was either making up the story, extrapolating from some remarks, or she was an incredible fool. A moment's reflection would have told her that she would not have received even $10. If I had been stupid enough to walk into such a clumsy trap and they had killed me, they would never have permitted a witness to live. Mary would have been killed at the same time. I doubt they ever had any such idea. Certainly Cassone had no authority to pull it off. He was a mere peanut, an errand boy in the small-town Syndicate. It was more likely that they wanted information and sent her to see what she could find out. Their talk was only gasconade to impress the poor goose.

I sent out my informants to see if they could learn what the hoods really knew about the girls. It turned out to be very little. The cop in North Pelham had apparently never checked the license number of my car. Inasmuch as we had temporarily curtailed our operations, the hoods saw nobody following them and became increasingly doubtful that there had ever been anybody.

Despite the danger signals, Anne wouldn't give up. She would casually walk up to an apartment house, enter, and stand in the doorway, back from the light, so that she could see the action without being seen. She was doing no tailing now, but it was amazing how much information she managed to piece together. Soon she had other girls doing the same thing. They watched known places from store windows or apartment lobbies. Before long they had a good idea of how the hoods were operating. Anne would call now and then with some exciting news, such as, "Oh, Fay! Today when I went shopping I stood in the Daitch vegetable department and watched out the window and guess what I saw! I saw WHK2345 meet YSA8976 and then be joined by old RDE4598." I always remembered to say something like, "Wow, Not RDE4598?"

Meanwhile, I was searching for money for the radios. I happened to meet Commissioner Carey on a few occasions and I decided to test whether his police force could catch bad guys. I told him about a certain bookie who operated out of a phone booth in a beach club. Within a few weeks an arrest was made on the basis of a wiretap. Another time I told him about a man who picked up a large amount of action in a certain industrial plant and took it to a drop during the lunch hour. Unfortunately, informants told me that the man learned he was being watched and, for the time being, gave up his work.

A friend who heard that I was trying to buy radios asked me if I had ever tried to get money from the National Council on Crime and Delinquency. I hadn't, because I thought that it was mostly interested in things such as prison reforms. The friend made an appointment for me with Milton Rector, the director of that vast and highly professional organization. After I had told my story, a wealthy man who was sitting in on the conference said quietly, "Give him anything he wants and send me the bill." I almost fainted.

That very day I bought a movie camera with an excellent telescopic lens and made an appointment with a salesman to discuss radios. The salesman tried not to show his surprise at a man in clerical garb trying to buy mobile radios and a disguised antenna, but it was hard for him. Through friends in Washington, we got the necessary license in shorter time than normal and sat down to wait for the radios to arrive.

The wait would have seemed interminable if it hadn't been for the camera. We began to take pictures of the "pass." It was great fun. We found someone with an office in the Medical Center building and arranged to film the pass from there. On the third day the blue station wagon came over the hill on schedule and swung into the lot just as the green cab arrived from the opposite direction. I trained the camera on the station wagon and began to grind away. The car stopped, up drove the cab—and my camera stopped. It was at the end of the roll of film!

The girls took the camera, too, and went in search of fun, but they were almost always in the wrong place at the wrong time. All except my wife. One day Grace went to the Medical Center. The blue station wagon promptly came over the hill like an obedient puppy. Grace had two handicaps: she knew nothing about cameras, and she can't shut one eye at a time. She had to hold one hand over her eye and hold the camera with the other, in a somewhat unsteady grip. Then when she saw the cab draw up beside the wagon, her hands began to tremble. The pictures came out clear, but one needed to do headstands to see them. "Gosh," said Rosalind, "you can see her heart beating in those pictures."

We got another good break about this time. The same friend who had borrowed the radios for us managed to get hold of an old truck equipped with special one-way glass that police officers had used for surveillance. I drove the old clunker around to various hood hangouts and got more pictures.

The real excitement, however, came after we got the radios.

CHAPTER TEN

I pulled into the shopping center lot and found my contact immediately. He was sitting there with his motor idling, his arm hanging
out the window. As I drove up, he reached under a coat thrown
loosely over the back seat, drew out a brown paper bag, and surreptitiously handed it across to me. As I took it, he said, "Better
watch it, there's a car with a couple of women in it over there.
I don't think they could be following me, but you never know."

I nodded, backed out rapidly, and headed for the exit. As I drove
past the women he had mentioned, I saw Belle and Honey os-
tentatiously trying to look the other way while watching me out
of the corners of their eyes. I swear I even heard them giggle as I
passed. Their car didn't move as I left the lot and headed onto
Quaker Ridge Road. The only movement I saw was Honey leaning
forward and putting her head down slightly, at the same time rais-
ing a shopping bag, as if she were talking into it.

As I passed the Flying A station on Quaker Ridge Road, a car
with two women in it who looked suspiciously like Anne and
Vicki pulled out and attached itself to the rear of my car, so close
that their front bumper appeared to be bolted onto my rear one.
I had to put myself through the humiliating experience of waving
them back. They didn't find it humiliating at all; they waved back
and giggled.

When I made the turn at the top of the hill, they were suddenly
gone and I thought for a minute that I was alone. Then, at the first

intersection, there was another car with two women in it. They, too, looked vaguely familiar, even in the nondescript clothes they were wearing. After a block my suspicions were confirmed; they were following me. It was Sue and Alice in Sue's little blue car, with three little boys tumbling back and forth over the front seat while their mothers tried to concentrate on me. Accelerating to lose them, I screamed around the corner on two wheels. They let the distance lengthen, but didn't quite lose me. I did two quick turns and came out on Pinebrook Boulevard. I breathed a sigh of relief. Nobody was behind me now. The work beside me on the seat was safe.

It was a beautiful spring day, and I relaxed as I headed for my second rendezvous, with the pickup man who would take the work to the bank. A quick glance in my rear-view mirror made me hesitate. A car with two women in it had entered Pinebrook from a side street and was just ahead of me. It was Belle and Honey again. I did a quick turn off Pinebrook onto Overhill and left the girls traveling east on Pinebrook. I chuckled at their naïveté in getting ahead of me and turned again on Trenor, heading for the rendezvous. I had given them the slip! As I made my turn, however, a car pulled away from the curb behind me. I glanced in the mirror and saw Anne waving at me again. I gave up and drove home.

Within minutes all three cars pulled up behind me. The girls came in for a cup of tea and a critique of their tailing skills.

"Well, girls, aside from obvious things, like not waving at the man as he makes his pass, I have to admit that you did rather well in tailing me."

"It's just that you looked so cute in that ridiculous little cap," Vicki said. "It's just like the one the cab driver wears."

"Listen, you idiots! A few things you must learn before you can become pros. One is that you must hang back farther. Don't get so close or he will be able to recognize you, and if he sees you again that day at another stop sign or something, he'll know he's being tailed.

"The second thing is that you must be careful not to wear any bright clothing. I noticed that when Sue first started to tail me she had on a red headband that flashed in the sun and caught my eye. Later, when she had picked me up the second time, I noticed it again. Always wear dull clothes and drive the most nondescript cars you can, and also *don't* try to look attractive. Men notice women, and since you are all raving beauties they'll notice you

179

more than other women. So wear bulky clothing and try to look like frumps."

"That'll be hard for me, but easy for Vicki," said Belle. The others laughed.

"Anne, shouldn't we tell each other exactly where the car we are tailing is every minute?" Sue grabbed at her young son, who was pouring Coke on the living-room rug.

"Yes, that's something we must remember. A couple of times someone said, 'I have got him,' but didn't tell us where he was at the time."

Alice said, "I want to ask about these radios. They're beautiful and make all the difference in the world, but does someone else have our frequency? I can hear other voices over it."

"Yes," I explained, "the frequency is not ours exclusively, but nobody in this immediate neighborhood has it. It does mean that, if someone wanted to get a receiver and listen in, he could hear us. So we should be careful about what we say."

"That means that you'll have to stop swearing at us when we boo-boo, Anne," said Belle.

"And there'll be no more telling smutty jokes over the air."

"Please, what kind of a Ladies Aid is this?"

The girls settled down to plans for picking up the surveillance of Dino the next day, thrilled at the prospect of getting back into action. They were still boiling about the way he had scared them off. Their plans were meticulous. The cars would be more carefully hidden, the strategy was more thoroughly thought out, the tactics more sophisticated. They were ready.

After handing out the radios, I saw them off with some anxiety that afternoon. They treated the radios gingerly, knowing they were expensive and that we had worked hard to get them. The way they were carried out of the church house was important, because we knew that occasionally the church had been watched. There wasn't much danger of the girls being identified as surveillance teams, because women came in and out all day long. North Avenue has a daily nursery school to which women bring their children, the women's association has many midweek meetings, and there are a Garden Club, a Mother's Club, and various committee meetings. For a time after the girls were "burned," I had amused myself with thoughts of mobsters sitting across the street and keeping track of all the women who went into the church, jotting down hundreds of license numbers and trying to tail them all. How funny it would have been for some dowager queen of New Rochelle to be tailed after delivering her potted plant to the flower show.

The girls had decided to carry the radios in shopping bags, which would also serve as perfect camouflage on the front seats. As they walked to their cars, toting the shopping bags, dragging their children and panda bears, and carrying their boxes of Oreo cookies, for a fleeting moment I thought I had gone insane and was dreaming it all.

Those had been busy days for me. Norman Stanton had left for another job and we had for weeks sought a replacement. The church committee had settled finally on Douglass T. Lind, a young man who had graduated from Union Theological Seminary three years before. He had married a girl from New Rochelle and gone off for three years of work with the Fifty Million Fund, a Presbyterian fund-raising organization. He was still with the fund and could not come to North Avenue until the first of May, but his wife, Penny, was to arrive that day to supervise the redecoration of their manse and start moving in.

Penny drove up as the girls drove out, waving and laughing. On the way up the stairs, she said, "Say, I hope you don't mind if I ask this, but who were those shabbily dressed girls with all the children who waved at you as they left?"

"Why," I said, "those are the girls helping me fight the Mafia."

"Help you fight the Mafia?"

"Yeah, great gals, every one of them. And you ought to see the hoods when they know those girls are after them! Boy, do they panic."

I realize now, months later, that the look in her eyes had been that of a person struggling to give the appearance that she thought my remarks were perfectly rational, even though she knew I was crazy.

"The Mafia is afraid of them?"

"Well, I guess it's pretentious to call these pickup men the Mafia. Actually, they're bums, tools of the Organization. But we know that they are employees of the Cosa Nostra, so we refer to what we're doing as fighting the Mob."

"Oh, I see."

I thought for a moment that I saw a look of panic cross her face, but she recovered her composure quickly. We discussed the color of paint she wanted for the living room and the repairs that had to be done on the house. The conversation was mundane, and

Penny seemed to regain her confidence. After a few minutes of staring silently out the window, she said, "Did—does—Doug didn't mention to me anything about the Mafia when he told me he was going into the ministry."

It dawned on me for the first time that they had not been told during their interviews about my fight against Organized Crime. I was appalled.

"Didn't the committee tell you about crime? I mean, about the crime work I'm in?"

Her eyes clouded a bit, but her voice was steady. "I don't recall the committee mentioning your crime."

"Heavens! I am embarrassed. You don't know anything about those arrests or the bomb plot or the undercover agents or—."

"Well, maybe they told Doug about the bomb when I was out of the room, or maybe it was mentioned in the dossier on the church—."

"Well, then, no wonder you were confused when you saw the Ladies Aid Society leaving down there to go on their mission."

"Your Ladies Aid has its mission work, too?"

"I'll say they do! It's unorthodox and it requires a lot of commitment, but it is more appropriate than the activities of most ladies aid societies."

"Oh, it sounds wonderful! Really. But what is it they *do?*"

"Well, they'll be back in a minute and they can tell you themselves. Meanwhile, why don't you go give my secretary your list of needs for the manse. And don't worry about this criminal work—it's fun. I'll bet you'll be in on it yourself soon."

She went into the outer office and chatted with my secretary for a few minutes. Before long the girls could be heard coming up the stairs. First Anne and Vicki burst in, their children trailing behind, drinking Cokes and looking tired. Then Rosalind and Belle, and finally Alice and Maureen. They were all talking at once and their children were crying, screaming, or sucking their thumbs. The office was a madhouse. Penny, who had no children and who was very beautiful, very young, and immaculately groomed, looked on in politely controlled bewilderment and horror as the girls sat on the floor, on tables, and on the arms of chairs to tell their tales. They were dressed according to instructions and looked exactly like washerwomen. Their accents were those of young Westchester matrons, but they talked like cops.

"Wow! Fay, do those radios make a difference."

"He never knew we were there."

"I'm not so sure of that. We were behind him longer than I wanted to be, and he looked in the rear-view mirror twice. I'm afraid he may have made me."

"No, he didn't. He was just casually glancing in the mirror, I'm certain."

I coughed delicately. "Girls, when you think he has identified you as someone following him, couldn't you say he *burned* you instead of—."

Belle looked at me in wide-eyed innocence. "But Tom always says that his subject *made* him when he has spotted him tailing."

Anne interrupted before I could explain. "Belle, you little phony, you know perfectly well what Fay is driving at. From now on the official verb is *burned*, OK?"

"So what happened?"

"Let Anne tell it."

"We got into position as planned and, sure enough, Dino came up from the direction of the west side, parked with his motor running, and dashed into the luncheonette.

"He was late for some reason. At any rate, he came out in a hurry and drove off toward Church Street. The car across Main picked him up in no time and we soon caught up. Belle, you tell the next."

"We saw him pull up to the cab, so we drove into a driveway where we could watch and alerted the other girls to wait farther back. They had hardly pulled up when that beautiful brown bag went flying through the air and landed in the front seat of the cab."

"You should have heard Belle telling about that scene. I was sure she was going to have a baby there in the front seat."

"So, as usual, the cab with the work left early, and Dino sat there and watched. We let the cab pass us and radioed back to Anne, who was waiting in exactly the right place."

"Well, we picked him up going like a bat out of hell and stayed right on his tail for about three blocks, when he made a sudden turn and we dropped back and let Maureen and Alice take him. He headed all the way across town, into the Rochelle Heights area and then through City Park."

"And then he pulled a fast one. He hit a light turning from yellow to red and kept going. We were stuck and sat there while he disappeared. But he wasn't suspicious, I'm sure of it. He was just in a big hurry because he was late."

"We drove all around that area near Larchmont. He came back along Fifth Avenue, just as casual and relaxed as you please. So we knew that he had dumped the work, and it had to be some place near City Park where he met his contact."

"The radios make all the difference."

"They're great. We'll get them this time, I know it!"

Penny was sitting in the background with a couple of cookie-covered kids crawling all over her. She never lost her ladylike composure, although she did jump a little when she realized that the two-year-old on her lap had wet his pants, and her, too. She was nice about it. A little stiff, but nice.

"Oh, girls, I didn't introduce you to Penny Lind, the wife of our new assistant minister. He won't be here for another two weeks, but she has come early to get the manse ready. She is dying to know all about your work and to join the mob."

Penny smiled bravely. "I certainly want to do *my part* in the Ladies Aid."

Anne picked up the situation immediately and said, with a straight face, "Penny, we're glad to meet you and to know that you're with us. My father was a minister, but my mother didn't like to do some of the things required of a minister's wife and it held my father back in his career. I'm glad *you* are willing to be a good minister's wife."

Belle never lifted an eyebrow as she said, "But don't worry, we don't come into your home while you're gone to see how you do your housework, like some church women do to their minister's wife."

"That's right," said Rosalind wryly, "in this church all that's required of ministers' wives is that they can drive fast and dodge bullets."

Penny licked her lips slightly, and brushed a strand of hair off her forehead, and said, "Well, ladies, I certainly have enjoyed this meeting of your circle, but I have to get along to my mother's house in Greenwich now. I'll be seeing you later."

I really didn't know whether to say anything to her, but I was sure that Doug knew of my anticrime activities and would be able to set her straight. I decided to let it go for the moment.

"Penny, seriously, I have to call Doug today about some papers

I want him to read before he comes, and if you have any messages I'll give them to him."

She licked her lips again, delicately, and said in a level voice, "Why, Fay, I'll be calling Doug tonight, *I am sure,* and I'll be glad to give him *your* message."

"I hate to have you go to the expense of calling him. Are you *sure* you'll call him?"

"*Quite sure.*"

I later learned that Doug had been even more mystified by her tale than she had been. By some incredible oversight, the church committee had neglected to tell him anything about our anticrime work. Doug told me weeks later that Penny had been close to hysteria that night, and he had become almost as hysterical as she. Tentatively, they decided to stick with it, for a few weeks, anyway.

The next day another squad of girls gathered at the church. They were driving different cars, but otherwise the operation was to be the same. They came back elated again. They had failed to stick with the cab long enough but were certain they would find that third man next time. As they were talking, Penny came in. A good night's sleep had helped her. I had warned the girls that we mustn't tease her too much, and this time they spent some time telling her quite seriously what we were doing and what our purpose was. Her expression changed from horror to interest to fascination. By the time she left, she had agreed to drive her car the next day. She was a peach and did good work from the beginning. She also raised the already high level of pulchritude in the group several notches. In fact, they were so attractive when out of their frumpy clothes and in something decent that Marv said, when he met them all, "All right, all right, Fay, I'll convert. Make me a Presbyterian!"

The girls made no headway for two days. The solution, they believed, was to be more aggressive about tailing the cab. This talk made me nervous, and I strictly cautioned them about taking chances. They were sure that with the radios, they could stick closer without taking any chances. They didn't count on the bad luck they were to have that day.

They picked up Dino as usual, stuck with him through his series of checks, found him handing off the bag of work to the green cab, and started after the cab. Belle and Grace were so close to it that they could read a poster on the side window.

The cab driver headed down Main with Belle and Grace close

behind, determined not to lose him at a red light. Once they shot through a yellow light right behind him, and he looked at them long and hard in his rear-view mirror. He then did a sudden screeching turn into a side street, and the girls wisely decided that he had become suspicious. They radioed back for another car to pick him up and pulled over to the curb to wait for instructions. Suddenly, out of the side street opposite them, the green cab appeared. When the driver saw them, he visibly gasped, did another screaming turn, and sped toward Larchmont. The girls figured he was heading for a certain parking lot in the Larchmont area. They left the other two cars to smoke after him and drove leisurely by another route toward the general area where they thought he would be meeting number three. As they came over the railroad bridge, they met him again! His eyes jumped out of their sockets, and he roared away again. He had long since lost the other two cars, so all the girls came back to report the gloomy news.

"Well, Fay, we had another bum break," Anne said. "Just like Helen and Cassone. Grace and Belle couldn't lose the bum wherever they went. I guess we botched it bad this time."

"Look, kids, don't be upset about it. This kind of thing just happens. But we *have got to play it cool* and stop all tailing for at least a week."

The girls groaned. They wanted to close in for the kill. They finally agreed that the only thing they would do the next day would be to have a car posted up the hill on Lincoln to see if the cab left on time. We also agreed never again to use the car the cabbie had spotted. Give him a few days of looking nervously behind him and he would think he had been dreaming about somebody following him. Then we could begin again.

The next day Vicki and Helen sat in Helen's car and watched. The cab never left the lot, but a gray Thunderbird did. The girls paid no attention to it; they were watching the driver of the cab chatting with some other hackies. They shouldn't have. He suddenly walked up the street toward them and made an obscene gesture. They drove off in a huff and came back to the office. They were still red-faced when they told us what had happened.

Meanwhile, another girl was waiting where we expected them to meet. Up drove Dino in his blue station. The green cab didn't come, but a heavy-set Negro in a gray Thunderbird did. There could be no doubt that the cabbie had been suspicious of the girls and had sent the Thunderbird instead. It also occurred to us that the car Helen and Vicki had used was the same car in which Helen had "chased" Tommy Cassone around Pelham. That was its last trip for our team. We also called off all surveillance, except when the girls could be completely hidden, for the next two weeks.

A day or two later Helen's car began coughing and spitting and suddenly it stopped in the middle of the street. A mechanic found sugar in the gas tank. We were never sure that it was anything more than a coincidence, because someone else in her neighborhood had had the same thing happen. As far as we knew, the hoods did not know where she lived, but it was possible that they had tailed her home or had happened upon the car by chance.

The day after the sugar incident, I got a telephone call. The voice was familiar, low and with a slight upturn of inflection at the end of a sentence. It was Mary, the double agent.

"Can I come in and see you?" she asked.

"Sure, got some information for me?"

"Sorta."

She came into the office in worse shape than ever, smelling of liquor and with every pore in her body oozing grime. Her brown hair was darkened with dirt. She had lost one job after another and was now on relief. She stared at her tennis shoes, her face reddened, and she cracked her knuckles. "Revren? You ain't got nobody riding for you, have you? Huh?"

"*Riding* for me?"

"Yeah, you know. Driving cars around after guys in the rackets?"

"Sure! I told you before, I have 76 cars full of women out there following the hoods around. They never do a thing without me knowing it."

"Come on, Revren, be serious. You ain't had no women tailing a green cab, have you?"

"A green cab? What's so important about a green cab?"

"He's the guy with the work now."

"No! What does he look like? A typical Italian? I'll have someone get on it right away."

"No, he ain't no Italian, he's a colored guy, but don't get nobody out, he's not doing it anymore."

"Who's doing it now?"

She realized she had said too much and lapsed into silence. We discussed other matters for awhile, and then she left. As she went out the door, I told her again that she was absolutely right, that we had been tailing the green cab and Cassone and every other major hood in town. She grinned slyly and left. I got on the phone immediately and called all the girls to tell them the story. I cautioned them to stay out of the way of the hoods for another two weeks. They agreed with uncharacteristic swiftness. It was a bit frightening.

Anne, Grace, and I once more discussed whether to call off the entire operation. But the more we thought about it, the more convinced we were that we did not need to. The hoodlums would be suspecting every car on the road with women in it, and during the time they moved the work the streets were full of women, driving children to school, shopping, and going to meetings. What were the hoods to do? Hit all of them? We figured that, in spite of our bad luck, we were reasonably safe if the girls laid off for two weeks and then showed more caution.

The surveillance didn't stop, however. The girls stood on corners at bus stops to watch the pickup schedules. They also posted girls in houses, stores, and in parked cars to watch the meeting places we knew about. In that way, we kept track of them during the layoff. We were worried about Anne, however, because she was out almost every day and because she was strikingly attractive and distinctively blond. We suggested that she wear a kerchief, but she did us one better: she dyed her hair reddish brown and continued her surveillance.

On at least two occasions, we had seen the green cab turn onto the Thruway toward New York. We decided we ought to watch the Thruway at the appropriate time, but could find no vantage point from which it could be easily observed. Belle told us to leave the problem to her.

The next day she parked on the shoulder of the Thruway and observed. As she was about to drive away, a state trooper pulled up and asked what the trouble was. Without a moment's hesitation, she replied that she had been stricken with a terrible coughing fit and had been afraid to drive. "I don't want to cause an accident," she said, looking at him levelly. He agreed that she had done the right thing and stayed long enough to be sure she had recovered properly. She did not see the cab.

I had one way to keep up on things in Heavy Eddie's during the layoff period. I asked Pete to find out who was carrying the work. He reluctantly agreed. To be certain I was getting accurate information, I also asked another informant, a woman, to do the same. Pete called first, to say that Dino was still carrying it out, and the woman confirmed this.

Now we had to get someone in there to bet and introduce a Treasury agent. I began to cast about for ideas, and one night got a beauty. I had once met a man who drove a soft-drink truck and was a gambler. For some reason, he was angry at the hoodlums, even though he bet with them constantly. He agreed without hesitation and immediately began to bring in important information. Because of his job, he was able to bet in half a dozen places and was willing to do introductions. He turned out to be a tremendous find.

The two weeks came to an end and the girls met again in my office. We pooled all our new information and plotted our next move. We were determined to get up the "pickup ladder" to the number three man, who, we were sure, delivered the work to the bank. Our observations had told us that, for the last two weeks, Dino had been carrying out the work on foot. He left his car across the street at a gas station, went into Heavy Eddie's, got the package, came out immediately, walked toward Main, and vanished. We planned to have all our cars across Main, ready to tail him. We knew he would be meeting that green cab or the Thunderbird somewhere.

About the time the girls got into their cars that day, it began to rain. When they arrived on their posts, it was pouring buckets. Along the street came Dino, in his usual lightweight jacket and shirt, with neither raincoat nor umbrella. He was drenched. To protect the policy slips in their envelope, he put his hand inside his jacket and held the package there, looking like a lanky, bedraggled Napoleon. He walked to the parking lot beside the Salvation Army building and stood there waiting for his contact. Before long Dino was kicking the fence and obviously mouthing cuss words. Alice got to feeling so sorry for him that she wanted to drive up and have him sit in her car to wait. When eventually the cab showed, Dino handed the driver the work and, on what seemed to be an impulse, got into the cab and had it drive him back to Heavy Eddie's—tailed by three cars full of girls.

The cab turned onto Huguenot. The girls were after him, but he lost them. They came upon him again, however, leaving the Pelham railroad station, and they also noticed a green 1950 Plymouth sedan leaving the station ahead of him. Anne, who had developed a good nose for such things, observed to herself that the driver of the Plymouth looked like a hood. By this time, the pass had obviously already taken place.

The next day was a bust. One flaw in our operation was the girls' independence. If a girl decided that she'd like to tail one man instead of another, she just might go ahead and do it. That day their discipline broke down completely. I took Anne aside and scolded her. I said that she had to take command, snap out orders, and not take any guff from anyone. Poor Anne! Her eyes became moist. She suffered, for all her poise, from a lack of self-confidence. She suggested that someone else be named commander. But Anne knew more than anyone else and had to be the boss. She agreed to continue, although with much fear.

I also scolded the girls, and told them that only with a coordinated effort could we reach our goal. They all agreed to obey Anne's orders. We turned to planning the next day's work, fairly certain that the pickup men would meet this time at the Medical Center parking lot. Some of the girls would be around the corner on Lockwood and others on Van Guilder. One car would be parked in the lot, its driver and the girl "riding shotgun" inside the building with me while I tried to film the meeting and radio to the other cars which of the thugs had the action. Because the girls had been a little nervous, especially after the cab driver looked over one of our cars suspiciously, we had decided that we needed some men to help. It was difficult to find them, not only because most of them work during the day but also because men tend to be more timid than women. I had tried once, unsuccessfully, to enlist some at a meeting of a neighboring Rotary Club. At last we lined up a couple, including my friend Sam Gordon.

Maureen, Claire, and I stood impatiently in the doctor's office until the green cab appeared and parked in a corner of the lot. "Tell Anne that the green cab is here, but not the blue wagon," I said.

Maureen passed on the information over her radio. Anne acknowledged the message. A blue car came down the hill and I snapped at Maureen to tell Anne that the other car was coming. But I realized almost immediately it was the wrong car and snapped at Maureen again to correct the information. She did.

Then I saw a blue Thunderbird come over the hill. I trained my camera on it and told Maureen to report to Anne that it apparently wasn't going to be Dino but the T-bird. The T-bird wasn't the right one, either, and I had to correct the message. Maureen looked at me in cold contempt. "Fay," she said, "why don't you just shut up and let us girls run this operation? I think we know more about it than you do."

I shut up. Eventually, over the hill came a two-tone 1950 Chevrolet. The driver had his arm hanging out the window just as Dino did when he drove. We watched it carefully. It slowed down at the entrance to the lot and swung in. It *was* Dino. He was late, and we suspected that he had had trouble getting his own car started and had to borrow another. He pulled up beside the cab and lazily handed over his big bag to the cabdriver. I got some magnificent pictures of the pass. The bag glinted in the warm sun as they passed it.

Maureen described the scene to Anne. The green cab pulled out to the Warren Street entrance and swung toward Lockwood. Then we heard Anne take control. She snapped out commands like a sergeant major. The air crackled with orders. One car roared into action and burned rubber down the street—right past the green cab that had the work! It was Anne and Sam Gordon. Over the air we heard Belle say mournfully, "Dino just passed us. You said we should follow him, but the cab left first. What do you want us to do?" Maureen and Claire looked at each other in blank amazement. Anne was furious and cracked out another order. "Of course, you follow him! That was my order, now get moving." We saw a car roar off after Dino, who was innocently on his way back to the luncheonette to have his coffee. Two cars tailed him there while Maureen and Claire tried vainly to find the cab. I drove back to the church alone.

Belle and Henry, our other male member, were the first to arrive, Maureen and Claire next, and then Anne and Sam. Anne was livid with rage. I took her arm and said, "Anne, what's the matter?"

"The matter? Why, all these blockheads got things so confused that we lost the rascal."

I tried to think of a tactful way to tell her that she had misunderstood our message. I broke the news to her gently that it was her orders that had fouled things up. She began to cry. "I *knew* I shouldn't be the chief! I can't give commands. I mess up everything I do!"

We calmed Anne down and persuaded her that she was the

only one in the world who could run the operation. As she stopped sniffling, I said, "I guess we should have told you the license number of the cab. Then there'd have been no confusion."

We lost both our male spies after that. Henry was nervous about being seen with one of our girls in what might be mistaken by his friends as a compromising situation. Sam had been wonderful, but we couldn't use him often because of his own work. So we went back to using only women, and Anne gave orders henceforth with no slipups.

Our newest recruit was Penny Lind. Doug was still winding up his old job, but Penny had returned to New Rochelle while the manse was being refurnished. She had talked to a few people about our crime work and had come to realize that it was not as crazy as it sounded. In fact, she had decided, it sounded like fun.

Her first day out proved to be quite a time. The girls took up their positions on Huguenot, on Main, and in a parking lot. Anne stood on the corner watching the luncheonette, ready to let the others know when Dino appeared. The blue car never showed up, but a black rental car did. Dino got out of it and went into the luncheonette while the driver waited in the car. Anne, realizing that she must give a quick explanation to the girls, ran for her car just as the black car roared toward her. She yelled at Helen, who was parked in the lot, "Dino is in a black rental car, and here he comes right now. Go tail him quick!"

Anne dashed for her car on Huguenot. As she ran, she saw Helen reach for the ignition switch so abruptly that her lighted cigarette hit the steering wheel and went flying into Ruth's lap. Ruth screamed as the hot cigarette hit her hand, and two passersby ran over to see what was wrong, but they had to jump out of the way as Helen gunned the motor and roared past them. She called to them as she flashed past, "Sorry, but I have to catch that car."

The black car shot down one street after another and then into a dead-end. The girls didn't fall for it that time, but they did worry that the man had been alerted. In a second he came out, looked around, and drove off toward his rendezvous, a shopping center parking lot. He met the cab, passed the work, and headed for home, while the cab sped toward Larchmont. Two of the cars were still following Dino, but they lost his trail in the City Park section. Then they met him coming toward them. They were sure he had made his contact only seconds before and looked frantically around for suspicious-looking cars. All they saw was an old green car in the distance on the entrance ramp to the Thruway. Could it possibly be the same old green Plymouth they had seen at the Pelham railroad station? They couldn't be sure, but it looked good.

That was Wednesday. On Thursday they gathered in my office again and prepared to leave. Belle appeared wearing a loud, striped dress. "Belle, you *know* you shouldn't appear here in such a dress," I told her. "One look at it and a hood would recognize you anywhere on the eastern seacoast."

"But I'm going to wear my raincoat zipped up to the throat. I had to dress decently. I have a doctor's appointment as soon as we're finished. My husband thought the dress was inappropriate, too. He said, 'That's a funny dress to wear when you are doing the Lord's work.' You know, I never thought church work could be so much fun. When I was a kid, I used to think that the dullest work in the world was being in the Ladies Aid, but I like *this*."

They were gone for so long that I was sure something was up. I was relieved when I heard their familiar voices, the screams of the children, and the clatter of toys being dropped on the stairs. They were so excited that they could hardly talk. Rosalind promptly gave me a big hug and kiss, and then delivered me in turn into the arms of Anne, Penny, Alice, and Sue.

"What did you get this time, you crazy kids?"

"We did it! We did it! We did it!" Anne was singing in ecstasy as she poured Coke into Rachel's paper cup.

"Oh, Fay, you should have seen it, you should have seen it!" Alice was almost hysterical with joy. "That green cab did about seven checks, but we stuck with him, trading him off from one to the other and running about six red lights and ignoring stop signs. When he thought he was alone for sure, he hightailed it for that Larchmont diner and pulled into the lot."

"Grace and I went right in after the guy," Rosalind interrupted. "We were determined to see the pass, and he wasn't looking at all. He pulled into a slot beside an old green Plymouth with a bushy-haired kid sitting in it. We drove into the first parking place and they never even looked at us. Grace, smart kid that she is, got out and stood against the car as if she had just come out of the diner and seen a friend there and was chatting. I looked right past her and saw the cab driver hand a big, fat, yellow bag to the kid and then get into his cab and drive away."

"And we were waiting outside, and when Rosalind said that the kid in the green Plymouth had it, we picked him up the minute he came out of the lot." Anne was trying hard to be professional.

Sue said, "But could that guy drive! Right through red lights. Suddenly he turned left onto a road that runs through a residential section between the Post Road and Palmer Avenue."

"For awhile we thought we had lost him," Anne said, "but then there he was, standing outside his car at a gas station on Palmer. We drove on past and radioed back to the others to wait up above on Palmer.

"But he didn't wait long. He seemed to be waiting for someone who never came. He jumped in his rattletrap and hit the light at Stephenson and was gone before we could get him. We know now who number three is. No doubt. We got his license number and everything."

For the next day's venture, Claire was to walk her two poodles along Palmer at the time the kid might reappear, although we had no confidence that he would run the same pattern. From what we had learned of their habits, it was more likely that the pickup men would do something different. The other girls were to pick up Dino at the luncheonette again. I scotched Grace's going out again because she was looking so pained and pale.

A late telephone call capped the day. It was our old friend Bob again.

"Seen her yet?"

"Have I seen who?"

"Dolores."

"How could I see her, when she, ha-ha, is in Columbus?"

"No, that's just the bit. She left me and went to New Rochelle. If you see her, take care of her for awhile, I'm on my way."

I broke out in a sweat that drenched my pajamas within seconds. With Bob around, anything might happen.

"Do you have any money, Bob?" Foolish question.

"No, she took all I got and I owe a month's rent. But I'm leaving all my clothes and furniture here and coming tonight."

"Bob! Don't do that. Wait! Think what might happen to you if you were to return to New Rochelle. Stay there and I'll see if I can find Dolores."

"Naw, I'm coming."

"But where'll you stay?" Foolish question.

"Well, I don't know—I wondered if . . ."

"Bob, I'd love to have you, but my wife is sick. It is absolutely impossible, and I am broke or I'd send you some money.'Wait there until I see if I can find her."

Bob wept. I almost did, too. That strange young man—sensitive, intelligent, moral in his own way, tough at times—loved his wife, even though he fought with her most of the time. I promised that I would try to find her the next day and he finally hung up. I have seldom been as close to tears of desperation as I was that terrible night. Grace was hardly moved by the call because she was so torn with pain again. I lay there thinking of the impossibility of trying to find Dolores and not knowing what I would say if I did find her. Then my mind would shift to Grace lying beside me in pain so intense that every time I turned over in bed she would wince. It was a long night.

Grace saw the doctor the following morning and felt better after taking some new medicine. I was feeling worse. I tried all the stores where Dolores used to shop and the homes of her friends, without luck. I knew Bob wouldn't wait long. If he returned, there could well be unpleasant threats from the hoodlums, and there was the remote possibility of his being beaten. What was certain was that he would again be in our hair, expecting money, dependent, probing, omnipotent. We didn't have any money to give, and no one we knew was interested in supporting a perfectly healthy young man.

The girls gathered at the church house again and came upstairs for their radios and a briefing. As Anne was giving her instructions and the others were taking their children to the bathroom, Helen rushed in, with both fury and fright registered on her face. "Do you know what I saw, just now? A Negro man came up from the parking lot and walked over to the peep truck, looked inside very carefully, obviously took down the license number, and then brazenly stood there and watched each girl go into the church house. I watched him to see if he was just curious or what. He walked right over to the taxi headquarters and started talking to the green cab driver."

The room was sickeningly quiet except for an occasional squawk from a youngster. Anne let out a quiet "Wow!" and sat down, staring silently at me.

I whistled. "Well, girls, we should have known better than to leave from here, after they burned us that time. We'll move our equipment to somebody's house and leave it there from now on."

"What about today?"

"I rather think that they'll have that blue T-bird drive today. They obviously think that we're tailing the cab from here."

"Then we can still go out?" Belle's eyes were dancing in anticipation.

The other girls ranged in expression from anticipation to anxiety. Anne said, "Well, let's do a very loose tail from Eddie's and see what happens."

"OK, Anne, and I'll move that old peep truck out of here."

"You can put it in my place until you're ready to use it, or until you're ready to take it back," said Rosalind, who had a large house with a triple garage.

Off they went, while I sat and sweated. When they didn't return immediately—which meant they were on the trail—I went out and took the truck to Rosalind's. By the time I returned, the girls were back. They had had no trouble picking up Dino, who seemed asleep at the wheel. As we suspected, he met the blue T-bird, and the two drivers had a long chat before the T-bird left with the work. He was obviously suspicious, but the girls managed to follow him to Larchmont again, only to get stuck at a red light. They got to the Thruway entrance just in time to see the green Plymouth driving onto the highway. The lead car had gunned onto the entrance ramp, stopped to pay the toll, and dashed after the Plymouth, but it had vanished. There were three exits it could have taken, and it was impossible to tell which one. It was frustrating to have lost the number three man again, but at least we knew he was carrying the work regularly. We believed it was only a matter of time before we could follow him all the way to the bank. We were exultant. The girls chirped and chatted and kidded each other.

Then the telephone rang. It was Dolores. My heart sank.

"Dolores?"

The girls gasped and went into various forms of shock. Anne sat down quickly. Helen sat down slowly. Belle stood as if frozen. The others stared in terror.

"Uh, hello, Reverend. I hear from my friends that you know I am in town. Did Bob call you?"

"Yes, he did, Dolores, and he is simply sick with worry about you. He so dearly wants you back. He says he is coming out to get you."

"Well, he won't find me. I'm hiding with some friends and I

won't even tell you where I am so you won't have to lie to him."

"Dolores, are you, uh, *sure,* that this is the right thing to do? To be here with both little children? How are you going to live while you're here?"

"He doesn't love me at all, and I thought maybe you could help me a little if I—."

"Dolores, I don't have any money, and it is the duty of a woman's *husband* to support her."

"Yeh, but he doesn't do it. I guess it was just too much to suppose that a Christian minister could help out a woman in distress with two little babies. I would be glad to work, but—."

"Have you tried welfare?"

"You want me to beg, Reverend? Anyway, I can't get any money from welfare for three weeks."

I was trapped and I knew it. I also knew that, unless I could persuade her to go back to Bob, he would come and try to find her. Anyway, he was only looking for an excuse to leave Columbus, where he was obviously bored, and return to the city where he had had the most exciting time of his life. He was sure I would support him. After all, hadn't I already given him lots of money? And wasn't the church rich? To his way of thinking, and hers, there was no excuse for my not taking care of them. I made one more try at getting her to go back to him before agreeing to give her some money.

The girls were speechless.

"You idiot! What are you going to give her money for? Make her go to welfare."

"Well, she says she can't get anything from them for three weeks."

"Baloney! She's just going to take you for a ride. Tell her you'll only give her money to go back to Bob."

I looked for a long time at Vicki, who had said that. "Would *you* force anyone to go back to Bob MacPherson?"

She dropped her eyes and sighed. The others did the same.

"And this has to happen just as we are about to make it all the way," Anne moaned. "Do we have to stop now?"

What a mess.

It was imperative that Bob not know what we were doing. He was so unstable that in a moment of hysterical anger he might sell us out. He already knew too much for comfort.

"Well, let's not cross that bridge before we come to it. It may be that we'll be done before he comes or that I can get Dolores to return. Or maybe we can go ahead without his knowing it."

It was a gloomy group of girls who left that day.

The night was still young when the call from Bob came. He had been trying to sell some of his pathetically few belongings to raise enough money to come for his wife. I urgently advised him to stay in Columbus while I tried to persuade Dolores to return to him. I finally had to agree to persuade her to phone him.

The next day, a Saturday, Dolores came for her money and refused adamantly to return to Bob. At midnight the phone rang. It was Bob, and he was in New Rochelle! He had not slept for 48 hours and was sick with fatigue. He asked me what he should do.

"Well, Bob, I think the most important thing would be to get a hotel room and get a night's sleep."

"Yeh, but I ain't got no money."

"Oh, well, have you tried the Salvation Army or the YMCA."

I felt like a stinker for suggesting such a thing when he could have come and slept on our couch, but I knew perfectly well that he would stay for several weeks and that, if he found his wife and two children, they would join him. Grace was half crippled and deeply discouraged by the constant pain she felt. To have Bob and his family in our home would destroy her. And I was not sure it would be of any real help to Bob. Some time in his life he had to grow up and take the responsibility for his actions. He had to stop making impulsive decisions. And if he were made miserable enough now, perhaps he would remember the next time he and his wife were about to have a fight.

"Try some friends," I said to him, "and see if you can't stay with them. You see, this is the reason I told you not to come out here. In Columbus you had a job and a place to stay. I don't know what to tell you now. But call again tomorrow morning, and I'll let you know if Dolores has called."

"Well, I'll try to find a bench to sleep on." With that he began to weep and hung up.

I turned to work on the sermon that I was in the process of finishing. The telephone rang a half hour later.

"Yeh, hi. I'm in a bar. If you want to do something to clean up this town, then take a crack at *this* place."

I said, "I've been so busy this year I haven't had much time for crime."

"Yeah? What about the girls? Are they doing anything? Maybe one of them will take me in for the night."

"I doubt it. Vicki has moved out of town, Anne is away for a few days, and the others have lost interest in crime."

I got two more phone calls from Bob that night. Then, between the nine-thirty and eleven o'clock services Sunday morning, I found him waiting outside my office, unshaven, red-eyed, dirty. I suggested that he go into my office to clean up, and then sleep in the chair there or on the floor until the service was over. He was obviously on the point of breaking out in one of his hysterical tantrums. I thought of calling the police, but I had doubts about how sympathetic they would be. As I rose to begin my sermon, I saw Bob enter the sanctuary. I was terrified, but he sat through only half the sermon and left again. When I arrived at the coffee hour, a woman who was helping serve said, "There's a man here who says that he hasn't eaten in 48 hours and that he is one of your undercover agents on the run from gangsters. He's over there." She looked at me accusingly, as if I were a monster who hired people to risk their lives and then abandoned them to their fate.

I found Bob regaling some of my members with stories of the time he had worked in the J and J. I got him upstairs amid many disapproving looks. There was nothing to do but give him some money. I dug into my pockets. The church has special emergency funds, but I didn't feel justified giving Bob any of that money. I was still $3,000 in debt from Grace's previous illness, and fighting off creditors every week, but I gave him what little I had in my wallet. He slunk off with a thin smile on his lips. He must have called 50 times in the next few days, each time hinting that he needed more money. Eventually, he did find Dolores and they moved into a rented room on welfare money.

On Monday, Bob or no Bob, the girls assembled at Penny Lind's and prepared to go out again, this time to "make the kill." They had no success. In fact, that whole week they did not see the green Plymouth, which they had dubbed the Green Pea Kid. On Friday I decided to go out with them. They objected that I was too well known and was sure to be spotted by someone. I insisted, however. I bought a plaid cap and sunglasses and hunted up a worn-out old shirt. In that outfit, I figured, no one would recognize me, especially because I usually wore clerical garb.

Anne and I were going together, she as the commander, I to drive. Grace would go with Honey, and Alice with Sue. There was a definite air of excitement that day. We were determined to get to the bank. And we were afraid of running into Bob, who we heard was driving a cab. When the children had all gone to the bathroom, the girls began taking their turns, and then they asked if I weren't going to go, too. I scoffed, but they laughed and said, "You wait. You'll have to go so badly you'll be fit to die. You're already excited. Look at how flushed you are."

I gave it a second thought and went. When I returned, the girls asked me if I wanted to pray before we left. Laymen often ask that of ministers, but this kind of piety has never appealed to me. It seems to me that we should say our prayers whether or not we are in tense situations and not make of them special petitions for favor, not try to use God for our own purposes.

We went off without the benefit of orisons, although I did suggest that it would be permissible for each girl to say a brief prayer for her own safety and that of the others.

The opening chapter describes the success we had that day. We followed the blue station wagon to a supermarket parking lot, where the work was handed to the heavy-set Negro in the blue Thunderbird. We tailed him to the place where he handed it to the Green Pea Kid. We followed the Green Pea Kid to Yonkers. It was a glorious day, and not even Bob MacPherson's presence in town could dampen our enthusiasm. We had made it, after all the hours, days, and weeks of frustration!

CHAPTER ELEVEN

All the girls were assembled except Claire, who was vacationing on the Riviera. Rosalind was languidly draped over the arm of the couch in my office. Vicki was sitting properly in a straight chair, her eyes as big as saucers, her little boy playing at her feet. Sue with the trim chin and the quick smile listened to Marv intently, turning aside only long enough to separate her two boys, who fought intermittently. Alice and Helen smoked silently, happily. Belle perched on the edge of her chair, her eyes twinkling, her somewhat sardonic smile occasionally dissolving into a laugh. Penny was there, too, still awed by the presence of the Treasury agents. Honey, Barbara, and Maureen sat across the room listening quietly.

The atmosphere was electric. It always was when Marv was there, with his Jewish humor and his incisive mind. With him for the first time was another T-man, Jerry, as different from Marv as anyone could be, quiet, sober, Irish-Catholic, unexcitable. Only the absence of Myron and Tom, who were away on other assignments, dulled our happiness. The person who most pleased me was Grace. She was much better. The pain was gone and she looked fine.

"OK, kids, give it to me slowly," Marv began. "I am still not sure I can believe what Fay told me over the phone. Start back at the beginning when you first began to tail this guy from Heavy Eddie's."

Everyone looked at Anne. Nobody else deserved the honor of telling the story to Marv. It was she who had organized the project, memorized every significant license number that crossed her path, harangued and goaded and wheedled the girls into going out when they had other things to do, and kept our records and wrote up the results of the surveillance each day. She had not had much confidence in herself before beginning the project. Now she knew that she did have ability and leadership qualities.

When she had finished her narrative, Marv stared at her and wordlessly turned to Jerry. The chunky, tough, experienced veteran of many a battle with the Mafia, the cool-headed, unemotional Jerry said, in the office of a Presbyterian minister and in the presence of 11 young church matrons, "Jesus Christ!"

"We're out of jobs!" Marv said.

"Not if we keep it quiet," Jerry quickly retorted. "We'll just let them go out and do our work for us and we'll sit in the office drinking coffee and then go out occasionally and make the arrests."

"Yeh, but how'll we explain it to the boss?"

"We won't. We'll just say that we have a secret weapon."

Marv shook his head in disbelief, staring at his shoes. "My God, think what would've happened if he had organized the ladies of Hadassah. We'd have Frank Costello behind bars."

Jerry looked vacantly at me and then at the girls, one by one. "Who can beat God and motherhood?"

We gave them coffee, to bring them out of their state of shock, and then asked what their plan was.

"We want to go out in our car and tail this guy Dino, just to get the feel of the thing," Marv said. "We'll then pick up the second guy and watch him hand off the work to the third man. We have to do that to be sure that you all aren't seeing things."

"Are you going to tail the Green Pea Kid all the way to Yonkers then?" Vicki was impressed at how easy Marv made the tailing sound.

"Well, not necessarily, but if we get a chance we may."

"You'd better take one of us with you to show you the way around town. These one-way streets will drive you crazy." Anne was a little annoyed at their confidence in themselves, and it showed in her voice.

"We've been to New Rochelle before, haven't we, Marv?" Jerry was nettled at Anne's suggestion that he needed a guide.

"Well, I only meant that we know all the streets and the places they go to, and if we miss them one place we just take a stab at it and often pick them up again."

"Girls, we can't take any of you with us. If we had an accident and something happened, well, we're insured, but you wouldn't be, and it is better if we are alone."

"Well, do you want us to stay out of the way today or do you want us to do something?"

"We want you to give us one of your radios and let us be your third car," Marv said. "You stand at the bus stop as usual and give the signal which way he is going, and then we'll all see if we can stick with him for awhile."

Marv and Jerry picked up Dino as the girls had said they would, tailed him through his usual checks, dropped him when they got too close, and watched one of the girls pick him up. Then they got into trouble. They turned down a New Rochelle street that had no intersections for a long way and found themselves in Pelham. They gave up the chase and drove directly to Yonkers. They recognized instantly, from the number of men hanging around and from the traffic, that they were in the middle of a collection point. They also spotted a well-known hoodlum, whom they had arrested several years before. He seemed to be directing the collection. They didn't dare linger, for fear of heating up the place, so they came back, delighted. There was no longer a shred of doubt that we had stumbled onto something important.

"Boy, were those girls something!" Jerry shook his head. "They talk all the time on the radio. They chatter like magpies. And they don't have any idea of the right language to use over the air."

"Right language! Wow! I tell you, the language they use! You should get after your parishioners, Fay! Once Anne said over the air that Dino was headed north, and this Belle says, sadly, 'Which way is north?' And you should have heard what that prim-looking little Anne said to her."

"Yeh, but what singed my ears was when Anne was standing on the street corner and Belle came over the air to ask Alice whether or not Anne had seen anything, so she says, 'Able to Baker, do you read me?' And this Alice snaps, 'You're Baker, I'm Able!' Only you should have heard the words she used! Phew!"

But where were the girls? There had been no word from them. We began to feel uneasy. Jerry lit another cigarette and said nothing. Marv bummed a cigarette and smoked it. I twisted in my seat.

"Didn't they say anything over the air to indicate where they were going?"

Marv thought for a moment. "Well, we got down below the hill and didn't hear much of anything after that, but I did hear a sentence about some cab, but . . ."

"Well, then they got the number two man at least. Remember? That's the cab driver."

"Look, Fay, Jerry here is the best wheel man in the Treasury Department. If he lost the bum, those girls couldn't keep with him."

"Yes, but, as Anne was trying to tell you, even when they lose a guy they know the spots they use and they just go to the one it seems the bum is headed for and they often pick up the guy."

Suddenly we heard the door open at the foot of the stairs and children's voices. There was the whirr of the Coke machine, and then in they came.

"Hi, fellas!"

"Where have you crazy girls been?"

"Been? Why, to Yonkers, of course. Tailing the Green Pea Kid and watching him take in the bag to that bakery shop across the street from—."

"You tailed him all the way through to Yonkers?" Jerry's face was beet red.

"Of course," said Anne airily. "After we saw you go down that little road that keeps on going until you get all the way into Pelham, we knew we had to do it alone. So we dashed over to the parking lot behind that bar where we thought they would make the pass and sure enough—."

"Why didn't you radio us what was happening?" Marv was strangely flushed.

"Well, I did, but you didn't answer. I guess you were in Pelham by then." Anne's eyes were large and green and innocent, but the corners of her mouth curved upward the tiniest bit. "When we saw the cab coming out of the lot, we knew he had the work already, so we tailed him to the Pelham railroad station. We called you on the radio then to tell you we had the cab."

"Yeh, we heard something about a cab."

"He drove in, met the Green Pea Kid, gave him the package, and the Kid came right out and drove onto the Hutchinson Parkway. We followed him into Yonkers on the same route."

"Anne was great the way she kept trading places with us so as not to arouse his suspicions," said Belle.

Jerry put his head in his hands. Marv said, "Gee! It sounds as if you girls really know how to tail! Listen to them, Jerry, and learn something!"

"This is the second time I have seen that car pull up at the curb and the Kid get out," Anne said.

"We were over there, too, and saw some action, but we didn't dare stay," retorted Jerry a little testily.

"Yes, we saw you driving up the hill. But we didn't think we should wave to you."

After a few more minutes of red-faced discussion, the agents agreed to meet the girls again the next day. As Anne started out, Marv called after her, "Anne! That was good work!"

She gulped, said, "Thank you," and left.

"You know," Jerry said to me, "when I heard the way they used the radio I thought they were pretty amateurish. But the way they handled the tail, and went to a known location when they lost the scent, that was professional stuff."

The boys turned up every day after that to go out with the girls. And every day they learned more about the patterns, the places the hoods used, the Yonkers personnel, the cars involved. After several hauls, Marv and Jerry announced that they were calling off the tailing for awhile and were going to Yonkers to see what was going on there, in the streets and the shops where the work was being collected from all of Westchester. Occasionally they came by to tell us how things were going or to ask for information about an individual or an automobile.

Both Marv and Jerry came in jubilantly one day. They had been able to do a thorough survey of the scene in Yonkers. Everywhere they looked they had spotted old friends—Frankie the Pug, Teddy Bear, Foxy, Big Henry, Ikey the Cat. It was like old home week, and they had to be extremely careful not to be seen. It was clear that this was an enormous operation. Even Jerry was smiling, and Marv was so unusually evasive that I knew he was pleased. I say evasive because he could report only certain data. Other bits of information had to be kept confidential, a fact that never ceased to annoy me. But that was the rule, and they kept to it.

They did have some bad news, though. We had our hearts set on the bank and dreamed of the day the raid would take place: Treasury agents would find millions of dollars of work and the Syndicate would be paralyzed for weeks. Marv's news was that we had not, after all, found the bank, but only a collection point. The bank might be miles away, or only a block away. There was reason to believe it was nearby, because one man who did a lot of collecting could drive away and be back in minutes. I suggested trying to tail this man, but the agents hesitated. It would be hard in that area and, furthermore, the man might merely be parking the car with work in it and leaving it somewhere for five or six hours. They doubted that they could ever find the bank.

I was devastated, but Marv and Jerry were as happy as clams. Even to find such an area was too much to hope for. They could observe for weeks and, when they had enough pictures of the work being passed and enough information, they would raid the collection area and be satisfied with what they got.

After they left, I sat at my desk, fuming, for half an hour before calling Anne. When I told her the news, she was just as determined as I was to go all the way. She agreed to get the girls together for another session, and the next morning we met in my office. By that time I had more bad news for them. Marv had to testify in a trial that might keep him off the job for two weeks. We bit our lips but decided that the trial might be fortuitous. It would give *us* an opportunity to find the bank.

That afternoon, there were an unusual number of young women on the streets of Yonkers, sunning themselves and watching their children play. Anyone who looked carefully might have noticed that every now and then one of them would seem to speak into a shopping bag beside her. A still sharper-eyed person might have noticed that this speaking occurred when a stubby little man got into an old car and drove away. And someone trained to notice such incidents might have seen that another car up the street, driven by a woman and with children in the back seat, pulled away from the curb and followed the little man.

The girls flooded the streets with observers and soon came to know all the hoods in the area. One thing that bothered them the very first day—and continued to bother them for some time—was that they never saw the Green Pea Kid come with the New Rochelle work. We surmised that he was going directly to the bank. For days a delegation of New Rochelle women dressed in old clothes and left their beautiful homes to drive to Yonkers. They became completely familiar in the neighborhood, and soon the residents and the hoods were looking right through them. They had become neighborhood fixtures. Several times I went along. I usually dressed in an old shirt, put on my cap and dark glasses, and drove one of the cars that did the tailing, although I also did some "street work" during the crucial half hour when the work was presumably delivered. Many times I would be holding a meeting at the church and quickly jump up, put on my outfit, pick up some of the girls, and drive in a rush to Yonkers, do the half hour of surveillance, drive back to New Rochelle, slip out of my shirt and cap, put on my backward collar and my suit jacket and be dropped off at the hospital for sick calls, all in the space of an hour. It was a wild two weeks, trying to find the bank before the agents came back on the job. We identified most of the individuals who were bringing in work and took lots of notes, but we consistently lost the car with the work. Tailing was almost impossible. The streets were narrow, winding, and one way, full of red lights.

These days had their amusing sidelights. Anne's little girl, Rachel, started saying to her doll, "Do you read me, Annie? Do you read me?" A lady in my congregation reported to another that she was worried about me because she had seen me driving through town dressed in old clothes and dark glasses, with a blond beside me. When she saw how many whispered conversations I had with the same girl at the Sunday morning coffee hours, she became even more worried. But it was Anne who suffered the most. She stood on the street corner at the bus stop so often that people who knew her and knew she had a car started a rumor that she must have a lover.

The big break came the Saturday before the end of our two weeks of grace. Anne was late getting to Yonkers and arrived alone. None of the other girls could make it, and I was busy working on my sermon. Just as she turned to head down the hill to the collection point, she almost ran over the Green Pea Kid, who was walking! She slammed on the brakes, pulled up a few spaces, and parked. He walked into a bar on the corner and came out seconds later. He walked back to an empty lot, got his car, and headed for New Rochelle. Anne had found it!

I called the Treasury office early on Monday with the news.

"Uh, Jerry, you, uh, you were *right* about that bank not being down there at the collection point." I tried to be casual, to hold in the excitement I felt, to be as maddeningly professional as the agents were.

Jerry took a long time answering and when he did he swore. "You found it! I can tell."

"Oh, uh, well, I guess—."

"I'll bet it was that damned Anne. I knew the minute I saw how she handled that lost scent that she was a pro. How did she do it?"

I was honestly stunned. He had picked out the one who was a natural detective. All the girls were good, intelligent, observant, but Anne had that rare sixth sense. She could tell a hood from the way he carried himself. Good cops have that sense, and she had it. Jerry had caught it in her bearing and words. One pro knew another.

"Well, Jerry, if you want the truth, she *did* find it," I said. "We have flooded the area with girls for the past two weeks, and we have a good idea of how the entire action is worked. And finally, just this last Saturday, she saw the Green Pea Kid arrive *at the top of the hill* and go into that old bar there. He was out in seconds and went directly home. Now we know why he doesn't always come down to the street. He goes directly to the bar. I imagine that the actual room is in one of the apartments above the bar, or in the basement."

Jerry swore again and then said, in respect, "That damn Anne."

Anne agreed to drive to Yonkers, park her car several blocks from the critical area, meet Marv, and go with him to observe the bar. She would point out which people she thought were bringing in the work. Alice would meet Jerry somewhere else and point out all the known hoods coming into the collection area. With what they had already picked up from their own observations and what the girls could now add, the agents would have a good picture of the operation. It was heady stuff for the girls to be working with two special agents from the Intelligence Division of the Internal Revenue Service, even headier to be told that they had been "professional" in doing their surveillance and had accumulated some tremendously important information.

They saw all the right personnel arrive on time with their little bags and surreptitiously pass them to a man standing beside a car. When the man got into the car and drove away, Jerry, who was a true genius at the wheel of a car, and Alice, who had the ride of her life, managed to stay on his tail. By a circuitous route, he arrived at the top of the hill, got out, and carried into the bar an enormous shopping bag bulging with smaller bags. Alice almost fainted with excitement and a thin smile even creased Jerry's granite face. Anne and Marv saw the same sight from their vantage point and had to restrain themselves from whooping out loud. Almost immediately, up drove the Green Pea Kid, who parked his car in the lot and sauntered into the bar and out again. Why he sometimes went to the collection point and sometimes to the bar, we never discovered. He got into his old Plymouth, waved to someone, and drove away toward home.

The four of them made plans to go out again the next day, before lunch, in order to scout around when nothing was happening. The girls promised to bring food. They also decided to change partners. Jerry, the wheel man, needed Anne's encyclopedic memory of license numbers to spot the right cars.

Off they went, two very excited women and two slightly embarrassed agents. They did their scouting, then had some time to wait before the action would begin. They pulled to the curb a few blocks away, but still close enough to see cars entering the area, to eat their lunch. Anne doesn't ordinarily talk much, but that day she was excited beyond containment and anxious to transfer all the information she had accumulated during those two weeks into Jerry's brain. While he chewed his sandwiches and drank his thermos of coffee, impassively watching the street, she chattered on and on. She told him everything she knew about the operation, and then about her children and their school work and about her husband's work and her father and the church and about her neighbors and about the little town in which she had grown up, until she realized that he was peering intently at a car down the street. "What's the matter? What are you looking at?"

"I'm wondering about that little man in the Oldsmobile."

"I just told you a few minutes ago that he is only a delivery man from a dry cleaner's. Didn't you hear me? I'll bet you haven't been listening to a word I've said."

He looked at her in amazement. "Were you saying something? When I'm on surveillance I can't concentrate on anything but what I'm looking at."

Marv was having an unusual time, too. Alice is a kind person who's meticulous about herself, her home, and everything she does. She is also feminine to a fault. When lunchtime came, she got out her basket, extracted two dainty little egg salad sandwiches with the crusts cut off, unwrapped them, and laid them on a Kleenex on the seat beside her. Then she pulled out a little packet of stuffed green olives wrapped in aluminum foil, which she opened to form a cup. Beside that she put slivers of carrots and celery and a tiny packet of salt in waxed paper. She put out two paper-thin cookies lightly dusted with sugar. After that came two china cups and saucers and a thermos. The last thing to come out of the basket was another thermos and two paper cups. "Marvin," she asked the T-man, "would you like tea or apple juice with your lunch?" Somehow those words penetrated his busy brain.

"Tea or apple juice?" He slowly repeated her words as he turned to look at his lunch. "Tea or apple juice?"

"Well," she said in alarm, "you can have *both* if you want it."

Her words were lost on Marv, who was staring at the dainty little luncheon laid out on Kleenex.

"Where are the lox and bagels?" he said in mock outrage.

"Why, why, I, forgot that—I mean, I—." Her face was flaming red. Marv burst out laughing, and he laughed and laughed, finally stopping to apologize and to admit that he had expected a bottle of beer or a thermos of coffee and roast beef sandwiches.

The airwaves cracked as the two cars talked back and forth over the walkie-talkies. Anne rattled off license number after license number. As Myron and Tom before him had been stunned, Jerry sat openmouthed while she showed her complete ignorance of the difference between a Plymouth and a Ford, but she had memorized the license numbers of every suspected car in Westchester County. It was a superb day all around . . . until the very end.

The day's work over, Anne got out of the convertible that Jerry was driving to get into her own car, the Pink Poodle, which she had left parked on a Yonkers street with the top down. As she reached for the door handle, a man came out of a shop and called out, "Hey, Anne, hi! Who's that guy you were with, a 'good friend'? Ha-ha." It was someone who lived in her apartment building. She panicked. If she stopped to talk, she would have to explain why she was getting out of a strange car in the middle of Yonkers and who the man was. If she didn't, it was tantamount to admitting that she was carrying on an affair. She stuck her chin in the air, ignored the call, got into the Pink Poodle, and drove off. Behind her the man stood mystified, scratching his head; he snickered and re-entered the store. A few days later the same man ran into her in the laundry and said, "Hi, Anne, get back from Yonkers all right?" Then he snickered again. She tried desperately to act surprised but her face flamed and she obviously overdid her innocence. The man winked and whispered, "Don't worry, I won't tell Art." Anne gritted her teeth to keep from driving her spiked heel into his instep. "I don't know what you're talking about." Later that day Art said to Anne, "What's going on around here between you and that idiot in 312? He just passed me in the elevator and said, 'That's some wife you have there, Art,' and winked. What is that dumb clown talking about?" When Anne explained, Art wanted to punch him in the nose, but at her insistence he dropped it. Unfortunately, this was not to be the last blow to Anne's reputation.

The next day was an important one at the church. On that Sunday our new assistant minister, Douglass Lind, participated in the service for the first time, and he was ordained in the afternoon. After the ordination, there was a small reception at Doug and Penny's manse. As I chatted with first one and then another of his guests, Doug brought over a young man who worked for *Look* magazine. He said, "I have been hearing some of the darnedest things about you. Is is true that you've been carrying on a war against the Mafia and that you're even using women in the campaign."

I explained some of the things we had been doing, and some of what the girls were doing about the bank. He said, "My God, that's fascinating. Would you consider letting *Look* do a story on it? I'm sure they would pay you something for it."

"No money for me, thanks. I have kept this fight clear of any personal motives and I want to keep it that way. But if you want to do a story, I will see if it can be done."

I asked Marv to check on the law and policies of the government and to see what the Treasury Department thought about the idea. The answer from his superiors was that the agents could have nothing to do with reporters while they were working on a case, but that we could do as we wished with what we had developed. I telephoned *Look* and made arrangements for a reporter and photographer to go out with us a few times and to interview some of my undercover informants. In return *Look* would make a generous contribution to the "crime fund" that financed our operation. The magazine's contribution was fortuitous, because we soon needed all the money we could get. In the midst of the bank operation, we had developed an undercover man who gave us marvelous information. Harry was remarkably clever and had been in the rackets himself, but not for long. One arrest had cooled his ardor for easy money. He retained his old acquaintances and contacts, however. Over the years he came to see how evil the men who ran the vast gambling enterprise in Westchester were. He saw men murdered and beaten and towns corrupted as the hoods tried to widen their operations or protect what they already had. Eventually he came to me and offered to help.

He was great. He knew many men we had been unable to touch before, and also some we had had arrested but who were back in action again. He spent many weeks working for us. But he had to be bankrolled for his nights on the town, and that was enormously expensive. Soon we had information we had never heard before, information that left Marv and Jerry thrilled, if disgusted. Harry told us of a city court clerk in a Westchester community who was a friend and confidant of the hoodlums and spent hours with them. The clerk was reponsible for making out search warrants and warrants for arrests. It was small wonder that when the raiding police arrived they almost always found the places in that city closed or innocently carrying on their front business.

Harry got one of our observers into a notorious tavern where he was able to watch the clerk and the hoodlums. Because of technical legal difficulties, however, we were not able to get enough observations to bring about an arrest or civil service hearing without endangering Harry.

Through him, too, we found that one of the editors of a Westchester newspaper was betting heavily on athletic events with a big bookie, and we discovered the personal bookie of a Westchester judge, a jurist notorious for the light sentences he handed down to minions of the Mob. Harry also helped us with a ruse by which we got evidence on a number of bookies in and out of town who were later arrested by IRS agents. The money from *Look* paid for Harry's work, and it was worth every cent.

Meanwhile, the weeks wore on and still the agents were not able or ready to make their move. Getting the necessary warrants was difficult, because the agents had to be able to show the existence of a pattern of activity that made it certain the men were indeed gamblers and not old cronies who met for a chat every day. The Syndicate kept changing men, cars, collecting places. We could do nothing but sit and sweat as we waited for the case to develop. The girls by now were going to the beach with their children instead of tailing hoods. We seldom saw the agents. They were either in court testifying on other cases, being pulled off our case to go on raids, or working in Yonkers. Only on the few occasions when they came over to work on something Harry had developed did we see them.

Then one day, Marv called. Would I get some of the girls together? He wanted their help again. As women, they could do some things the agents couldn't.

It was hard to assemble them this time. Some were away on trips or were getting their kids ready for camp or planning graduation parties for them. Moreover, a few of the husbands had clamped down on their wives' activities and insisted that they not get so involved this time. We managed to round up five girls, excluding Grace, who was again ill. When I muttered something angry about husbands not understanding, Marv cocked his head and thought for a moment. "I don't know, Fay. It seems to me that they have been pretty understanding already. If my wife came to me and said, 'Hey, Marv, the rabbi came to me today with a funny idea about going spying,' I don't know what my reaction would be."

Jerry exploded, "I do. I wouldn't allow it!"

"What?" Anne was aghast. This was the man who had called her a pro, the man with whom she had gone out tailing hoodlums.

"Absolutely not," he said firmly. "A woman's place is in the home. If you let your wife get out and do something like this, would she ever be satisfied at home?"

Marv stopped the conversation before it got into more dangerous water and told the girls why he had called the meeting. The agents were getting ready to make their move and they wanted to begin at the beginning in New Rochelle, at Heavy Eddie's luncheonette tailing the first, second, and third pickup men and heading right through the collection point to the top of the hill. Then he dropped his bombshell.

"And I have some bad news for you. Even the hill is not the bank. We suspected so earlier, and now we know so. It is a sort of 'sanctuary area' where they come to 'cool' the work. They gather it together, drive up there, and take it either into the bar or into a room off the alley next to the bar, or on some occasions they leave it in the car while they sit inside and drink beer. Shopkeepers stand around outside and watch the street. If all seems well, they move the work. But on this leg they take unbelievable precautions, doing a dozen checks. So far we have been unable to follow them and we doubt that we ever will."

Our faces showed our dismay. "Cheer up," he said. "You did great work. You found an area we knew nothing about and you put us onto a tremendously complicated policy operation. We'll hit the hill and take all kinds of men. But we won't get the bank."

After a few more minutes, we got our chins off the floor and agreed to help on the tail. When Marv asked if Dino was still carrying the work from Heavy Eddie's, Vicki said, "I guess so, but is he a mess! My husband and I stopped at a bar for a drink the other night and who should be at the bar sitting all by himself but Dino, smashed and getting deeper in all the time. He just sat there and drank and drank. Once when he said something to someone next to him, the man said, 'I know you have a problem, Dino. Have one on me.'"

Belle was full of sympathy. "What sort of problem does he have?"

I interrupted Anne, who started to speak, to say "He is in debt up to his eyes to a loan shark and could get killed for it."

"Doesn't he have family trouble? Maybe that is the reason he gambles and drinks so heavily.'

I exploded at that. "He has trouble, all right. He drinks and gambles away all his money and his wife has to work to support the family. His children are all perfectly delightful. *He* is the family trouble."

Marv was grim as he said, "Well, he's going to be even more trouble to his family after we arrest him."

The thought of this nice family suffering because of a no-good father saddened us momentarily, but we had to make our plans and get started. Anne explained that during the last few days she had observed that Dino was no longer giving off to the cab driver. He met the Green Pea Kid himself, and the Green Pea Kid then drove to a diner in the Bronx, parked, went inside for 20 minutes or so, came out, and went right back to his haunts in New Rochelle. Apparently he was passing the work to someone in the diner.

We got four cars out that day. Dino did his lazy checks, sped to the Pelham Shore Road, met the Green Pea Kid, and gave him the work. We tailed the Kid, but he didn't go to the Bronx. He went directly to the collection area on Old Broadway in the Italian section of Yonkers. Alice jumped out, took Chucky by the hand, and followed the Kid as he walked out of the parking lot and down the stairs toward his rendezvous. When he reached the sidewalk, a tall man caught his eye and nodded. The Kid stopped, nodded back, turned around, and started up the stairs toward Alice. She had seen the shake-off and wondered if it was to warn the Kid that he was being tailed. Then she figured that the Kid must be late and was being told to take the work directly to the hill. She boldly snapped her fingers as if she had forgotten something, turned around, and ran back up the stairs behind the Kid. She was afraid he would hear her, but had to get word to the other cars that the Kid still had the work and was going to another rendezvous. She climbed into the car where Belle was waiting and radioed to the rest of us to be on the lookout.

We caught the Kid as he came out of the lot and, by leapfrogging cars, managed to tail him while he did a slight check. Then he parked at the top of the hill and went into the bar. Parked directly in front of the bar was one of the cars we knew took work from the collection point. So far, so good. We had taken it all the way from New Rochelle to here. Marv was cooing with happiness. But the minutes dragged on, and the men in the bar who should be taking the work to the bank did not come out. "Yesterday we sat here watching that same car for four hours and nobody came," Marv said. "They either used some other car or they suspected something and waited until nightfall before moving. It's impossible to know. If you go into the bar, you see several doors, and when we checked we found that they open out into other hallways or into an alley that would allow a man to carry the work into any of several places—even pick up a different car out there in the lot. It's like the Casbah. You'd have to have a dozen men sitting at various points to catch all that could go on in this place. And yet if you have a dozen men around who are strangers, the hoods get scared and sit on the work for hours. In fact, we'd better move to another spot. That little shopkeeper is giving us the eye."

By the time we found new parking spaces, the car we had been watching was gone. Frantically we fanned out through the area trying to find it, but it was gone. We had lost again. And the more I studied the area and the problems, the more certain I became that Marv was right. It was hopeless. We would never get the bank. We were sad people that night, but we agreed to try again the next day. Marv asked Anne to have the girls organized and to give them their orders, because he and Jerry would be arriving late.

When I got home, Grace met me at the door. "Well, I have a nice problem for you. Joanne called to ask if she could give Kristin a ride to the party tonight."

"What can we do? If we refuse, he is likely to suspect something, and if we let him . . ."

"Well, what can *he* do? After all, he is no Mafia gunman."

"Yeah, but it gives me the creeps to think about him taking Kristin to that party in his car, the same car we have tailed so many times."

"But Kristin is already asking what's wrong. We must either let her go or tell her the reason."

That evening Dino pulled up in front of our home, just as we had seen him pull up next to the cab and the Green Pea Kid so many times. Kristin kissed us goodbye and ran out. We watched them drive off. I was to pick up the youngsters and bring them home, and it was a relief when they came running out to the car three hours later. When I drove Joanne to her house, the familiar station wagon was nowhere to be seen. Apparently the man with the problem was out getting smashed again.

Anne was determined for everything to go well that day. She wanted her troupe to impress the agents with their professional skill. Because some of the girls had not worked on the case for weeks, she had typed out their instructions in detail, with the license numbers to watch for and a description of the way she expected the work to move. She handed out the instructions, and Marv and Jerry entered to find the girls reading them.

Marv took one of the papers, read it, and said, "What do you want us to do, chief?"

Anne laughed nervously, colored a little, and apologized for her superefficiency, but the agents didn't laugh. They knew professional ability when they saw it. They made a joke out of it, teasing her mercilessly, but from that time on she was the "chief" to them, and when new agents occasionally came along she was introduced to them as the "chief," and the newcomers were instructed to jump to attention when she entered the room. In the weeks ahead, they never failed to enjoy their little joke. Marv would slap a new agent on the shoulder and say, "Get up, you slob. Don't you know the chief when you see her?" The grizzled agent would frown, jump up, do an elaborate bow, and apologize, saying that he had never met "the chief" before and didn't realize who it was. "That's no excuse. You should be able to tell by the aura around her that she is The One. Don't let it happen again." Anne may have tired of the buffoonery, but she never let on. She knew it was a mixture of respect for her and laughter at themselves for being involved in such a venture.

Despite the elaborate instructions, the day's tailing was largely a bust. We got Dino all right and tailed him to the Green Pea Kid, who drove to the diner in the Bronx. Marv jumped out and went inside to see who took the work from the Kid. We were supposed to watch the car, to be sure that someone else didn't come and pick it up. I saw the Kid go to the telephone inside the diner and make a long call. We waited and waited, but nothing happened. We knew that in a few minutes all the work would have been collected on Old Broadway and on its way to the hill. Jerry and Anne drove off there to see if they could get a break on the car that had the work. The Kid stayed on, drinking one and then another cup of coffee. I sat waiting for Marv, wondering if the Kid had known we were behind him, if he had given the work to Dino and told him to give it to someone else, maybe Cassone, to take to the bank.

When the Kid finally came out, we tailed him all the way back to New Rochelle, where he went into a bar and settled down for a long stay. How he got rid of the work, if he ever had it, we never found out.

Back at the church, after an hour of anxious waiting, Jerry and Anne returned. He was grinning from ear to ear. Anne's green eyes were burning with emotion.

Marv could hardly believe it when he saw Jerry's face. "What did you get, you bum?"

Jerry smirked, "Oh, not much, just the bank!"

Marv stopped dead in his tracks, glaring at Jerry. "You son of a gun. You didn't! You didn't!"

"Well, to be honest, I didn't. Anne did."

"Oh, Jerry, if it hadn't been for *your* skill at driving and the way you knew just about where he was going, we would never have—."

"Look," said Marv, "if the bum wants to give someone else some credit, let him. By the time he gets back to the office, he will be telling everyone that he did it. You tell the story, Anne."

"Well, we drove around through the Old Broadway area, but the action was over, so we went up to the top of the hill. There sat the car that usually takes the action, right in front of the bar. Nobody was in it, so we decided to watch it for awhile. But nothing happened, and we had to move, and of course the moment we did the car took off. As we came around the corner, we saw it disappearing through a red light. By the time we got on our way, it was gone."

"And Anne was so gloomy I suggested that we stop and have a Coke somewhere before going back to the church, and we parked at this drive-in."

"Jerry had a Coke, but I had a root beer float because I like a little ice cream in my soft drinks. And he was finished with his before I was, so he was just starting the car when I looked out at the traffic and saw this familiar license number flash by. I screamed at him—."

"She screamed, spilled her float, pounded me, and almost jabbed out my eye as she pointed down the road. And, Marv, you know what she said? She says, she says, 'Hey, there goes old WSV2871.' Now, Marv, you know that I can see a car once and memorize every dent and scratch on it and recognize it any time I see it again. But license numbers? So I says, 'What's WSsmiltch?'"

"Only that is not the way you said it, Jerry," said Anne, her eyes twinkling. "You used some language that wouldn't be fit to repeat in this office in front of a minister."

"*You* should talk. I learned those words listening to you girls on the radio."

"All right, all right, so you had a break and caught the car on the fly," Marv interrupted. "I suppose you lost him two blocks later."

"Jerry wouldn't have lost him if he had had to handcuff his car to ours," Anne said. "He played it beautifully. I learned so much from him about how to tail someone. He hung back just far enough until he got on the Thruway, then played it really loose, kept behind him when he got off at the first Tarrytown exit, and then wove in and out of traffic right behind him."

"It really wasn't very hard, because they were sure they were clean and they were asleep. They just drove right on through town, and when they came to Wilton Street, they—."

"Jerry was so good there," said Anne, and she came the closest to squealing that I had ever heard her. "He said, 'Now I'll bet he turns that corner and goes to Marchetti's Tavern,' and before I could catch my breath he turned there and, sure enough, he stopped at Marchetti's Tavern."

"Marv, it was gorgeous. Catching them on the fly, they were just yacking away to each other and paying no attention to anybody. And this fat guy jumps out and runs into the bar, and comes out with another big bag full of work, and another guy who gets in with them. By that time there was five guys in the car. So we sat back half a block, but kept on their tail until they pulled up in front of the apartment house there on Main Street. And you should have seen the bags they took out of that car. Three big shopping bags full of little bags. I never seen anything like it."

"I got so excited that I squeezed Jerry's arm until he screeched, but I had to do it or I would have died."

Jerry rolled up his sleeve and showed us four red indentations. "I thought someone had shot me. But I didn't even care. Now I *know* we got it."

"Yeh, that's it," Marv said. "There's no doubt about it. That is the bank. It's perfect. We have a lot of work left to do, but that is it."

We sat there savoring our success. Marv got a sudden idea and called his office. "Give me Charlie," he said, and Jerry broke into guffaws. He turned to us to explain.

"We used to have a squad of guys that did nothing but look for banks and Charlie was its head. He told us we'd never find one. And when he heard we were working with a minister and a bunch of women, he laughed us out of the office."

"Hi, Charlie, old friend, old buddy," cooed Marv.

"This is called the setup," Jerry explained.

"Charlie, you know that bank we're never going to find? You were right. Treasury agents could never find one in less than months, you guys proved that. So we sent some girls and a minister out to find one for us, while we drank coffee and told stories, and now we have got it."

There was a skeptical squawk from the other end. Marv told Charlie the whole story. When he finished, there was nothing but silence. Marv waited a minute, then said, "I guess he fainted," and hung up.

Anne had to leave, to get some shopping done before the stores closed. Marv, Jerry, and I sat around enjoying it some more. "You know, that dame is something," Jerry said.

"Dame? Dame?" Marv screamed at him. "You mean the chief? Be respectful."

Jerry didn't even argue. He inclined his head in agreement and continued, "She has that sense, that feel for the work. She caught that car going by us at 40 miles an hour. I can't believe it was the license number she saw, but she says it was. And even before that, during the rest of the time, she has been great. She can look you right in the eye and describe what someone is doing across the street from her. I have been doing tailing for 12 years now and I've had only two partners I liked working with. One was an old New York detective and the other is that—the Chief. Some dame!"

Before they left, we agreed to send Anne some roses, with a card reading "To our favorite blond, the chief, from her admirers, the Indians." Art, her husband, told me that when she received them she lost her cool for a brief minute and wept, smearing her eye makeup terribly.

That was the beginning of a fine friendship between the chunky, tough, impassive Treasury agent and the pretty, sophisticated young matron. From then on, whenever they were in the same group, Anne and Jerry would soon be quietly telling of their most recent adventures or discussing their families. As they came to know each other better, they also became teases and would save up ways to chide each other. Sometimes the teasing took on an earthy nature. Once, as he left a conference in Anne's apartment, Jerry noticed that the door to a notoriously nosy neighbor's apartment closed quickly, and he called back, "We had a great time, Anne. Can I tell all my friends?" Poor Anne's reputation was already deteriorating rapidly, and that almost finished it. Her husband had to endure pitying glances for a time after that, and to this day a few people are convinced that she is a loose woman.

The discovery of the bank led to more observations, more complications, and more problems, as well as more opportunities. The girls were still of value because they would not heat up the area nearly as much as the Treasury agents would if they were recognized. Once Belle and Alice parked their car in the municipal lot above the street where the work was being collected, spent some time on the street, and returned to their car to find that the "manager" of the "street action" had parked his Cadillac beside them and that a bevy of thugs were sitting on the fenders and leaning against the side of Belle's car! Without a moment's hesitation, they walked up to their car and she said, with undisguised annoyance, "Excuse me, please! This is *my* car and we have to go." Those words and an angry glare sent the hoodlums scurrying. When they moved Belle saw something that made her gasp. The "manager" was sitting in his Cadillac counting money, piles and heaps and gobs of money. The front seat was covered with greenbacks. The girls got in their car and drove off, glaring at the cringing racketeers.

Many weeks had now gone by since we found the collection area. The prospect of arrests was fading into the far distant future. The picture was complicated, and the possibilities so rich, that the T-men had decided to do more observing. Furthermore, in order to get warrants, they had to have several observations of the same persons. Because the Organization was forever changing cars, people, and meeting places, it was difficult to get the necessary evidence. We were living a life of unbearable tension, waiting, wondering, unable to do anything substantial to help. And then it was time for me to go to Portland, Oregon, for the General Assembly of the Presbyterian Church. I was on the nominating committee and had to attend, but never was a member of that committee so reluctant.

I was at my hotel in Portland when a message came that a reporter from *The New York Times* was trying to reach me. I was sure something had gone wrong. If the raid had been held, Marv or Doug would have called me. But if one of the girls had made a mistake and been hurt, and had told about our operation, then the reporters would be calling me. I was sick. The phone rang. It was Doug. He explained that somehow *The Times* had gotten hold of the story that a Presbyterian minister had a lot of housewives tailing hoodlums all over Westchester County. *The Times* wanted the story. That put me in a delicate position with regard to my obligation to *Look* magazine. But the worst of it was that, if *The Times* printed a word of what we had been doing, it might blow the entire operation, months of work would go down the drain, and the big raid would never be held. Doug hadn't known what to do and had referred the reporter to me. I spent the next few hours trying to dodge the reporter's calls, feeling certain that he wouldn't write a story until he had talked to me. By evening, however, he had caught up with me. I explained the situation and promised that I would talk to him as soon as I returned to New Rochelle. Grace called to say that she had been pestered and that the girls were scared. I told her to tell the girls to keep their mouths shut.

Doug's trials were not over. The man who had gotten me the peep truck wanted it back. Doug drove over to Rosalind's house and tried to start the truck. He was dressed in his clerics, and the picture of a handsome young man with a backward collar, toiling in the hot sun over a recalcitrant old panel truck, with seats for two observers to watch criminals through its one-way windows, that picture still gives me amusement. Doug had studied in the finest seminary in the United States and had worked at learning the personal skills with which to perform his ministry, but no one had ever told him that his wife would join a Ladies Aid that investigated crime, or that he would one day be driving a peep truck into Manhattan. After drying the spark plugs, he got it started and coaxed it onto the highway. He had driven about five miles when he smelled something. The engine began to cough and belch black smoke. He pulled over to the side and got out to investigate, not that he knew enough about engines to know what to do, but he faithfully looked under the hood. The engine was fiery hot, and a pool was spreading under the truck. It was water from the radiator. The pool didn't grow much bigger, however, because the radiator was already almost empty. Apparently there was a hole in it. A state policeman suddenly pulled up beside him. He saw his reflection in the window, and knew instantly that it was one-way glass, that the truck was a peep truck, and that it was being driven by a clergyman! He asked Doug for his license. Suddenly Doug realized why the policeman was being so poker-faced. "Oh, ha-ha, of course! Here is my license. You want to know how it is that I, I mean, about the peep truck and how come, I mean, well, I, uh, you see, it's this way. I just got out of seminary three years ago and this is my first parish. I mean, I am an assistant in a church for the first time, and the Ladies Aid is doing some spying for the pastor—I am the assistant minister—and he is in Oregon and I have to take back his truck."

Doug handed the officer his Social Security card, then, realizing his mistake, fumbled for his driver's license and couldn't find it. He dropped all his credit cards on the road before he found the license. The officer read it and his suspicions eased slightly. He asked to see the registration on the truck. I had forgotten to tell Doug that it was in a little compartment above the windshield. He stammered that he didn't have it, but if the cop wanted to call me or a Treasury agent he was sure one of us would know where it was. His very naïveté was probably what convinced the officer that, although someone was obviously insane somewhere, it was unlikely that anybody was breaking the law. Either that or he was so confused already that he let Doug go rather than hear any more.

There wasn't much of anywhere for Doug to go. The engine wouldn't start until he could get some water and cool off the radiator—and that meant a long walk down the dangerously busy Thruway. He made it in half an hour. Unfortunately, the heat had apparently enlarged the leak. As he poured in clear water, rusty water poured out onto his foot. Finally, by driving a short way, stopping for water for his truck while people stared in disbelief, and repeating the process over and over, he got to his destination.

The reason for *The New York Times'* sudden interest was not just normal reportorial curiosity, but derived from a story that had suddenly broken in Mount Vernon, the city between New Rochelle and the Bronx. A few people there had been working on the problems of urban renewal but had given up in disgust. A professor of sociology at nearby Sarah Lawrence College who had been working as an adviser resigned, saying that one reason the city couldn't get any action on renewal was that the Organization, the Mob, resisted all efforts at progress. The thought of Organized Crime throwing monkey wrenches into efforts to clean up and reorganize a city was intriguing, and *The New York Times* headlined it.

There was an immediate furor, with the usual charges and countercharges, and one of the most interesting chapters in the history of Organized Crime in Westchester County began. The district attorney of Westchester, Leonard Rubenfeld, was highly skeptical of the charges and defended his county and administration. "The Mafia has been blamed for many, many things," he declared, "but this is the first time I've heard of interference with urban renewal. That is utterly ridiculous in this county." He went on, "Westchester is the cleanest county in the United States." County Executive Edwin Michaelian agreed with his district attorney, adding that county authorities were putting down all attempts by Organized Crime to operate in the county.

United States Attorney Robert Morgenthau disagreed. He called Westchester "one of the major problem areas for law enforcement" because of the entrenchment of Organized Crime, and said that he was continuing his investigation of rackets there.

Two days later a top Mafia leader and one of his aides were tried in federal court, convicted, and given prison terms and heavy fines. Treasury agents had arrested them for failing to pay the $50 gambling tax. The United States Attorney charged that the Mafioso was a member of the Carlo Gambino family and the head of a vast gambling organization that operated in the Bronx and Westchester County. A florist testified that he had given bets to him, and a federal agent also gave testimony that led to the conviction. Then came one of the tragic events in the fight against Organized Crime. The Supreme Court handed down a decision stating that the law under which federal agents had been making gambling arrests was unconstitutional and useless, making the conviction of the Mafia leader certain to be dismissed. A few days after the Supreme Court decision, two thugs walked into the florist's store and beat the old man half to death.

It was in the beginning stages of the Mount Vernon furor that *The New York Times* heard about our work in New Rochelle and called me in Portland. I managed to hold off comment for several weeks. Back home, I was "out" when reporters called or "forgot" to return their calls. The immense publicity from Mount Vernon was already making the hoodlums unusually skittish, even the New Rochelle hoods. Anne's encounter with Dino is an example. She was driving down the street one day and saw Dino ahead of her, but paid no attention to him because she knew it was too early for him to be carrying her work. She passed him and a few blocks later he pulled up beside her at a red light. He leaned on the door of his car and said, "Hi."

She thought he was being a typically obnoxious masher, so she gave him her most frigid look and said, "Hello."

"That's a nice little boy you got there," he said. "You'd better be careful or he'll get hurt."

Anne thought he meant that the door was unlocked, so she reached over and pushed down the latch, but he repeated his warning.

"Yeah, you better be mighty careful, or that kid'll get hurt."

The warning sank in. Anne wasn't particularly frightened. The thought of that weak, alcoholic lackey hurting even a woman was so improbable that it caused little more than derision, but it did infuriate her, and it did serve as a warning that the hoods knew she was one of the women who had been following them.

The reporter from *The Times* finally told my secretary that he wanted an interview or he was going to go ahead and print a story about me and my women tailing hoodlums! I had not expected such blatant threats from *The Times*. I agreed to an interview, telling him what we had done in the past and how my efforts were then bent toward the founding of a Westchester citizens' crime commission that would have a staff of professionally trained investigators to do what we had tried to do so amateurishly. I told him that our present work was secret and that any attention to it would interfere with an official investigation. He pressed me about the girls, and I soon saw that he knew a good deal about them. Someone in our little organization had talked. We agreed that his article would concentrate on what we had done in the past, making it sound as if we were finished. We parted on that note, but I had a sinking feeling that his article would say things that would jeopardize what we had been working on for months. Doug and I jumped in the car and drove down to New York to see one of the editors of *The Times*. He bluntly told me that he knew I had a deal with *Look* to give them the story, that this wasn't fair, and that he intended to print a story about our work. I was stunned. The thought that a great newspaper, possibly the greatest newspaper in the United States, was willing to destroy a criminal investigation by federal officers in order to get a jump on a story was too much. I argued, pleaded, snarled, threatened, and finally wrung out of the editor a deal that he could run an article on us if it clearly gave the impression we were all washed up, and if it did not mention any activity by the girls or any of the movies we had made.

When the article appeared the next day, I almost wept. One of the headlines was, "U.S. Given Movies on Gambling in New Rochelle." The article told the story of Anne being threatened and had several other mentions of the use of housewives to keep track of the hoods. The editors did, however, stick to their agreement not to say that we were doing anything now. The article also quoted Commissioner Carey as saying, "There's no organized crime in this city." And it quoted City Manager Fuerst as saying, "I don't think there ever was organized crime here. Not to my knowledge. There are no bookie places here now."

I was devastated by the article. Not only would it give the hoodlums a hint of what we had been doing, but it might also endanger Anne's life. Dino may have just thought she looked like one of the girls he had seen around a lot, but if he read the article he would know for sure that he had identified one of the girls. The chance of real physical danger was remote, but it was greater than it had been. I was also sick about the bitterness I would have to face for having been the subject of an article that could jeopardize an important operation. Yet I didn't know what else I could have done.

I hardly had time to think about it. I had barely finished reading the story when the telephone rang. It was a radio station wanting to interview me about the article and about crime in suburbia. I refused to say anything. All through breakfast, the telephone continued to ring with requests for interviews. I was amazed. In the early days, when attention from the influential New York papers would have given us leverage in gaining action from City Hall, we couldn't attract any interest. Now, when we wished to heaven they would all shut up so the agents could finish the investigation and make their raids, we were deluged with publicity!

When I arrived at the office, I found my secretary already overcome with calls. She said, "NBC-TV and CBS-TV and Channel 5 have called, and so have two radio stations, and a federal narcotics agent wants to talk to you about drugs in New Rochelle."

I made a dash for the telephone and called Marv. He was great as usual, disappointed about the article but sympathetic. He did point out how I could have avoided all the trouble by simply saying that the report about my using housewives was nonsense. No one would have dared to print anything then. I hadn't thought of it because I don't find it easy to lie. I wish I had.

Most people thought the article was just fine. They called to congratulate me and to wish me luck. Parishioners on Sunday morning told me how proud they were. Everywhere I went people commented on it. I was thunderstruck. The one thing I had tried to avoid, personal publicity, was the cause of their congratulations. Where before I had been the object of much suspicion and mistrust among the citizens of New Rochelle, after that unwanted article I found a subtle change. Apparently being the subject of a feature story in *The Times* had given me a sort of legitimacy.

It did, as expected, create problems for Marv and the other agents. The collection area quieted down and the pattern changed. The T-men let it cool and turned to work intensively on some of Harry's information. Harry had outlined a way to use some old customers as patsies to get agents into a few places. With the work in Yonkers at a standstill, Marv and the boys got busy on this new angle.

There was an old score to settle, too. Michael Carchietta's trial was coming up. One of the original nine men we had gotten arrested, he operated the Lyn Sue stationery store, the place where Hazel had introduced a Treasury agent as her husband. We had hoped he would plead guilty so that she would not need to testify, but he insisted on a trial before a judge. When the day arrived, I went along with Hazel. Carchietta sat glowering at her as she crisply told of going into his store on many occasions over a period of several months and repeatedly placing bets. The defense attorney tried to shake her, but he only made things worse. He asked her, with obvious sarcasm, why she had made bets in the store, evidently trying to imply that she was a gambler who had changed her spots. She calmly replied, "I made them because my pastor asked me to help him, and because I hate Organized Crime." The attorney asked few question after that. The judge took about 30 seconds to find Carchietta guilty and directed him to return later for sentencing.

There must be thousands of these trials of numbers operators before judges each year, but this one made history of a sort. *The Times* devoted a 17-inch story to it, and *The Standard Star* put it on the front page. Hazel had become famous. The reason for the unusual attention was, of course, the tremendous debate about the existence of Organized Crime in Westchester. The story had human interest and was timely.

It wasn't only federal agents who were active. Men from the office of District Attorney Rubenfeld suddenly raided a bookie establishment in Mount Vernon and caught four men. The D.A., a man who had deprecated all talk of the Mafia and Organized Crime in Westchester, now said that the arrested men were members of the Milo Syndicate in Westchester. *The New York Times,* in its story of the arrests, reported that the FBI had identified one as being a member of the Vito Genovese family. Rubenfeld insisted, however, that the arrests had nothing to do with the current controversy, but had been planned months before. "We might have come up with more without all the publicity," he declared. "The bigger boys we wanted to get with the slips weren't there."

While Marv and his agents were working on Harry's evidence, there was another development in the unfolding story of Organized Crime in Westchester when an official of a refuse collection company was arrested by state police and charged with using coercion and threats to keep a competitor from expanding his business. This was an important arrest for a number of reasons. First of all, it had long been known that 90 percent of the private carting industry in Westchester County was controlled by gangsters. The official was tied in by Rubenfeld with the activities of a Mafia family that "go right to the highest echelon of organized crime." It was active, he said, in legitimate businesses, such as amusements, hotels, bars and grills, jukeboxes, and motels, and had also been cited as the heads of policy and bookmaking operations throughout Westchester.

The Mount Vernon story was only beginning. *The New York Times* shortly carried a story stating that a Congregational minister, Martin Duffy, had proclaimed from his pulpit that his city was controlled by a vicious group of gangsters who acted through their servants in City Hall, on the police force, on the school board, and in both major political parties. The system, he declared, couldn't operate without police protection.

One night, Reverend Duffy's wife and daughter went out for a walk on Third Street. At an intersection, they noticed a white car parked, facing east. When the light changed and Mrs. Duffy and her daughter began to cross the street, the car suddenly roared away from the curb toward them, tires screaming as it ran through the red light. Mrs. Duffy jerked her daughter back to the curb as the car sped by. She was too shocked to get a good description of the car, nor was she able to see the driver or license number. Duffy immediately telegraphed the governor to ask for protection for his family and himself. This was not the first instance of threats or harassment of someone who had dared to speak out against corruption and the rackets in Mount Vernon. Others had experienced the same thing.

The citizens of the county debated the incidents for some weeks. Anybody who had driven through Mount Vernon could see that the stationery stores and luncheonettes were obvious fronts, and they read constantly of federal and state authorities making arrests in their fine city.

Meanwhile, Marv and his friends, waiting for things to cool off, were working on Harry's leads instead of the bank. One day I returned to the office and found him and Jerry waiting for me. They grinned, and I knew that only an arrest could have caused such glee. They had just hit one of New Rochelle's best-known gambling establishments. A federal grand jury handed up a five-count indictment alleging a $1 million-a-year horse bet emporium had been operating at the downtown luncheonette. According to Assistant United States Attorney Edward Meyer, an undercover agent laid bets of $20 to $40 a day in taxpayers' money to get the goods on the pair, and even picked some winners. From 7 AM to 7 PM the place was open, with as many as 7 bettors in 5 minutes ducking in during the peak hours of 11:30 AM to 1:30 PM. A raid on the back room produced bet slips, scratch sheets, and other paraphernalia, with the chief cache an old camel's hair polo coat hanging on a peg in the corner. Its pockets were stuffed with bet slips. United States Attorney Robert Morgenthau said the investigation was spurred by a tip from me. The two men arrested were old friends; they were among the original nine arrested in our first successful operation.

The summer, a heady one for us, was not over by any means. A couple of weeks later, the agents struck out of town and grabbed three men who were conducting a $2-million-a-year action. A few days after that, they arrested a New Rochelle man for conducting a gambling operation and credited my little band of volunteers with the information that led to the arrest.

As the fruits of our work ripened into successes, the subtle change I had noticed in the way I was treated by local business-men and politicians continued. One politician after another would coyly congratulate me and tell me how surprised he was to learn of all the gambling activity. I could certainly be assured of his support and admiration. Would I care to come out with a state-ment supporting his candidacy, inasmuch as we stood for the same thing? When I suggested that in return said politician should show his opposition to Organized Crime by coming out publicly in support of my work, he would get red, hem and haw, and drop the subject. Businessmen who for the first time began to treat me with respect did so, I believe, not so much because the arrests and the recognition I was winning were proof of my allegations, but because they were afraid of what I might do next. All over town I was being treated with kid gloves. No one any longer attacked me or claimed that I was full of beans. I was just avoided like the plague.

Not everyone ignored me. Certain luncheonette owners were known to spit on the floor when I walked by. One stationery store owner once came outside his store after I had passed and made obscene gestures to my back. He never did so to my face.

Then there was the time I had to go into a restaurant where hoodlums gathered to meet a friend. An automobile salesman was so infuriated at my daring to enter their sanctuary that he loudly proclaimed—after I had gone—that, if he had had a gun when I walked in, he would have shot me.

The heat finally cooled down enough for the Treasury agents to think about the bank routine again. They checked in Yonkers. Things had returned to normal. After a few more observations, they came back to New Rochelle and again began to tail Dino and his contact. They missed the pass a few times because of bad breaks and made it a few other times. They had almost enough observations when a friend called to tell me that Dino had been arrested by the local police. I was furious. The thought that they had let him operate freely until the federal agents came to town made me wonder if the police had not seen the agents following Dino and made the pinch to steal their thunder.

Whatever the reason, that one arrest completely scrubbed the operation from the New Rochelle end. The agents would have to start all over again with the new pickup man. They threw up their hands in despair and decided to try something from the Yonkers end. That was the last I saw of them for weeks. To me and the girls, Dino's arrest was a particularly bitter pill. All our movies were worthless. The months of surveillance were wasted— except that they had led to the bank. They did not lead to a single New Rochelle arrest. We had two undercover people betting with Heavy Eddie and the agents could have arrested him, but there was little point. It would have meant the undercover men having to testify, and it hardly seemed worth it. I went on vacation the day after the arrest.

The entire month of August I searched the papers for news of a raid on the bank or headquarters in Yonkers. Nothing appeared. I called Doug several times to see if anything had happened, or if he had heard from Marv or Jerry. Nothing. Never have I spent a more miserable summer vacation. Had we lost everything we had worked on? I called Anne to see if she had heard of any arrests. She had not. We stewed in our cottages and motels as we traveled and waited.

Back home again, Marv called one day to say that his men were going to strike soon, but that they were not going to be able to get the bank. The pattern had changed so much that there was no chance of hitting it. The T-men were going to hit the hill and take what they could get there. If they waited, they might lose what they had. I was brokenhearted. We knew where the bank was, but we could do nothing. The one thing we had wanted the most, the one thing we had worked the hardest for, was going to be lost.

Soon the agents did hit the bar at the top of the hill, arrested five men, and got a lot of policy slips. The work came from as far away as Connecticut and was part of the most sophisticated policy operation in Westchester's history. The United States Attorney credited the girls with providing the information that led to the arrests. Newspapers, radio stations, and TV reporters called again, but I was too disappointed to give anything but perfunctory replies.

It may be that my disappointment and the deep frustration felt by Anne and the girls were uncalled for. In the first place, the agents had cracked into an area until then immune to arrests and raids. Also, the monkey wrench they put in the works caused quite a disruption in the Syndicate. And they had shaken the confidence of the hoods in the invulnerability of their hill sanctuary.

Most important of all, we had shown irrefutably that, where there was a will, there was a way to catch professional criminals. If some housewives and a Presbyterian minister could do it, then policemen trained in criminal investigation and working full time should be able to do it, too. Newspapers throughout the nation shouted the story, and the Syndicate in Westchester became a laughingstock. Now, when hoods walked by, people snickered and made humorous remarks. The *Look* magazine article capped our triumph. There were the photographs we had taken of the most secret of the Syndicate's operations.

Shortly after the article appeared, Dino was apparently fired by the Mob and a kid took over his work. The county executive, who had virtually denied the existence of Organized Crime in June, announced in November the creation of a special task force to combat the Organized Crime that didn't exist. We had *not* failed. We decided to celebrate and have a party.

CHAPTER TWELVE

It was going to be a blast. Claire, Grace, Belle, and Alice took over the planning and Alice volunteered her home, because her living room was large. Anyway, we were hesitant about going to a restaurant or hotel. There was too great a chance that a waiter or patron would become aware that these were the women who had made monkeys of the Mafia, the infamous North Avenue Irregulars, or the "Lace Pants Mob," as the *Look* writer had called them. That could lead to tire slashing, nasty telephone calls, or rocks through windows.

Husbands would be invited, as well as the *Look* writer, the Treasury agents, a writer from *Ladies Home Journal,* which was also going to do an article, and the friends who had helped me to get the funds for the radios from the National Council on Crime and Delinquency. Alice, Belle, and Grace went to see a cateress about the meal. They chose the menu, the napkins, the liquor, and the silver. In the middle of their enthusiastic planning the cateress said, "My, this is a *nice* party you are giving. Do you mind if I ask what the *occasion* is?"

There was a deathly silence. Alice delicately cleared her throat. Up popped Belle. "Oh," she said, "it's the anniversary of our Ladies Aid Society."

I was still being deluged with requests from radio and TV to bring some of "my mob" to the studio and tell of our work in chasing the hoodlums. We had become immensely popular, at least with everyone except the hoodlums. Once a friend and I were waiting at a traffic signal when the friend said, "Fay! I think that man is swearing at you!" It was Mickey the Blob, who had just gotten out of jail.

Another time, Honey, walking along Main Street, saw two of New Rochelle's minor thugs come out of a well-known bookie joint. She paused for a moment and thought of following them, in case they were doing some pickup work.

Just then a couple of young women pushing baby carriages came around the corner and walked toward the thugs. The men stopped dead in their tracks, whitened, turned around, and bolted back into the safety of a stationery store.

Such experiences convinced us that we didn't dare let the hoods know who the girls were by putting any of them on television. We turned down all requests until after the *Look* article appeared, and then I accepted a few at *Look's* request. But it was not I whom they were interested in. It was the girls. It made me sad that they couldn't have the fun of telling their story on TV and receiving some public recognition. The danger, however, was too great. If one of them were ever publicly identified, she would worry every time she went out alone at night or a child was late coming home from school.

Another person interested in the girls' work was Bob MacPherson. He called me the moment the story hit the papers and offered his services. He also gave a little new information he had picked up. He was still good, and had accumulated some good data. I dutifully took it all down, without knowing what to do with it. He offered to introduce an agent into a place where he said he was betting, but later backed out. In fact, he offered and changed his mind several times, and I never knew if it was because he was lying about being able to bet in the places or because he was being sulky. I saw him only one more time.

I had reluctantly agreed to appear on the "Alan Burke Show" at the request of *Look*. I walked onto the set and was met by a girl who was the assistant producer. "Mr. Hill," she said, "you know we announced for the last two evenings that you were going to be on this show tonight, and that announcement caused someone from New Rochelle to come. He says that he used to work for you and that he is willing to ask a question from the audience." I had no doubt who it was. Bob was the first one to reach the microphone and ask a question. Actually, he made a statement in which he disclosed to millions of viewers that he was "part of Mr. Hill's organization." Among those watching were special agents of the Intelligence Division of the IRS, who looked on with disbelief as an undercover informant blew his cover in such a dramatic way. Of course, Bob had already blown his cover when he gave testimony in federal court, but this was flaunting it before the Syndicate. His appearance on TV made the hoods look like fools.

Within a few days I began to receive calls from Bob that he had been threatened, fired from his job (because, the owner said, he was a "rat fink"), and followed when he left home. I didn't know what to believe, but by then it wasn't my problem. Bob had also begun to call virtually everyone in the IRS and at the federal courthouse to demand protection. Fortunately, he and his wife had already made plans to leave the country for an extended visit to her parents overseas, and we had to endure his instability for just a few days before they left. We have heard from him only indirectly since. I fervently hope that he has found some employment that gives him satisfaction, and that his personality has begun to stabilize.

The period of intense publicity led to many fascinating incidents. The usual complement of pathetic, unstable people called or wrote to offer information about the Mafia in their areas. One lady told me that the man across the street from her was a hoodlum, and she knew so because he looked at her in a strange way as he backed out of his driveway.

The publicity also caused me to acquire some valuable if sometimes eccentric informants. One old man turned out to be very good, except for one minor handicap. He was stone-deaf. He would scream into the phone his information on bets he had placed, payoffs he had witnessed, gangsters he had followed. I tried to shush him, but it was pointless. Once I said, "Look, why don't you go back into the bookie joint and—."

"GO BACK IN? THAT'S WHERE I AM CALLING FROM NOW. WHAT DO YOU WANT ME TO DO?"

How the man kept from getting killed I don't know.

Another valuable informant was a fundamentalist minister. He would enter my office and say, "Praise the Lord, Brother Hill. With the guidance of the Holy Spirit, I was able to bet in another place this morning." His eyes burned with zeal for the Lord, and yet as an "undercover agent" he would look a bookie in the eye and swear like a sailor about a horse that did not come in.

One of the most interesting of my new agents was a young man who calmly walked up to my house one day to offer his services. He reported that he was ready to spend a great deal of time on spying and knew several places where he could begin. He was exceedingly intelligent and motivated by the highest ideals. However, the kind of work I could permit him to do was limited by the fact that he was nine years old.

Everywhere I went I picked up new informants. One day's calls at the hospital brought me two new men who hailed me from their beds to offer their services. Others telephoned anonymously with information. It was manifest that these calls were made under great stress, and that the callers were certain they were giving information so hot that their lives would not be worth a plugged nickel if it were known they were divulging it.

We continued to plan the founding of a citizens' crime commission similar to one set up in Chicago. One necessary step was to gain the support of several citizens' groups in the county. I visited one group after another seeking to enlist their support. One turned out to consist entirely of little old women. They were fascinated, but also alarmed. One dear soul of 85 said in a quavering voice, "Mr. Hill, you wouldn't want *us* to become part of your North Avenue Irregulars, would you?" The old dears couldn't shake the conviction that what I really wanted was more members for "my mob." When I asked them how they proposed to fight Organized Crime, one determined little lady said, "Why, we'll have a tea and ask the district attorney to speak."

The bright spot in our lives finally came—the party. The girls looked gorgeous. Anne was coolly beautiful in a new white dress and Vicki looked stunning. Claire was ravishing, Penny radiant, Belle funnier than ever. Helen emerged from her self-deprecation long enough to enjoy herself. Alice was a charming hostess, and Sue, Ruth, and Maureen helped her to welcome guests. Rosalind was poised and confident, Barbara smiled through the grief she still felt, and Honey was dazzling in her black gown.

We had invited Myron, of course, but he was out of the state on a secret mission. Tom came, and Jerry couldn't have stayed away if he had wanted to; his "partner" insisted that he come. The two of them, the cool, stunning Anne and the chunky, tough agent, spent half the evening in animated conversation.

Marv, the rascal, was also there. I say rascal, because we later learned that he hadn't wanted to come. He had assumed we would serve tea, little sandwiches with the crusts trimmed off, and maybe some jellied consommé and cottage cheese. When he saw the bar, all the husbands refreshing themselves at it, and then the delicious meal, he cheered up considerably.

We loudly relived our experiences, shared the movies we had taken, and Marv regaled us with stories. We had a glorious time.

Still another happiness came our way in a few days. The NCCD had selected me to receive its Carl M. Loeb Jr. Award for Citizen Valor. With the award came a $5,000 check that was to be presented by the Attorney General of the United States. I would be able to pay off some of the debts that so weighed on me during the past few months. Bob's imperious demands, other needs of our crime work, an extra pledge to the church's expansion fund campaign, and the endless medical expenses for Grace had plunged me hopelessly into debt. The award would permit me to break even. I was to receive the check a few weeks later at a banquet. It was something to look forward to.

The days were filled with speaking engagements. I went everywhere I could to tell the story of our work and the proposed crime commission. Some of the invitations were amusing. One good friend, a woman who had given me some money for Bob, asked me to speak at her Episcopal church. There was a brisk debate when she announced I was coming. Some in the congregation didn't think I was "spiritual" enough, but the strongest challenge came from a dowager who said, "That man is going to get himself killed, and if you invite him here, he'll get us killed, too." A compromise was finally reached. I would be invited to speak, and the police would be asked to guard the church. The members were so excited at the prospect of such a notorious and controversial speaker that they invited the public—and an extra three persons responded.

Another time, a friend in the Junior League of Pelham, a rather exclusive little community contiguous to New Rochelle, and also the town where many of the pickups took place, asked me to speak before her group, and I accepted. My friend was so enchanted by what the North Avenue Irregulars had done that she suggested to several of the Junior League matrons that, inasmuch as they did civic things, they might form a similar group in their town. One of the older members, however, scotched the idea. She haughtily drew herself up and said, "Oh, my dear, that would *never* work in *Pelham*. We try to be *positive* here!"

The Woman's Club of New Rochelle is a charming organization

whose meetings consist of book reviews and spirited discussions of burning issues, such as how many potted plants the hospital should put in its lobby. It also publishes a monthly magazine. The editor called one day and said she would like to have one of the Irregulars write an article for *The Candle*. I was flabbergasted. Then I remembered that they had long ago endorsed my campaign, and I decided I had misjudged the ladies. They must not be typical women's club types, after all. After Anne wrote the article, however, I received a call from an officer of the club who said that the editor had made a mistake and that the article was not the type they usually used. I read through a few issues of *The Candle* and decided she was right.

A reaction provoked by the *Look* article was a visit by officials from North Pelham. They had read about the cop who chased Grace and Rosalind away from the hoods and were cut to the quick. Three of them came to assure me that they were indeed anxious to rid their city of any criminal element. It was hard for me to keep a straight face, because I knew that a relative of one of them ran a big policy and horse action in their town, and informants had told me of comments by at least two of the officials to the effect that, if they chased the local boys out, Syndicate gamblers would come in. Just how that would happen or why they thought their "community" bookies were not affiliated with the Organization baffles me. I told them what I knew about gambling operations in North Pelham, and they left with more assurances of their eagerness to wipe out crime in their town. Informants later told me that the town was as wide open as ever.

The girls, in the meantime, were chafing a bit. They were bored with the PTA and the Garden Club. They wanted more action. So I decided to unleash them again. This time they went to North Pelham, sat in the sun, drove around, and tried to identify the pickup routine. Within a few days they had it! I was astonished. There could be no doubt that they were pros. They would sit on park benches and read newspapers—Claire once took her maid along on a stroll down the street—and they saw everything that went on. Before the week was out they were tailing people all over town and had identified all the men involved in the action. They had license numbers, descriptions, schedules, and contacts. They found the center of operations at a tavern, and saw our old friend Dino turn up, with Cassone following him. We even got an undercover informant inside the tavern and heard the hoods giving orders to each other. All our girls were in on it, their cars criss-crossing through town and radio messages crackling out. Rather, everyone was in on it except Grace, who was now spending many hours in bed.

The information on Westchester's Crime Syndicate flooded in day and night. New informants called daily, including my deaf old man. He got my son David on the phone one night, and began to shout at him the news he had to report. David tried to interrupt several times, but it did no good.

"AND SO, REVEREND HILL, I SAYS TO THIS MAN, I SAYS, 'I'LL BET YOU NUMBER THREE-OH-SIX COMES IN TO-MORROW,' BUT HE SAYS, HE SAYS—."

"Sir, SIR! I'll call my father and—."

"OF COURSE, I WENT FURTHER. I MADE SEVERAL BETS ON A COMBINATION. AND THEN—."

"SIR! SIR! You *mustn't*—."

"NO, THERE WAS NO MUSCLE AROUND ANYWHERE EX-CEPT THAT DIMPS FELLOW, AND HE DOESN'T COUNT BECAUSE—."

David finally put the phone down and came to find me. When I got to the phone, the old man was still shouting into it.

"THIS GANGSTER COMES IN THAT I KNEW FROM THE OLD DAYS AND I SAID—."

"WHY DON'T YOU COME IN TOMORROW AND TELL ME ABOUT IT THEN?"

"NO, HE'S NOT VERY *THIN*, IN FACT—."

"NO! I'M NOT TALKING ABOUT THAT. I WANT TO SEE YOU TOMORROW."

"NOT ON YOUR LIFE! YOU CAN'T BORROW ANY MONEY FROM ME."

"NO! I WANT-TO-SEE-YOU-TOMORROW!"

"YOU WANT TO SEE ME? WHY DIDN'T YOU SAY SO? I WISH YOU COULD SPEAK UP. I AM A LITTLE HARD OF HEARING, YOU KNOW."

The day of the presentation of the award, my father came from California. It was given to me at an official meeting of the NCCD. Senators and many other important people were there and the Attorney General, Ramsey Clark, made a little speech. It was exciting.

That night I got a telephone call from a new informant who offered to go after some information about the higher echelons of the Syndicate in our county. When he finished I sat there with my mouth hanging open. He was supplying almost the last bits of information on corruption, loan sharking, and the take-over of legitimate businesses that we needed to crack the Syndicate wide open. If we moved fast, we could really get the goods on the hoods, because they were now involved in something that made them highly vulnerable. I called Anne the next morning and she oohed and aahed as I pointed out what we had. She sent out her teams that same afternoon to check on what we had been told was happening. It was accurate. I could hardly believe it. After all our hard work, heartbreak, and frustration, we had it! But we had to be exceedingly careful, because someone could get hurt at that level.

I told Marv the news. He listened quietly and then swore to himself. His department was so shorthanded and had so many other important cases going that it might be weeks before Treasury agents could return to Westchester. I did something outrageously daring. I called the Attorney General of the United States, outlined as briefly as possible what we had, and said that, if he would give us a "task force" to work on our leads, we could deal Organized Crime in Westchester a crushing blow. He quietly suggested that I come to Washington and talk to Henry Peterson, chief of the Organized Crime and Racketeering Section of the Justice Department. I was elated, so confident of the value of our information, that I was certain my request would be granted.

The information we had went far beyond gambling, but it all depended on gambling. Federal agents would have to do the investigating, and they did not have jurisdiction over all kinds of crimes. But they could use the gambling excise tax law to make large-scale arrests. Some of our county and municipal officials would at last have their connections with the hoodlums unmasked.

I savored the prospect. It was difficult to get through the rest of the day. I tried to make notes for a sermon, but my mind wandered. I went to visit some shut-ins instead. As they discussed their ills or their past lives, my mind again and again wandered off to our incredible good fortune. I was ashamed for not paying better attention to the shut-ins' problems and memories. It was like a dream. They sat in their wheelchairs or lay in their beds, reminiscing, telling of the battles they had fought, of their families, their jobs, their struggles. The poignancy of it finally caught me up and melancholy replaced my excitement. How long before I would be in a wheelchair, remembering the struggle in which I was now so deeply involved? How many of the gangsters would soon be inside oxygen tents while nurses felt for a pulse? Soon, sooner than any of us dared to think, the Irregulars would be old women telling their grandchildren about their adventures. And young ministers would call on them and smile absently at their tales.

My thoughts turned to Grace. A doctor was seeing her that night. What would be find? I felt tired and lonely. I was back in my office now. I picked up my Bible and began to page through it, aimlessly. I am not one who turns to the Bible every time of stress. Nor do I look to it for magical phrases that will give me comfort in difficulty. I believe that the proper use of the Bible is to read it regularly and absorb its meaning, take its point of view of life, submit to its message.

As I leafed through it, I found myself muttering an incoherent prayer for Grace. Yet that, too, is against my principles. I do not believe in any magical power of prayer. Although I do believe that in some circumstances God in His infinite mercy and wisdom will decide to turn aside the course of nature and spare someone from death, I do not believe that we can coerce Him into it by believing with all our power. Nor do I believe that there is a technique of prayer that will nudge God into doing something contrary to His will. Many good and pious people have died before their time despite great faith, and many people are afflicted with serious diseases despite the fervent and honest prayers of their loved ones. Prayer is no assurance that we will be immune from trouble. To me, the proper attitude is for us to say our prayers, to honestly state to the Eternal our deepest fears and desires, and then to get up and be obedient in whatever circumstances we find ourselves. If that means being faithful to His commandments as a rich man, then be a responsible rich man who struggles with all the problems and temptations associated with being rich. If you are a sufferer, it is up to you to suffer with faith and to deal with all the problems and temptations associated with suffering. There is no scriptural justification for believing that if we are good enough, or if we have enough faith, or if we say the right prayer, we will be spared trouble.

I hadn't intended to say a "crash prayer" for us. Other families had gone through more and retained their humanity and, if our faith meant anything, we should be able to do so, too. I didn't think I could wheedle God into doing me a special favor. The anguish I felt had simply emptied into these vague, muttered prayers. And strange, superstitious fears crowded my mind. Was I being punished for not being the sort of minister I should be? Was God going to use Grace's pain to force me into being what I ought to be? Could it be that the Omnipotent would use this to show me that my proper role in life was one of compassion and redemption, not of trying to get evidence to imprison some men and perhaps disclose the venality of others to the public? I was sick with fear and confusion. Was I just a troublemaker? Would it have been better to shut up and ignore the corruptions I had seen? Should I have devoted myself to tenderly loving the bookie in order to change his heart?

I am, however, a skeptic by nature. Superstition has no place in religion, and I was able to reject the idea of God thinking me so important that he was making my wife suffer to force me to stop doing something. My confidence began to return. Then I came across a reassuring passage of Scripture. It is Proverbs X:10:

"He who winks the eye causes trouble but he who boldly reproves makes peace."

After that I felt fine and I rose from my reveries sure that I was right in my determination to see the drive against crime through to its conclusion. I felt reassured that Grace would be all right, that the pain was only sciatica. Her mother had had it, and it was a common affliction. I was certain that her special diet had kept the cancer from returning, that our fears were groundless. The pain would disappear and our crime drive would be successful. By the time I reached home for supper, my spirits were high.

At the doctor's that evening, Grace was apprehensive, but I radiated confidence. I idly paged through a magazine while she went in for her examination and X-rays. When the doctor suddenly appeared he wasn't smiling. "Your wife's cancer has reappeared in the pelvis," he said. I was shaken.

Driving home, I was blinking back the tears when she said calmly, with determination, "I am going back on that diet. It is the only thing I believe in. I can't stand the thought of any more operations. And the most those other things can do for me is stall the disease."

This time there was little likelihood that we could keep the news from the children. As we lay in bed that night, our hearts cold and our minds incapable of sleep, the memory of my earlier confidence was bitter, and all the superstitious thoughts and fears returned to mock me. My elation over the crime break was painful to remember. It seemed so inconsequential now. I slept very little that night. And I don't know how much Grace slept. She lay very quiet, but in the morning her eyes were dark with exhaustion.

The news frightened the children but they took it well. The three little ones didn't ask many questions, but the older two wanted to know why she had to chain herself to such an unpleasant regime. I took David and Kristin aside and told them the whole truth. From that day onward they would come home from school and look anxiously at their mother, wondering if she were better or worse, wondering how much longer she would be all right.

Whether I wanted to or not, I was unable just to drop the drive against crime. I had the appointment with the Justice Department and I had begun the drive to establish a citizens' crime commission. And the girls were planning to go out a few more times to get some last bits of information we needed. I met with them that afternoon. They were all there, in my office, and as we talked I realized how much their friendship meant to me, how much I admired them. Somehow I felt better with them around. We had done the impossible together, and now maybe Grace and I could do the impossible in another way. Apparently they noticed my subdued tone and the lines in my face, for suddenly the room was quiet, and then Anne said, "Fay, what's wrong? Is it Grace?"

For a long time I couldn't speak. I knew that if I said a word I would cry. I didn't have to say anything. They knew. Before they left, each one came over to pat me on the shoulder, say something comforting, or squeeze my hand. They were good girls, good friends.

I flew down to Washington to see Mr. Peterson. He listened courteously to what I had to say and answered that he would take it up with the proper people and let me know. I returned home encouraged by his attitude. Within a few days, he called to say that the authorities had agreed to assign a squad of men to work on the leads we had dug up. The agent in charge would be Marv.

Marv and I went over what I had pieced together and what we had by way of evidence. He whistled when I finished and said he would get his agents going immediately. He was soon calling regularly to ask for more information and to report that the operation was going better than he had ever thought possible. My heart lifted a little from its gloom.

And things at home improved a little, too. Grace began to feel better almost the moment she went back on the diet. Her eyes brightened, the pain lessened, and her spirits lifted. My work in the church continued to go well, too. We had almost finished our expansion fund drive and began to work on the parish house renovation. Life didn't look so bad after all. We were going to hurt the Organization badly and Grace was going to get well.

The investigation of the leads we had supplied to the Treasury agents went superbly. Marv and his boys were ecstatic about what they would be able to do. It would be the greatest triumph of all.

One afternoon, however, driving to the office, I turned on the car radio and heard the announcer say, "Today the Supreme Court declared unconstitutional the $50 wagering tax stamp law under which federal agents have been prosecuting gangsters throughout the United States. The Court stated that forcing a man to buy such a stamp forced him to give testimony against himself in violation of the Constitution. At the same time the Court also overturned the gambling excise tax law. When told of the decision, Henry Peterson of the Organized Crime and Racketeering Section of the Justice Department said, 'They have cut off my right arm, taken away the instrument by which I was most able to fight organized crime.'"

I was physically shaken by the time I got Marv on the telephone. "How bad is it, Marv?" I asked.

"It's a disaster. All our cases awaiting trial will be dismissed. The men we picked up in Yonkers as a result of your work, the men we got through Harry, all of them are free now. And it also means that we no longer have jurisdiction in the case we have been working on for the last few weeks. It's a complete ruin."

The girls telephoned one by one to say they had heard the broadcast and wanted to know what it meant for the cases they had worked on. They were devastated. None of the men whose arrests we had brought about would ever go to jail or even be fined. The hoods had won after all. They always won. They were invulnerable. All the cynics were right.

When Anne heard the news, she sat down and wept—and I would have, too, except that the past few weeks had emptied me of emotion. Of course, the government planned to submit to Congress substitute legislation that would put the federal government back into the business of suppressing gambling, but all our leads would be dead by then. There was nothing left, nothing to show for all our work. When I left for my office, I was so depressed and exhausted that I sat outside in my car and wept.

I had to stop at the post office. A local politician came up to me there and said unctuously, "Well, Reverend Hill, did that Supreme Court decision wipe out all your cases?" I told him that it did and he commiserated with me courteously, but I am sure I detected a slight smile on his lips.

And that afternoon, on my way to see a parishioner, I happened to drive past Heavy Eddie's. There was the familiar dented blue station wagon across the street, resting from its errands. The work had already been safely moved, and the men were standing outside in the sun enjoying the beautiful, unnaturally warm winter day. I didn't look at them, but the light turned at the wrong time and I had to stop directly in front of the luncheonette, with all their eyes on me. I could hear them talking about me and chuckling at the futility of my fight against them. Then the full humor of the situation struck them. There I was, stuck at a light, while they were comfortably sunning themselves. Heavy Eddie began to laugh. Mike the Mouse, Frankie the Bear, and even the sullen Dino joined in. They jabbed each other in the ribs and pointed at me. When I finally looked, they threw back their heads and roared, leaning against each other, holding their ribs, laughing, and whooping until the tears made streaks down their grimy cheeks. I still hear them sometimes at night.

As I write this, it is late spring again, and I think often of the days last year when we were driving all over the county tailing hoods. I think of how we made them so angry at us that we had to keep all the shades pulled at night and be careful about going out. Now there is no danger. The Mob knows I am helpless. The girls are back to their normal chores now, tending children and attending PTA meetings and ironing. Occasionally we get together and go out, mostly for old times' sake, to see if things are the same. We pick up the action easily, now that we know how it is done, and a few times we have done some scouting to see if the same people are still involved in Yonkers. There have been some changes, but not many. We have sat in the park there and watched the hoods collect the bags of work while the cops drove blissfully by.

Periodically, heartbreaking articles appear in the local paper proclaiming that federal prosecutors have moved to dismiss the case against someone we had helped to arrest. Big John is no longer under indictment. Patsy the milkman is free, and virtually all the others have had their charges dropped. Dino's case is still pending. Now and then I call Commissioner Carey or one of his captains to report some flagrant operation in town, and they raid the place. But there is not much we can do now. I try to avoid going past Heavy Eddie's place, but whenever I have to someone is there to smirk and point.

Marv is doing tax investigations now, but occasionally he or one of the other boys will drop by to say "hello" and reassure us that some day Congress will give them jurisdiction over gambling and they will be back at work on the leads we gave them. But we know the leads are dead, and the big opportunity is lost forever.

We are continuing to work for the establishment of the Westchester citizens' crime commission. If we succeed, we will have done something of significance against Organized Crime. Its main function will be to evaluate how well public officials are doing their jobs. At least Westchester County may improve, because we have a new district attorney. The one who insisted that we were the cleanest county in the nation has been promoted to judge as a reward for his years of faithful and ineffectual service. Our new district attorney is Carl Vergari, the former chief counsel for the SIC, and we have high hopes for him.

I don't often hear from my informants anymore. They know my claws are pulled. Even Pete rarely calls. He did roar at me over the phone just yesterday that he wanted me to do something about the filthy mess a local hoodlum, who is Pete's neighbor, is making by dumping garbage at the curb in "fragrant violation of the law."

I do have more time to spend with Grace. She has inched along until today she is remarkably improved. She is no longer bedridden and even drives the car on occasions.

I can't help but compare the two problems. Organized Crime is a cancerous growth. We will always have some of it, just as we will always have traffic violators, bank robbers, arsonists, and murderers. But it can be kept under control if government officials vigorously and imaginatively do the jobs we pay them to do. And they will do those jobs if we, the public, insist on it. I do not subscribe to the theory that the public is to blame for the existence of Organized Crime, but it *is* true that, if the public decides it doesn't want hoodlums operating in their society, they will be through. The public is the human body, the Criminal Organization is the malignancy, and the elected officials, the police, and the courts are the body's immunity system. When the law enforcement system doesn't function properly, the cancer grows. We in New Rochelle tried to goad that sluggish, almost inert immunity system into action. If we achieved anything lasting, it was to so embarrass local officials that they found themselves on the spot and had to do something themselves about suppressing crime.

If, all over this country of ours, people would awaken to the menace in their cities, if they would organize as we did, Organized Crime would diminish to manageable proportions. If the cancer is permitted to grow unchecked, it will destroy our nation. A city infected with gangsters is soon unable to deal effectively with any of its problems. Why, at a time when our cities face the massive problems of race relations, urban blight, burgeoning welfare rolls, clogged transportation facilities, and slums, are so many of their leaders cynical, often stupid men without any qualifications except that they obey their racketeering masters. The "fix" and the "pay-off" have become almost an accepted part of the modern American scene.

Organized Crime is growing today, rapidly and strongly, and I see few signs that much is being done about it. Legislators pontificate about "crime in the streets" and the rising tide of muggings and burglaries, but they say nothing about the Organized Crime that imports and sells narcotics to men who then burglarize our homes in order to get enough money to pay for their drugs. There is little political mileage to be made in acting against Organized Crime.

Soon, very soon, I hope, Congress will get around to passing a law that will permit federal agents to arrest gangsters on gambling charges. When the law does pass, we will again be doing our best to provide the leads. And we can do it. We have built up a good organization, and these people will work again as soon as the agents have jurisdiction. We already know the personnel in New Rochelle and throughout much of Westchester County. Our intelligence data is still accumulating and, although some leads are cold, we will get hot new ones! Because we live here, and every time I or any of the girls go shopping we check to see what is going on. Some day we will hit them again, hard. Not only because we want to stop this evil Organization, but also because it beats the PTA.

Was it, then, all futile? I refuse to think so, despite the continuing indifference of the public and the inattention of the politicians and the police. It is seldom in life that any battle is ever completely won. Certainly, the fight against Organized Crime is not like the television programs where the hero is frustrated for half an hour but soon finds out that the chief of the Syndicate is in reality the local banker, who is then arrested and the Syndicate smashed for ever and ever. We *did* dent the Organization and accomplish something of importance. Certainly never again will the police in Westchester County be able to plead that it is so very hard to catch these criminals in their activities. Not if 12 housewives did it! That great, massively lethargic lump we call the public is somewhat more alert to the situation than they were before we began our work. If for no other reason than that our work was so bizarre, they read and listened and learned. No longer can anyone in Westchester who is honest and who read the newspapers say that the local bookie is not part of a sinister Syndicate. Of course, some people, especially some politicians and some police, will continue to maintain just that, but they know it is untrue and only maintain it in order to excuse their own inaction, their own willingness to bet with bookies.

We did more than add a little knowledge to the public's store of information, however. We also built a little "organization" of people who will not give up their interest in Organized Crime. They continue to watch and learn and note. And because they are on the scene, not merely appearing periodically for a specific investigation, we build up intelligence information readily and thoroughly. Hardly a day goes by that the "Irregulars" don't acquire some new piece of information by surveillance or from our informants.

And then we have also begun the Westchester County Citizens' Crime Commission, which will hire investigators and provide the people of the county with objective information about the crime situation that will be above the angry outcries of citizens and the wounded defenses of public officials. If the commission hires as its director someone like Marv, who has served with the federal government and who has the necessary skills, it will be able to be of some real help to the county in ridding itself of gangsters. The Chicago Crime Commission, under the superb leadership of Virgil Petersen, has performed useful service for that blighted city for years. In fact, President Johnson's Commission on Crime was so impressed with the work of such citizens' groups that it urged their formation in every major metropolitan area. Our commission, if it becomes fully operational, will be of great assistance to Westchester.

Perhaps the most significant contribution we made was to stimulate the involvement of citizens in their own protection against crime. There has been a steady and deadly drift away from the wholehearted involvement of citizens in law enforcement. It is harder and harder to get people to give testimony in court or even to report crimes. Thirty-seven witnesses in New York City decided that it was none of their business if a young woman was being murdered; so she died. All over our nation, witnesses hurry from the scene of accidents or ignore a crime being committed so they won't have to "become involved." If we are to avoid a police state, then ordinary citizens must be willing to pick up the phone and inform the police that someone is illegally entering the house next door and even give testimony in court. I don't mean to suggest that we must snoop on each other, make nasty, anonymous calls to the police about neighbors, or "tail" others whom we may dislike and suspect of amorous liaisons. But I do suggest that a democratic society cannot survive if men speak only of "the establishment," of "them," of "minding one's own business." We must talk of *our* government," of "*us*," of "*our* neighbors," and "*our* city's" welfare as being "*our* business."

If we did anything at all helpful and of lasting benefit, therefore, it was to stimulate interest in responsible citizenship as related to the crime problem. After the newspaper and *Look* magazine publicity, we have received queries from people all over the United States about beginning such efforts in their own communities. One group in California is working on the narcotics problem. Another in New Jersey is applying itself to eliminating syndicated gambling. If this trend continues, we will not have done our work in vain. For the Organized Criminal is like a fish and the people are the sea. When the sea is no longer hospitable to the fish, it will die. So will it be with the gangster in our midst. When a significant number of people decide that they do not want him, he will perish.

Once when Marv and I were discussing our work and I expressed frustration, he said, "Fay, it is important that you don't overrate what your group has done, that you do not think you have wiped out the Mafia. *But there is no doubt that if enough groups like yours could develop all over the country and cooperate with authorities the Mafia would be doomed.*"